CONFIGURING
CISCO® AVVID

SYNGRESS®

solutions@syngress.com

With over 1,500,000 copies of our MCSE, MCSD, CompTIA, and Cisco study guides in print, we have come to know many of you personally. By listening, we've learned what you like and dislike about typical computer books. The most requested item has been for a web-based service that keeps you current on the topic of the book and related technologies. In response, we have created solutions@syngress.com, a service that includes the following features:

- A one-year warranty against content obsolescence that occurs as the result of vendor product upgrades. We will provide regular web updates for affected chapters.
- Monthly mailings that respond to customer FAQs and provide detailed explanations of the most difficult topics, written by content experts exclusively for solutions@syngress.com.
- Regularly updated links to sites that our editors have determined offer valuable additional information on key topics.
- Access to "Ask the Author"™ customer query forms that allow readers to post questions to be addressed by our authors and editors.

Once you've purchased this book, browse to www.syngress.com/solutions.

To register, you will need to have the book handy to verify your purchase.

Thank you for giving us the opportunity to serve you.

SYNGRESS®

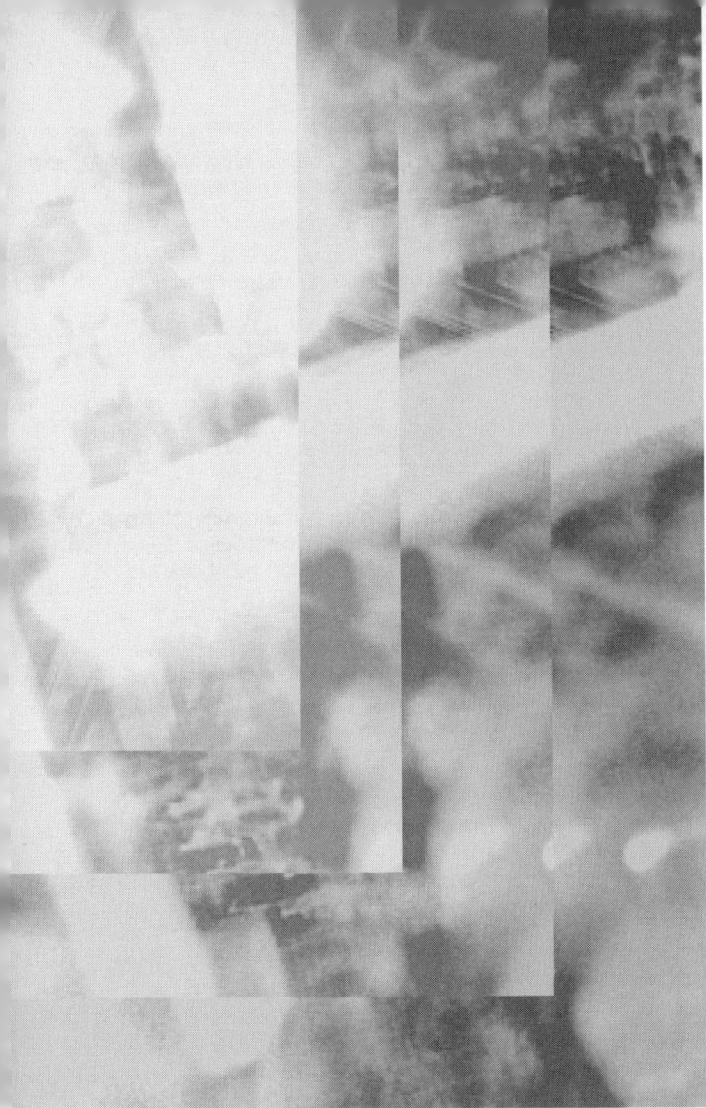

CONFIGURING
CISCO® AVVID

SYNGRESS®

KEY	SERIAL NUMBER
001	26PQ92ADSE
002	XBN74835C4
003	C3NML2LR4E
004	Q25C87BCJH
005	66PCA94DUC
006	PF6288AZ73
007	DTPF385K24
008	XRDXDR65T2
009	65YT9D94DS
010	SMG22WS2CN

PUBLISHED BY
Syngress Publishing, Inc.
800 Hingham Street
Rockland, MA 02370

Configuring Cisco AVVID

Printed in the United States of America

1 2 3 4 5 6 7 8 9 0

ISBN: 1-928994-14-8

Copy edit by: Nancy Kruse Hannigan
 and Adrienne Rebello
Project Editor: Mark A. Listewnik
Co-Publisher: Richard Kristof

Technical edit by: Wayne Lawson
Index by: Robert Saigh
Page Layout and Art by: Shannon Tozier

Distributed by Publishers Group West

Acknowledgments

We would like to acknowledge the following people for their kindness and support in making this book possible.

Richard Kristof, Duncan Anderson, Jennifer Gould, Robert Woodruff, Kevin Murray, Dale Leatherwood, Rhonda Harmon, and Robert Sanregret of Global Knowledge, for their generous access to the IT industry's best courses, instructors and training facilities.

Ralph Troupe, Rhonda St. John, and the team at Callisma for their invaluable insight into the challenges of designing, deploying and supporting world-class enterprise networks.

Karen Cross, Lance Tilford, Meaghan Cunningham, Kim Wylie, Harry Kirchner, Bill Richter, Kevin Votel, Brittin Clark, and Sarah MacLachlan of Publishers Group West for sharing their incredible marketing experience and expertise.

Mary Ging, Caroline Hird, Simon Beale, Caroline Wheeler, Victoria Fuller, Jonathan Bunkell, and Klaus Beran of Harcourt International for making certain that our vision remains worldwide in scope.

Anneke Baeten, Annabel Dent, and Laurie Giles of Harcourt Australia for all their help.

David Buckland, Wendi Wong, Daniel Loh, Marie Chieng, Lucy Chong, Leslie Lim, Audrey Gan, and Joseph Chan of Transquest Publishers for the enthusiasm with which they receive our books.

Kwon Sung June at Acorn Publishing for his support.

Ethan Atkin at Cranbury International for his help in expanding the Syngress program.

Joe Pisco, Helen Moyer, and the great folks at InterCity Press for all their help.

From Global Knowledge

At Global Knowledge we strive to support the multiplicity of learning styles required by our students to achieve success as technical professionals. As the world's largest IT training company, Global Knowledge is uniquely positioned to offer these books. The expertise gained each year from providing instructor-led training to hundreds of thousands of students worldwide has been captured in book form to enhance your learning experience. We hope that the quality of these books demonstrates our commitment to your lifelong learning success. Whether you choose to learn through the written word, computer based training, Web delivery, or instructor-led training, Global Knowledge is committed to providing you with the very best in each of these categories. For those of you who know Global Knowledge, or those of you who have just found us for the first time, our goal is to be your lifelong competency partner.

Thank your for the opportunity to serve you. We look forward to serving your needs again in the future.

Warmest regards,

Duncan Anderson
President and Chief Executive Officer, Global Knowledge

Technical Editor and Contributor

Wayne A. Lawson II (CCIE # 5244, CCNA, CCDA, NNCSE, CNX, MCSE, CNE, Banyan CBE) is a Systems Engineer with Cisco Systems in Southfield, Michigan. His core area of expertise is in the Routed Wide Area Network (WAN) and Campus Switching. He has provided pre- and post-sales technical support for various dot-com start-ups on redundant ISP access, failsafe security, content networking and verification for local premise, as well as geographical load balancing. His internetworking proficiency includes Layer One and Two, Layer Three, IBM & Voice Technologies, and Network Management and Monitoring Technologies.

Wayne received the "Top Performer" award at Cisco 2000 National Sales Meeting for achieving Cisco's highest level of technical certification. He has also contributed to Syngress Publishing's *Building Cisco Remote Access Networks* (ISBN: 1-928994-13-X). Wayne lives in Holly, MI.

Contributors

Randall S. Benn (CCIE #1637, CCSI, CCDA, CSE) is the President of Global Network Solutions, Inc., a network consulting and training services company. He has over 13 years experience building voice and data networks and holds an MBA from Old Dominion University and a Bachelor of Science degree in Mathematics & Computer Science from Bloomsburg University.

Randy currently specializes in designing and deploying converged voice, video and data networks. He also provides sales and technical training to Cisco Systems employees, partners, and customers with CCI, a Cisco Systems Learning Partner. He spends his spare time maintaining the popular Web site "Cisco

Systems In a Nutshell" (www.iponeverything.net). Randy lives with his wife Liza and son Jason in Herndon, VA.

Erik Rozell (MCNE, MCSE, MCT, CCNA, CCNP, CCDA, CCDP, CCA) is a Sr. Systems Design Consultant with WareForce, Inc. He has accreditation in a broad spectrum of computer and network systems professional specializations and over 12 years networking experience in computer systems, systems management and architecture, and Internetworking. Erik has implemented many solutions at several Fortune 500 companies and continues to be a widely sought-after authority on information technology throughout the industry. He has authored numerous books on subjects ranging from TCP/IP, to system optimization and routers, to Proxy Servers, as well as authored dozens of technical articles on data migration and tape technologies. He has a degree in Management Information Systems.

Erik continues to consult on cutting-edge infrastructure and systems issues, as well as to implement systems strategies and deployment for numerous hi-tech companies. He maintains a full schedule of lectures, presentations, and project management assignments with leading companies on all-things related to network systems and Internet-based technologies. Erik lives in Canoga Park, CA.

Sandy C. Kronenberg (CCDA, CCNA, CIPT) is the Chief Executive Officer of Netarx, Inc. and is the inventor of Netarx NMS, a patented system for remote monitoring of client networks. Netarx was recently voted one of *ComputerWorld*'s "Top 100 Emerging Companies to Watch in 2001." As a technologist, he spends much of his time improving the design of client systems and integrating best-of-breed technologies into Netarx practice. Sandy holds a Masters Degree from Georgetown University and a Bachelor of Science from the University of Michigan. He lives in Bingham Farms, MI.

Nicole Keith (CCNA, MCP, CIPT) is a Network Technician with Netarx, Inc. She provides Windows NT and Cisco consultation and technical support. Her specialties include Cisco routers and switches, Cisco firewall security, Microsoft NT and 2000, Exchange, AVVID design and implementation, strategic LAN and WAN planning, and network troubleshooting, recovery, and optimization.

John Deegan (MCSE, CCNA, CIPT) is a Network Technician with Netarx, Inc. specializing in network support as well as in enterprise deployment and integration of IT solutions ranging from AVVID installations to Wide Area Network implementations. John holds a Bachelor of Arts from Oakland University.

Clay Richards (CNE-5, CCNP, CIPT) is a Network Technician with Netarx, Inc. providing enterprise level design and network integration and systems monitoring for its clients in the Detroit area and across the country. Clay provides LAN and WAN integration as well as technical support for Netarx's clients. His specialties include Cisco IP Telephony, Cisco routers and switches, Novell NetWare design and implementation, and network troubleshooting and optimization.

Darrel Hinshaw (CCIE, CCNA, MCSE, MCP+I, MCNE) is a senior consultant with Callisma. He currently provides senior-level strategic and technical consulting to all Callisma clients in the south-central region of the US. His specialties include Cisco routers and LAN switches, Microsoft NT, Novell design and implementation, strategic network planning, network architecture and design, and network troubleshooting and optimization. Darrel's background includes positions as a senior engineer at Chancellor Media, and as a senior network engineer at Lucent Technologies in the Octel Messaging Division.

Contents

Chapter 5 Utilizing AVVID Applications and Software Solutions   167

Chapter 1

An Introduction to AVVID Technology

Solutions in this chapter:

- AVVID—An Architecture of Voice, Video, and Integrated Data

- The AVVID Vision

- An AVVID Overview

- The Converged Infrastructure

Introduction

I think that it's fair to say that throughout the 1990's, Cisco Systems has made a huge impact on how many companies and individuals do business. From the release of their initial Cisco router product through the design and development of their entire Catalyst switch product line, Cisco has developed a system to transfer TCP/IP traffic—the most commonly known TCP/IP highway being the World-Wide Web. In the late 1990's and now, in the beginning of the 21st century, Cisco has taken their TCP/IP equipment to the next level—the transmission of time-sensitive voice over TCP/IP. This new initiative is what is known to the consumer market as AVVID. AVVID is an acronym that you will hear quite often; in fact, it is an acronym that is changing the way the world does business!

AVVID—An Architecture of Voice, Video, and Integrated Data

AVVID is, quite simply, a Cisco Systems, Inc. acronym that stands for Architecture for Voice, Video, and Integrated Data. In practical terms, it is a network architecture made up of hardware and software to transmit your company's computer data such as e-mail, World –Wide Web traffic, and file transfers; voice traffic, such as a telephone call, say, from your Detroit office to the Dallas office; and your company's video traffic—for example, a video conferencing call or a video training session, over the same physical (and logical) computer network.

Over the past several years, the recommended and requested design by many was to implement three separate networks. A realistic example of this would be a single Frame Relay or Point-to-Point Wide Area Network (WAN) for all of your company's data traffic, a second network consisting of any number of analog or digital trunks and tie lines for voice, and a third network, usually ISDN (Integrated Services Digital Network), infrastructure for video conferencing. As you might expect with three separate networks, the hardware costs are quite high, as are the costs for the circuits, support, and maintenance associated with the individual networks. Cisco Systems, Inc. has developed the AVVID solution that reduces the "multiple infrastructure" approach by combining all of your infrastructures into a single, high-speed TCP/IP network. With this approach, your company's support and maintenance costs, as well as the cost for hardware, is decreased due to the fact that everything can run on one system.

The AVVID Vision

Imagine taking the three networks your company currently has and combining them into a single or *converged* infrastructure. That sounds like it would make managing, budgeting, and staffing somewhat easier, right? Well, that's only a small list of the benefits you'll receive when implementing a converged network. Throughout this book, you will be introduced to new and beneficial technologies that are available from Cisco such as unified and intelligent messaging and communications, and toll bypass. These components of AVVID not only save you hard dollars, but they increase your companies overall performance and response to customer and employee service and support.

Toll Bypass

One example of a cost-saving scenario is a toll-bypass solution seen in Figure 1.1. Let's say your company has two main offices, one in Dallas, Texas, and the other in Detroit, Michigan. Currently the two offices have a single Point-to-Point T1 data infrastructure in place, so they can send e-mail and files back and forth between the two locations. They also have a public telephone network in place. Currently, 80 percent of the calls made at the Dallas branch are long distance calls to the Detroit branch, which results in a monthly telephone bill of $3000 for each location. An example of a simplistic AVVID solution would be to implement a Voice-Over IP solution at each location. You would simply add a module into the router at each location, giving you the benefit of taking voice, converting the voice to TCP/IP, and shipping it across the data infrastructure you currently have. This is not a completely converged infrastructure, but it is the first step toward becoming a 100 percent AVVID network.

Figure 1.1 A Toll Solutions Bypass

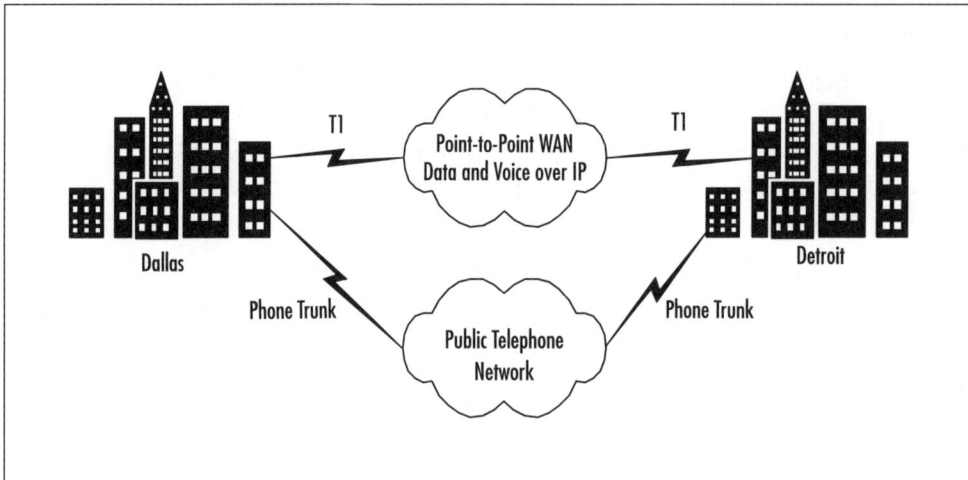

In the previous scenario, each location would still use the existing public telephone network for calls outside of the company, but all of the calls that are placed from Dallas to Detroit would traverse your Point-to-Point network—resulting in a "toll bypass" scenario. By implementing Cisco's QoS (Quality of Service) at each router, you are guaranteeing that the voice traffic maintains "voice" quality and your data traffic is still sent across the link in a timely, acceptable fashion. So, with virtually no impact to your data traffic, the company depicted would instantly begin saving $6000 a month on their long distance telephone charges.

Unified Messaging and Unified Communications

Building from our previous example, let's move on and talk about another beneficial technology that's available when implementing an AVVID solution—Unified Messaging and Unified Communications. Let's say that Kevin, in the Dallas location, was expecting a notification from Wayne, in the Detroit location, regarding a highly visible deal that was pending. By implementing a Unified Messaging/ Unified Communications solution, Kevin would be able to make the following scenario occur.

Kevin has to leave the office for his afternoon appointment, but is waiting quite anxiously for Wayne's notification. Kevin configures his Unified Messaging and Communications system to route all calls from Wayne to Kevin's cellular, but all other calls will be sent to voice mail. Also, Kevin programs his e-mail system to look for messages from Wayne. In the event that one arrives, that e-mail is converted to a voice mail (via text to speech) and forwarded to Kevin's cellular phone—leaving him the message. This way, Kevin is guaranteed a notification via whatever means Wayne used to get the information over to Kevin, whether it's e-mail or voice mail.

An AVVID Overview

When explaining the AVVID Architecture, we will be breaking down the pieces and parts that make up the entire solution set into hardware and software. It is important to understand that even though these hardware and software solutions can operate independently of each other, they are still considered a part of the AVVID family. This book outlines how each piece of hardware and each software application function independently, as well as how they interoperate with each other forming a completely converged solution.

Hardware

The AVVID architecture is currently made up of many individual pieces of hardware that can be used together to form and meet any business' required solution. The parts of AVVID range from the Cisco Systems, Inc. router product line, Catalyst switches, IP Telephony Phones, IP Telephony Call Manager Servers, Voice Trunks, Gateways, as well as the individual modules that can be integrated into these devices. It is important to understand that to build an AVVID network, you don't need a set number of pieces of hardware.

Let's review some of the hardware that can be used to construct an AVVID infrastructure.

Cisco Routers

Throughout the 1990's, Cisco has led the market share in the TCP/IP router marketplace. As the industry leader in router technology, Cisco Systems has continuously improved and added functionality to develop router technology. Today Cisco's routers can transmit time-sensitive data, as well as time-sensitive voice traffic over a TCP/IP network with an outcome that's more than acceptable! The Cisco router's new look—a "modular" approach—has increased the popularity of the, already, leading industries product. As a member of the AVVID family, the Cisco 1750, 2600 Series, 3600 Series, 7100 Series, 7200 Series, and 7500 Series all support a wide variety of voice modules that give you the functionality of Voice-Over IP technology as well as router-to-traditional PBX connectivity.

Cisco Catalyst Switches

The Cisco Catalyst switch product line has recently been expanded to support, not only high-speed data modules, but a wide variety of voice gateways as well as voice trunks. In addition, the proven data switches have also been redesigned to support special "voice" rated quality of service (QoS). The new models have also been designed to support a cost-effective "line power" model that allows the data switches to provide inline power to an IP Telephony handset over standard Category 5 cabling.

Cisco IP Telephones

At the endpoints, Cisco Systems is currently manufacturing and shipping a variety of Ethernet attached TCP/IP Phone handsets that convert voice to TCP/IP packets and run over industry-standard Category 5 cabling. There are multiple models of the Phone handsets to choose from, ranging from a basic, one-line waiting room handset to a six-line executive handset. The most recent addition to the IP telephony phone product line is an IP- based polycom phone.

Cisco Call Manager Server (MCS 7800)

The heart of IP Telephony is Cisco's Call Manager software solution. The Call Manager software replaces the traditional PBX and is run on Cisco's MCS Server hardware. The Call Manager software is currently running in the 3.x version, which has been much improved from the initial 2.0 version. The Call Manager server runs a modified version of Microsoft Windows 2000 on a Cisco certified platform and can be clustered to provide a larger call volume and a redundant telephone system.

Analog and Digital Gateways

To provide analog or digital connectivity to the PSTN, Cisco has developed an analog gateway device that can support any number of traditional PSTN analog and digital interfaces. The current offerings consist of a stand-alone VG200 Analog gateway as well as multiple modular solutions that interoperate and function within the MCS Server and several of the Catalyst switches.

Voice Trunks

To interface with traditional PBX technology, Cisco currently has a number of digital T1 and primary rate interface (PRI) trunks to choose from, ranging from modules that fit into routers and switches to individual modules that integrate into the Call Manager (MCS) server. Currently, there are a number of modules to choose from depending on whether you need standard T1 signaling, FT1 (fractional T1) or PRI support, but whatever option you're looking for, Cisco has a solution that will fit smoothly into your network.

Voice Modules

As mentioned previously, since Cisco has adopted the modular approach in their router and switch product line, there are multiple models of voice modules to choose from. The many Foreign Exchange Station (FXS), Foreign Exchange Office (FXO), and receive and transmit (E&M) (or ear and mouth) modules can be used in either a Cisco router or a Cisco Catalyst switch to interface with traditional telephony devices.

Software

Within the AVVID software portfolio, there are many, applications that we could touch on. Cisco has specialized in developing enhanced applications that focus on E-Commerce, Customer Care, Workforce Optimization, Supply Chain Management, E-Learning, and E-Publishing. In this book, we will focus on some of the core software products that are currently available. Those products consist of Cisco's Call Manager application, Soft Phone, Web Attendant, and the Active Voice messaging product. To find out more about Cisco's offerings in the software arena please visit the following URL: www.cisco.com/warp/public/779/ibs/.

Call Manager 3.0

Cisco's proprietary Call Manager application was developed as a means to provide functionality within an IP Telephony network. The Call Manager application provides the call setup and teardown functionality as well as call routing within an IP Telephony network. Currently, the Call Manager application runs on the Cisco MCS Server and can be clustered with multiple MCS Servers to provide a higher level of call volume or an added layer of redundancy.

Soft Phone

The soft phone application is an application developed to provide clients with a phone that runs within software. This application can be installed on any PC that connects to an IP Telephony network. Once installed, the end user (the person placing call on softphone) needs a regular handset to hear and speak, but dials the calls from a PC. The client or end user has the touch and feel of a regular handset except that it is running in software. This client can than receive and place IP Telephony calls over an Ethernet network infrastructure.

Web Attendant

The Web Attendant is an application that runs in conjunction with Call Manager, giving an office assistant a GUI/Web-based program that can be used for call pickup and transfer. Instead of the cumbersome hardware that some office assistance utilizes, the Web Attendant is a software application that runs on a desktop PC. When a call needs to be received or rerouted, the office assistant uses the "click and drag" method to successfully process the call.

Active Voice

Cisco has recently purchased a company by the name of Active Voice. They provide an enhanced unified messaging product that has been, and currently is, the industry leader. The Unity product provides a voice messaging and unified messaging (interaction with fax and e-mail) solution that functions on an IP Telephony network. This product, in conjunction with Cisco's IP Telephony hardware and Call Manager application, guarantees complete functionality of call processing, voice messaging and unified communications with interaction with email and fax.

The Converged Infrastructure

When discussing AVVID, it is important to understand what we mean by a *converged network*. It is also important to understand how a network can be converted from an "old school" infrastructure to a "new age" AVVID or *converged* infrastructure. When implementing an AVVID solution, most businesses or institutions are going to determine what is feasible based on resources and cost. They will review their annual budget and staffing to determine how quickly they can afford to move forward. There are some expenses that need to be addressed. If a company is looking to implement an infrastructure from the ground up, it is definitely cost-justifiable to implement a completely converged system. However, in a scenario where an existing (legacy) voice network, video system, and data infrastructure is in place, a migration approach is usually needed. Cisco has developed a phased approach that can and should be followed when converting to a converged infrastructure. Briefly, we'll take a look at the three stages that can be used when implementing an AVVID infrastructure.

NOTE

We'll be discussing AVVID implementations on a much more technical level throughout the rest of the book. The AVVID implementations illustrated in this chapter are intended provide a basic overview of how a converged infrastructure *can* be utilized an implemented.

Phase One—Legacy Voice System with Toll Bypass Benefits

The first phase when converting an existing network to a completely converged AVVID infrastructure focuses on your data network. In this phase, your existing voice network will remain in place, but you will be able to utilize your data infrastructure for benefits like toll bypass. Figure 1.2 is a diagram of an existing infrastructure that is not utilizing AVVID technology. It is a two-site network that currently uses a proprietary (legacy) voice system (as well as voice mail). There are trunks into the public switched telephone network (PSTN) for voice and video (BRI), and a T1 between locations for data-only traffic.

Figure 1.2 An Existing Infrastructure Before an AVVID Implementation.

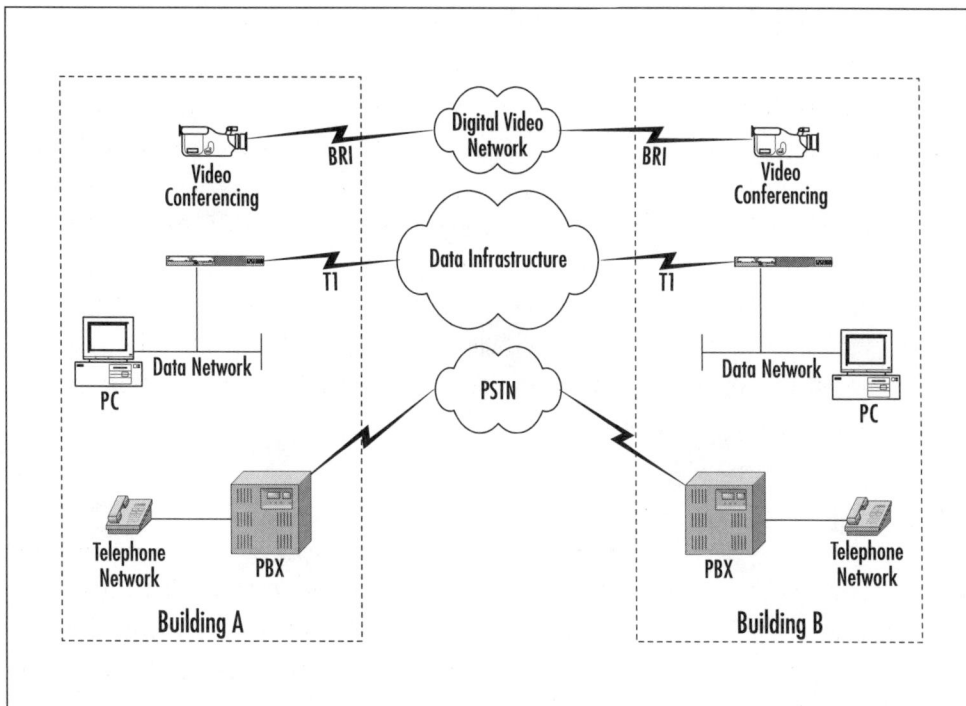

To begin the first part of the conversion phase (see Figure 1.3), the first step is to take advantage of Voice- and Video-Over IP. You will instantly gain the benefits of Voice-Over IP. This benefit is justifiable only if the two locations utilized PSTN long distance. This is done by implementing a gateway (module) into the Cisco router(s) or switch(es) located at the edges of the WAN. You will also need to convert your video network, which is usually H.320, into an Ethernet standard for video, which is H.323. The H.320 to H.323 conversion can be performed by implementing a device called a Video Terminal Adapter (VTA) at the edges of the existing video network. This lets your video system utilize the Ethernet network instead of utilizing your ISDN infrastructure.

Figure 1.3 Using Voice- and Video-Over IP

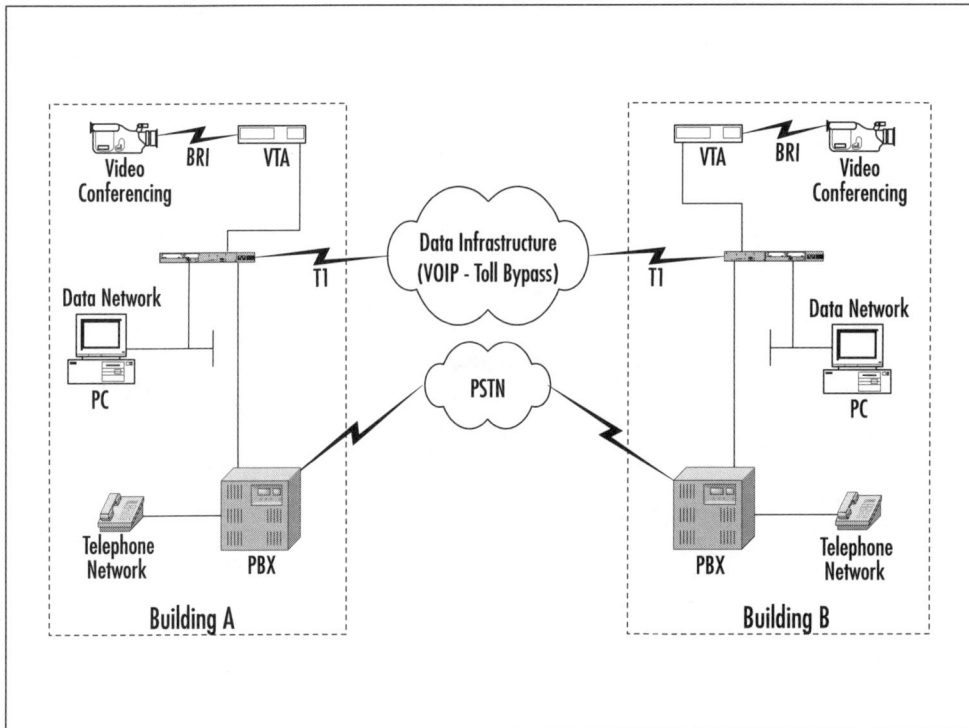

Phase Two—Legacy Voice System and IP Telephony in Parallel

The second phase in an AVVID conversion (shown in Figure 1.4) is to implement an IP Telephony network in parallel to the existing infrastructure. This is accomplished by adding a Call Manager server, IP Telephones, and an IP telephony gateway at each location. In this scenario, it is being displayed as a gateway/trunk module in a Layer 3 core switch. This phase allows you to utilize the IP Telephones and the Call Manager server for functionality, and allows you to maintain existing legacy telephones with their private branch exchange (PBX). This design still takes advantage of the toll bypass as well as gives the end user a migration path from legacy telephony to a complete IP telephony system. This phase and scenario will also require two separate voice mail systems—an Active Voice solution for the IP Telephony system and a proprietary voice mail system for existing telephones.

Figure 1.4 Implement an IP Telephony Network in Parallel to the Existing Infrastructure

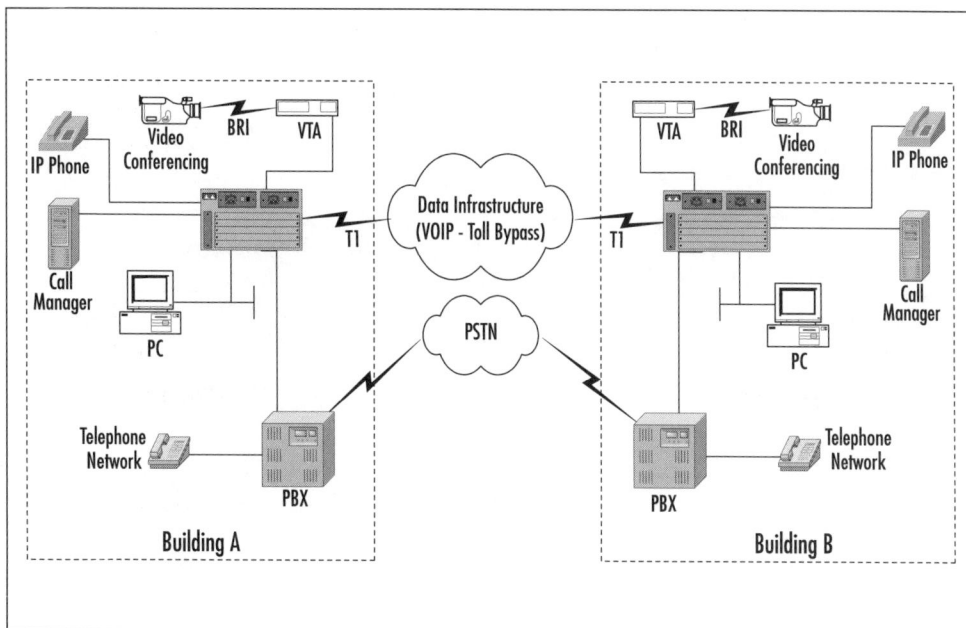

TIP

Depending on the type of existing voice mail system you had in place, it may be possible to interconnect the two systems together, allowing them to communicate with each other.

Phase Three—A Converged Infrastructure

The final phase is to remove the legacy voice system and utilize a 100 percent IP telephony/converged infrastructure. In Figure 1.5, we see a core Layer 3 switch with analog or digital PSTN access. We also see the Cisco Call Manager server (MCS) as well as IP Phone handsets and IP desktops. The video network is also being converted from H.320 to H.323 over Ethernet via the Video Terminal Adapter (VTA).

Figure 1.5 The Final Phase of an AVVID Migration

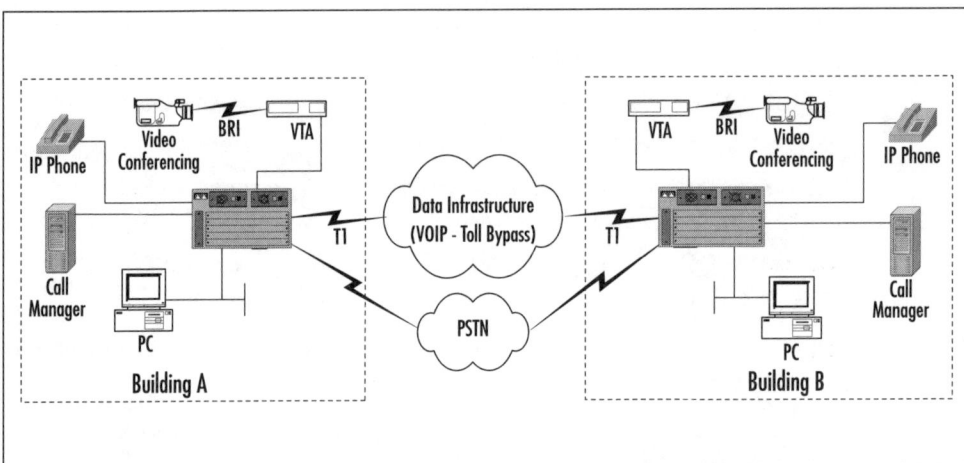

Summary

As you read through this book, you'll be introduced to different pieces of AVVID beginning with the hardware and then the software. It is important to look at the "bigger picture" and understand the overall solution to fully realize what AVVID brings to the table. There are many individual pieces to the AVVID family, but the real benefit is what a complete infrastructure will bring to your company or organization in the areas of reduced network redundancy, overall cost savings, employee productivity, as well as customer and employee satisfaction.

FAQs

Q: Do I need to purchase all new equipment to implement an IP Telephony network?

A: That depends on the model of routers and switches that you're currently using. If you are using models that have been purchased within the last 10 to 16 months, chances are that you're using a modular solution. In this case, you will probably only need a software upgrade as well as an additional module for voice support. If you are looking to power line phones, you can use your existing switched infrastructure, but you will need to provide an alternate method of phone power via the external patch panel or a standard power supply. You will then need to purchase the Cisco Call Manager application, the MCS Server that the application runs on and the number of needed IP Telephone handsets you require.

Q: I have heard the terms "IP Telephony" and "Voice over IP." Do they mean the same thing?

A: Not exactly. The term "IP Telephony" conceptually depicts a switched LAN, a Call Manager server and IP Phones within a building or local campus. "Voice over IP," on the other hand, is the term for taking voice traffic at one location, converting it over to TCP/IP packets and shipping it across a Wide-Area-Network (WAN) to another geographical location for the benefits of toll-bypass.

Q: Is anybody running Voice over IP or IP Telephony today?

A: Yes, in fact, statistics from Cisco, Lucent, and Nortel show that businesses or corporations that are in the process of implementing a new telephone system from the round up are choosing an IP Telephony solution because of the benefits in cost and support.

Q: If the Call Manager application is running on Windows 2000, what if the Operating System (OS) fails? We've all seen the "blue screen of death."

A: Cisco has developed a redundant model. If your system requires 100 percent uptime, a redundant Call Manager Server should be installed. Your phones can be configured to register and operate with multiple Call Manager servers anywhere in the network.

Q: If I have a two-site network with a Wide Area Network (WAN) connection between them do I need two separate Call Managers?

A: No, you don't *need* two separate Call Manager servers. As long as your IP Telephones have IP connectivity to the Call Manager (even over a WAN), your system will still operate smoothly. However, if the WAN link goes down, the remote phones will not be able to register and operate successfully.

Chapter 2

An Overview of AVVID Hardware Solutions

Solutions in this chapter:

- Understanding IP Phone Sets
- Cisco Routers (Voice over X Capable)
- Cisco Catalyst Switches
- Utilizing Media Convergence Servers
- An AVVID Video Hardware Overview
- The AVVID Telephony Infrastructure
- Web Cache Engine Technologies
- Maximizing Hardware Using QoS

Introduction

Although the AVVID solution is more than just hardware, this chapter outlines the routers, switches, trunks, gateways, and other hardware accessories that currently make up the AVVID product line. Cisco Systems, Inc. provides an innovative standardization of equipment, which can be assembled to interact with other vendors' solutions. As components that make up the architecture, hardware will typically dictate the interaction and capabilities of the services that it supports.

Whether referring to the physical linking of technologies, the ability to support a directed flow of data, or the capacity to stream-line the communications aspects of a business, standardization is too commonly overlooked and ignored. Unlike other vendors, which have entered proprietary solutions that addressed a single configu-ration or solution, Cisco offers an infrastructure by which all com-ponents specified by the AVVID design can interact. Traditionally, companies form partnerships in order to achieve this level of inter-action; however in this case, Cisco has purchased or owns most proponents of its technology.

When choosing a hardware solution, your considerations should go beyond the simple contemplation of a few desirable features. Frequently the optimal approach is to go with the solution that offers the best long-term usage. Take, for example, the number of companies that built the core infrastructure based on 3Com tech-nology. While an inexpensive and functional competitor to Cisco, 3Com simply did not have the capabilities to compete in the core infrastructure arena. Those with lagging technology now face having to migrate to a solution such as Cisco's. Looking to the future with the assumption that Voice over IP and video integration with data will be important, Cisco's AVVID is the right solution.

The hardware and functional capabilities of a device define its capabilities and acceptance within the user community. Selecting the right solution and equipment for a given job is equal in importance to the skills used to deploy them. To summarize, Cisco AVVID voice and video solutions enable you to do the following:

- Deploy IP-enabled business applications
- Implement a standards-based open architecture
- Migrate to a converged network in your own timeframe

Not to preach the word of Cisco, but a network architecture is not something that any company will want to implement on a regular basis. Cisco's AVVID is an innovative infrastructure that drives technology and expandability. To summarize, when selecting a technology solution, be sure to examine the company behind that technology to make sure that your investment is sound and that it has the capacity for enterprise design.

NOTE

The AVVID solution is continuously being enhanced and modified. It is important to realize that some of these products may be modified or replaced with newer technology as the AVVID architecture matures.

Understanding IP Phone Sets

IP-enabled phones provide unified telecommunications and data systems that can easily be installed, managed, and expanded by IT personnel. Unlike traditional phones, IP-enabled phones can be managed better according to routing protocols, available bandwidth, and inherent network fault tolerance. Aside from usage inside the office, using IP-enabled phones to extend the office with true call forward (by IP address) is another major factor in why you might want to choose an AVVID telephony solution. It enables a company to fully integrate field home users to their office without incurring additional expenses.

IP phone sets vary greatly between manufacturers. Cisco does produce its own, but many more manufacturers are in the process of creating compatible units. These units offer a number of promises that vary according to model. For instance, low-end models offer phone support with a built-in 10 Mbps hub to link a PC or other Ethernet device. Higher-end models support 100 Mbps perhaps via switch and may include a camera or optional USB interface.

However, without looking too far into the eventual technology, phones, regardless of their features, are now classified into two categories—those that use inline power and those that rely on an external source. Of these phones, Cisco supports a first-generation series by use of an external power source, while its second-generation phone can use either an inline or an external power source.

Cisco's First-Generation IP Telephones

Cisco's first-generation IP telephones have been discontinued; however, they can still be found in the market place. Overall, the first-generation phones are very similar to their second-generation replacements, with the exception of an inability to use inline power, less functionality, and a few minor programming differences. An import point to remember is that usage, troubleshooting, and compatibility remain constant between both first- and second-generation IP telephone sets and that an understanding of how first-generation equipment works is still valid for the second-generation equipment. One of Cisco's core technologies introduced in the first-generation phones is efficient use of network resources. For example, if neither person in a conversation is talking, no data is sent. To give the users the feel that the conversation is continuing and to sound less like a radio, however, Cisco deploys a comfort noise-generation technique that is enabled and disabled though voice activity detection (VAD) programming. On all Cisco AVVID phones, calls can be made to regular telephones or to an IP-enabled systems using applications such as Microsoft NetMeeting with support for H.323 protocol.

The first-generation IP telephone defines primary two sets—the 30 VIP and the 12 series, which both require the use of external power supplies. The 30 VIP phone is designed for high-intensity use, whereas the 12 series is meant to be placed in areas of lower use, such as in break rooms or for personnel who do not utilize phone resources as much as others. In short, these phones are very similar to each other with the exception of the number of buttons for convenience functionality, as explained in the following sections.

Cisco 30 VIP/SP+ IP Telephones

The Cisco 30 VIP IP phone represents the flagship of Cisco first-generation handsets. This phone offers 26 programmable buttons in addition to four fixed buttons used for transfer, display, hold, and redial. As you would expect, this phone is the ideal executive office and operator switchboard control for welcoming calls into your office. This unit boasts a number of additional features, such as a speakerphone (with acoustic cancellation), volume control, automatic redial, adjustable ring tone/volume, out-of band dual-tone multifrequency signaling (DTMF), a contrast-adjustable, 40-character 5/8-inch two-line display, and compatibility with both headsets and hearing-aid peripherals.

From the data communications standpoint, the Cisco 30 VIP IP phone appears as a device connected to an integrated two-port 10 Mbps Ethernet hub that offers support for RJ-45 cabling. One port of the hub is used directly for the phone while the other can be used for a PC, printer, or other Ethernet device. Regardless of the switch support that these phones plug into, if a PC is using the RJ-45 port on the phone, it will have a maximum throughput of 10 Mbps half duplex.

As a network device, the 30 VIP IP phone is IP enabled utilizing either a dynamic host configuration protocol (DHCP) address or one that is statically defined. Once on the network, voice traffic for this unit is processed through a G.711/G723.1 audio compression codec (coder/decoder) providing an efficient use of network resources.

Cisco 12 Series IP Telephones

The Series 12 (S, SP, SP+) IP telephone set is the junior version of the 30 Series IP phone. The primary difference between the two phones is the number of programmable buttons. The 12SP + IP phone is designed for use by common employees or office workers who do not need the additional functionality that 30 buttons provide. In some instances, these phones are placed in break rooms or lobbies for a cheap, compatible telecommunications add-on. Other than the buttons, there are no major differences between these phones.

Utilizing First-Generation Capabilities and Features

Cisco's IP phones require Cisco Call Manager to be installed on an IP network. Call Manager is the network equivalent of a PBX, which is used to direct calls and enable IP phone functionality. Because the phones can be configured via DHCP or statically, there is no need to co-locate all or any of the phones with the Call Manager system. IP simply allows telephone communications, provided a route exists.

In setting up an IP phone on a Cisco AVVID network, the most important step is either to define the phones to be automatically registered with the Call Manager system or to manually add the phones one by one. Phones that are added automatically will take the next available phone extension number. These configuration items that are designated to a phone can be modified, deleted, or re-added manually.

The first-generation phone will communicate effectively over any Ethernet media via switch or hub. Because the phone is a 10 Mbps hub itself, if the PC is to be coupled through the phone, there are no speed requirements for the network other than a minimum of 10 Mbps, although a switch is recommended. If a Cisco switch is to be used, the IP switch that manages calls should have PortFast enabled; otherwise, an extremely slow registration with the Call Manager will occur.

Testing and Troubleshooting an IP Phone

Once a phone has been plugged in, it will initialize its startup processes. During the startup phase, the phone will show a message, such as *Configuring VLAN*, *Configuring IP*, *Configuring CM List*, *Connecting*, *Registering*, and *Requesting Template*. Once the startup has completed, the phone will display the date and time along with the extension number assigned to the unit.

You can test the phone to verify that it is communicating correctly by pressing the star key "*" twice. If the phone is functioning correctly, you should see a status of 0x04800. If a phone is not registered in the Call Manager database, it will be unable to function resulting in an error, such as those listed in Table 2.1.

Table 2.1 Common Error Messages for Non-Registered Phones

Message	Issue
Resetting E3	Could not establish a TCP session with a Call Manager.
Resetting E4	Failed to obtain a DHCP address/No Stored address in phone's memory.
Resetting E5	StationRegisterRejectMessage request received from Call Manager.
Resetting E6	Invalid or damaged configuration file.
Resetting E7	Unable to resolve TFTP server Name (DNS).
Resetting E8	StationResetID request received from Call Manager.
Resetting E9	Received broadcast address via DHCP for DNS, default gateway, host, or TFTP.
Resetting 73	Same as E3, but indicates that the phone is likely trying to communicate to the secondary NIC not the Primary. This is an issue at the Call Manager.
Connected to Wrong Call Mgr?	This is not an error. This occurs when there is only a single phone connect to a call manager.

The issues that appear in Table 2.1 tend to be similar between first- and second-generation phones, regardless of the error message. Other issues with IP phones tend to be more logistically situated, such as the relocation of users. For example, if a user on the fifth floor of your building relocates to another office and takes his or her phone, the IP address, if configured statically, may be on the wrong network, causing a communications failure. You can verify this situation by pressing the star key "*" twice and looking for a status code of 04025. In the event that the static address was updated manually but still shows this status code, it is more than likely that the configuration did not take due to pushing an invalid key sequence.

Network issues also extend into oversubscription of lines. For this very reason, it is recommended that a management tool such as CiscoWorks be used. CiscoWorks allows an administrator to monitor traffic so that an overabundance of dropped packets, collisions, or bottlenecks does not occur. Network problems such as these could result in dropped calls or jitter that sounds similar to an echo but is more likely than not an issue with Quality of Service functionality on the IP network. Unfortunately, there are limits to CiscoWorks, and some items, such as phone functionality and correct routing, can be tested only by using a phone and dialing the extension to verify that proper routing (call) exists in the Call Manager. Depending on your hardware, you may also find that a call route is set up in Call Manager, but it fails to connect. In the cases where a route exists but communications fail, the issue is likely due to a codec incompatibility. For instance, the IP phone supports both G.711 and G723.1, but the Cisco IOS gateway defaults to G.729. In order to function with the IP phones, the gateway must use one of the codecs supported by the phone. Not all codecs are available in all versions of IOS. For further details about compatibility with a specific IOS version visit the Cisco Web site.

On occasion, it is possible that you will find a phone that exhibits a popping or crackling noise. In most cases, this is caused by inconsistent power. Cisco recommends trying an external power adapter to correct this type of issue. Sometimes the crackling noise is also an echo that appears on the line. As with a power issue, this is usually a hardware issue, such as a dirty line or interference in the line (usually cause by other high-powered equipment, such as a vacuum cleaner).

Further details regarding Call Manager software configuration are covered later in Chapter 4.

Using an IP Telephone

Use of an IP phone is just like using any other phone: The mute button mutes, the hold button places calls on hold, the SPKR button turns on and off the speaker phone. Special functions such as call park are activated simply by pressing the call park button and entering a call park number, which allows anyone on the IP network to take the call by simply dialing the parked number. A call can be parked for up to three minutes before it is returned to the extension that parked it. Typically this type of phone system is compared to a Nortel or Lucent system, where this functionality is quite common.

Other features, such as transfer and forward, work in a similar manner, with the receiver off the hook or with the speakerphone on: Simply press the related button and enter the extension to which calls should be sent. When call forwarding is enabled, a light will indicate this status. Simply pick up the phone and push the forward option to disable call forwarding.

Perhaps the only thing not intuitive about the use of these phones is the contrast adjustment of the LCD screen, which changes by using the volume button while the phone is on the hook. Table 2.2 shows a comparative functional comparison of the 12 series and VIP 30 series phones.

Table 2.2 A comparison between the 12 series and the VIP 30 series phones

Function	VIP 30 Button	12 Series Button
Select Line	1 to 4	1 to 2
Call Park	5	10
Redial	6 / Fixed	3

Continued

Table 2.2 Continued

Function	VIP 30 Button	12 Series Button
Speed Dial	8 to 13, 22 to 25	4 to 6
Messages Waiting	14	11
Call Forwarding	15	9
Conference	16	12
Hold	Fixed	7
Transfer	Fixed	8
Display	Fixed	Volume

NOTE

In second-generation phones, more functionality is controlled though the LCD screen rather than a dedicated button.

Cisco's Second-Generation IP Telephones

Cisco's second generation of IP telephones is built on the technology of their predecessors, incorporating standard features, such as hearing-aid handset support with ADA-compliant volume controls, support for standard G.711 and G.729a audio compression codecs, H.323/Microsoft NetMeeting support, and DHCP/BootP client capabilities. The main difference between first- and second-generation phones, however, is the fact that second-generation phones offer better programming capabilities and may be powered either though their CAT-5 cabled connection or with an external power adapter.

For second-generation phones, inline power functionality simply replaces the external adapter and supplies 48 volts of DC through the switch. Unlike a regular phone, however, which the telephone company (telco) powers, a switch must be enabled to do so with special hardware, which will be discussed later in this chapter in the section on inline power.

Cisco 7910 and 7910+SW IP Telephones

The entry line to Cisco's second-generation IP telephones, the 7910 and 7910+SW, provides a low-price unit for areas where phone usage and functionality are less of a need. Typical implementations of the 7910 series are placements in shop areas, lobbies, break rooms, and so forth. Unlike all other phones Cisco has offered, the 7910 series phone provides only the convenience of a call monitor button to listen to call progress and perform on-the-hook dialing. No two-way speakerphone support is offered.

The key features of this phone are a new wider 24-character screen, plus four buttons statically defining hold, transfer, call park, and end call. The 7910 and 7910+SW phones are identical, with the exception that the 7910+SW offers a two-port 10/100 switch rather than a 10 Mbps hub.

Cisco 7940 IP Telephones

The 7940 IP telephone is Cisco's midlevel device that provides all of the capabilities of the 7910 series phone with an integrated two-port 10/100 switch and adds programming capabilities. The integrated switch natively supports 802.1q and gives network administrators the ability to assign both the phone and the user's PC to separate VLANs.

In addition to those features it has in common with the 7910, the 7940 also boasts a high-quality full-duplex Polycom speakerphone, 24-user configurable ring tones, and a (EIA/TIA) RS-232 serial interface for expanding to more lines or add-on equipment. The 7940 is an advanced phone set that is similar in nature to a computer rather than just an ordinary phone. Like a computer, the 7940 can be programmed so that its keys function as macros to perform any number of tasks. Furthermore, a navigation control allows a user to cycle though the 4.25x3-inch LCD menu to control different functions in the phone.

The highly flexible capabilities of this phone are due in great part to its menu features and pixel-based display. With an integrated screen, these phones have computer-like functionality and, as required, may be updated with newer firmware to expand their features. Unlike a router, which operates with TFTP, these phones are updated through Call Manager. Currently, the 7940 supports the following functionality controlled though the LCD menu:

- Message notification and message storing
- Direct-dial callback to numbers with Caller ID
- Directory information, such as services by Lightweight Directory Access Protocol 3 (LDAP3)
- Configuration settings, such as display contrast, ringer tone, handset, headset, ringer, and speaker volume
- Network configuration including DHCP and TFTP settings and network status
- Call status
- Information services, such as those provided by the system administrator using Extensible Markup Language (XML), such as stock market quotes, weather reports, company information, and so forth
- Online help with any of the above described functions

Cisco 7960 IP Telephones

The 7960 IP telephone is essentially the same as the 7940 with the exception that it includes six lines or speed dial buttons rather than two and may be set up using Session Initiation Protocol (SIP) in place of Call Manager.

SIP is a standard developed by the Internet Engineering Task Force (IETF) to define multimedia/voice conferencing over IP.

Operating at the application layer, SIP takes full advantage of the underlying IP stack to establish, maintain, and terminate communications. In practice, the SIP protocol is used to overcome network boundaries, allowing multiple users to communicate using the common set of combined functionality between all callers in a multicast configuration. Moreover, SIP is an intelligent communications protocol that offers the ability to dial e-mail addresses rather than phone numbers and provides explanations such as *line busy* or *call not answered* responses.

The 7960 is designed more as a choice phone for remote offices than anything else. Unlike the traditional IP telephone communications architecture, the 7960 IP phone operating over SIP needs only to have a Cisco router configured with a voice gateway to communicate to the PSTN; it can be configured to interoperate with virtually any IP-enabled structure.

Cisco 7935 IP Conference Station

The 7935 IP conference station is Cisco's answer to corporate needs for an all-encompassing solution to service meetings and conference events. Composed of a desktop architecture, Cisco's 7935 provides features similar to those of the 7910 telephone. The primary differences are, of course, in design for a speakerphone and lack of a handset. Cisco's 7935 provides a digital Polycom-designed speakerphone that utilizes three microphones to service a room in 360 degrees.

NOTE

Polycom is a third party to Cisco, but it is well-known for its high-quality speakerphone systems.

Like other Cisco phones, the 7935 provides a pixel-based LCD display for providing information such as date, time, name (if available), and phone number dialed. In a conference room layout, only a single line is required for both power and connectivity of the 7935, as with all second-generation phones. Cisco's 7935 allows users, when making presentations, to plug a laptop or other PC system into the network without having to pull wires from throughout the room. This functionality is attributed to the integrated 10/100 Fast Ethernet port and the fact that speakerphones are generally placed in a dedicated position in the middle of a conference table.

Utilizing Second-Generation Capabilities and Features

Second-generation phones are extremely similar in nature to their first-generation counterparts. With the expectation of expanded pro-gram capabilities and the integrated LCD pixel screen, these phones experience many of the same issues and test considerations as those mentioned previously.

While error messages tend to vary, the issues will be consistent with those of first-generation products. With respect to program-ming, however, second-generation phones can be slightly more of a challenge. The LCD on the phone opens an entire can of potential worms that can best be reviewed in looking at Cisco's documenta-tion online. Note that the Call Manager and its delivered set of attributes tend to be a driving factor toward second-generation phone configurations. Programming features will vary greatly depending on software levels of the phone and what a phone admin-istrator places in Call Manager.

Inline Power

Home phones are analogous for use of inline power, with the excep-tion of those that operate as a cordless handset charger, answering machine, and so forth. By using inline power, the telco is effectively independent of the power company's services and is capable of allowing telephone handsets to be positioned in areas where adding power would be logistically awkward. The theory behind the design is that having fewer wires appears cleaner, is easier to install, and is less problematic. In keeping with these ideals, inline-powered phones provide a clean and convenient adaptation of telephony and networking topologies.

Cisco offers the *Catalyst inline power patch panel* to provide an inline power solution. Offering 48-volt service up to 100 meters over standard CAT-5 cabling, the Catalyst inline power patch panel replaces a common passive patch panel solution. Because the Ethernet 802.3 solution does not provide for inline power, Cisco's panel offers an auto-discovery solution that determines if power is needed. Aside from the obvious power wiring advantage of not having to plug the phone into a power jack, a key consideration of this technology is the ability for the Catalyst inline power patch panel to be linked into a data center's UPS. By using a redundant power system, a corporation's telephone system is protected from outages that could otherwise take the phone system down. This design extends to the corporation the type of availability inherent to the telco. When we consider the possibly adverse situations that power problems can incur, it is no wonder that 24x7 shops place all vital systems on a UPS.

The Catalyst inline power patch panel was designed to augment existing switches that lacked inline power faculties to power phones. Each Catalyst inline power patch panel provides support for up to 48 stations via 96 RJ-45 ports. Effective as an intermediary between the computer and an actual Catalyst switch, one jack is used to connect to the end station while another is used to connect the network (via the switch). The most common application for the Catalyst inline power patch panel is inside a wiring closet to support devices on switches, such as the Catalyst 2900 and 1900 series.

Additional information regarding inline power will be presented later in this chapter in the sections on the Catalyst 4000 and 6000 series switches.

Understanding the External Patch Panel Power Option

With the exception of a newer wiring technology or perhaps a switch/hub device (for example, 802.3af support) that has the ability to both provide voltage and data on the same lines, external power sources need to fill this requirement.

As with any other network device, a power source is a requirement. In many environments, especially in manufacturing, where additional power outlets are seen as a poor option, this is a major drawback to this type of phone solution. Inline power and higher speeds, however, will become more economically viable as network equipment is replaced and economies of scale begin to take hold.

Overall, we will observe that inline-powered versus external-powered phones share the same argument as internal versus external modems—no one wants to use an extra power jack or put up with an additional cable. Without regard to this, each phone type has its place and proper usage in the enterprise. Figure 2.1 illustrates the layout of a typical 2600 Series router.

Figure 2.1 Cisco 2600 Series Router Layout

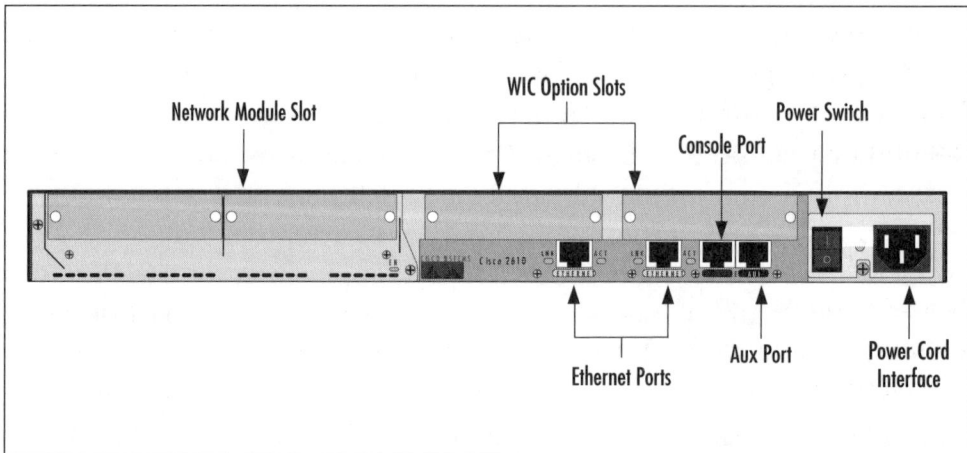

Cisco Routers (Voice over X Capable)

Cisco voice-enabled routers are more than simply IP-enabled devices that provide encapsulation and compression. In fact, these routers provide host capabilities to link both analog and digital telecommunication technologies together. Over the past several years, Cisco has made the commitment to expand its voice-enabled products onto many additional platforms. In the tradition of Cisco, as newer products become available, they will most likely follow the base design with improvements, such as better compression, variable samplings, emulation for incompatible phone systems, and so forth. The basics laid out in this section will remain a constant, though.

Cisco offers highly flexible solutions for which a modular router can support any number of interface types, software functionality, and protocols. This flexibility has made Cisco the world leader in network telecommunications technologies, but this market position has come at the price of consumer confusion. To address this issue, Cisco offers hardware support for consumers, resellers, and partners at 800-553-NETS as well as through the Internet.

Cisco's Web site offers a configuration tool to assist in selecting compatible router components and software. Cisco's configuration tool can be located at its Web site at WWW.CISCO.COM; click on *Order Information* and assistance, then select *Configuration tool* from the menu. The direct link to this Web page currently is www.cisco.com/pcgi-bin/front.x/newConfig/config_root.pl.

Before we can dive into Cisco's current voice-capable routers, let's first review the technologies behind the options so that as we examine each product, each add-on is fully understood.

Understanding Memory Usage

In the Cisco world of routing, there are essentially two types of memory that every router contains—flash and RAM. Flash memory is essentially nonvolatile memory similar in nature to a hard drive. This memory is used to store the IOS software image that governs the router. Various IOS images are available for each router. These software images include functionality ranging from simple IP to that which enables support for VPNs. Without knowing the future use and capabilities of routers or how a company's telecommunications will transition, it is impossible to give a predetermined size to the flash. Experience tells us that it is usually better to go with a larger flash size than recommended. A larger flash means you have the ability to store more information and creates an option if the router is to later utilize an image, which requires the additional space. Also, in some cases such as update validation, it is desirable to store multiple images; however, doing so requires additional space. The only solution is to work with a larger capacity flash.

Once an image is selected for its functionality, it is loaded either by Trivial File Transfer Protocol (TFTP) or via a very slow serial upload through the console port. When the router is then booted, it will decompress the image and load the router IOS software image program into RAM. The IOS program will then enable interfaces, load configurations, routing tables, and so forth. As with flash memory, there really is no true test to say how much memory should be used. Unlike Microsoft Windows, which has the ability to write to a swap file on a hard drive, thus extending its physical memory into virtual memory, a Cisco router either will have the memory to carry out its functions or will report failures. Because it is easier to purchase and install additional memory in advance of use, it is again recommended that a larger amount of RAM be used even if its use is not immediately foreseen.

In either case, when a router is purchased from Cisco or one of Cisco's authorized partners, the vendor will validate the purchase by running your configuration through a configuration validation tool. This tool will suggest a memory size. Regardless of this specification, it is highly recommended that the cost of the next-size memory module be examined. In most cases, the price differential is not prohibitive enough to warrant purchasing the leanest configuration possible.

Remember that one of the greatest considerations for your company should be growth. If, for example, Cisco releases a new IOS that corrects problems or stabilizes interactions with other vendors and that IOS update requires more flash and more memory, equipment will have to be replaced. Unless you are the gambling type or unless you do not mind replacing hardware in the event of necessary updates, more RAM and flash should be considered.

The Importance of a Modular Chassis

Part of the ever-changing world of networks is the technology that we use to interconnect our devices. As we consider the diversity of services provided by the telecommunications industry, where we have ATM (Asynchronous Transfer Mode), T1, ISDN (Integrated Services Digital Network) PRI (Primary Rate Interface), voice, Frame Relay, and other services, we quickly realize that fixed configuration devices are a poor choice. In some instances, such as where a specific task needs to be accomplished by a device, it is more than likely that an investment's protection far outweighs a small price difference for modularity.

As a company grows, it is often the case that a "fork lift" (cycle out all equipment) replacement is required to meet the needs of expansion. This problem is commonly due to having inadequate capabilities when utilizing existing equipment. For example, a router may come with an integrated 56K WAN interface; however, due to expansion, you might perhaps need fractional T1 features. With this said, a modular chassis provides a great advantage in adapting to these situations without requiring that you replace the entire piece of equipment. If multiple interfaces were needed and a router with multiple expansion slots were purchased, it could be stated that a modular device also supports scalability. Think of it in terms of a PC. When you purchase a PC, adding different cards, such as network adapters, augments its features and customizes the system much in the same way that a modular router does. When a component in a PC fails, typically that failed component is replaced. Likewise, in a router, it is just as effective to work with a field-replacable component rather than replacing an entire unit.

Cisco takes modularity one step further than a simple ability to exchange boards and scale equipment; it has also designed a number of its routers to operate with a common interface so that options are interchangeable. For example, Cisco 1750, 2600, and 3600 series routers share common boards that any of these routers can use. The advantage, of course, is that this feature helps to promote economies of scale, great availability of product, and lower costs. An illustration of the 2600 series modularity is shown in Figure 2.2.

Figure 2.2 The 2600 Series Router Modularity

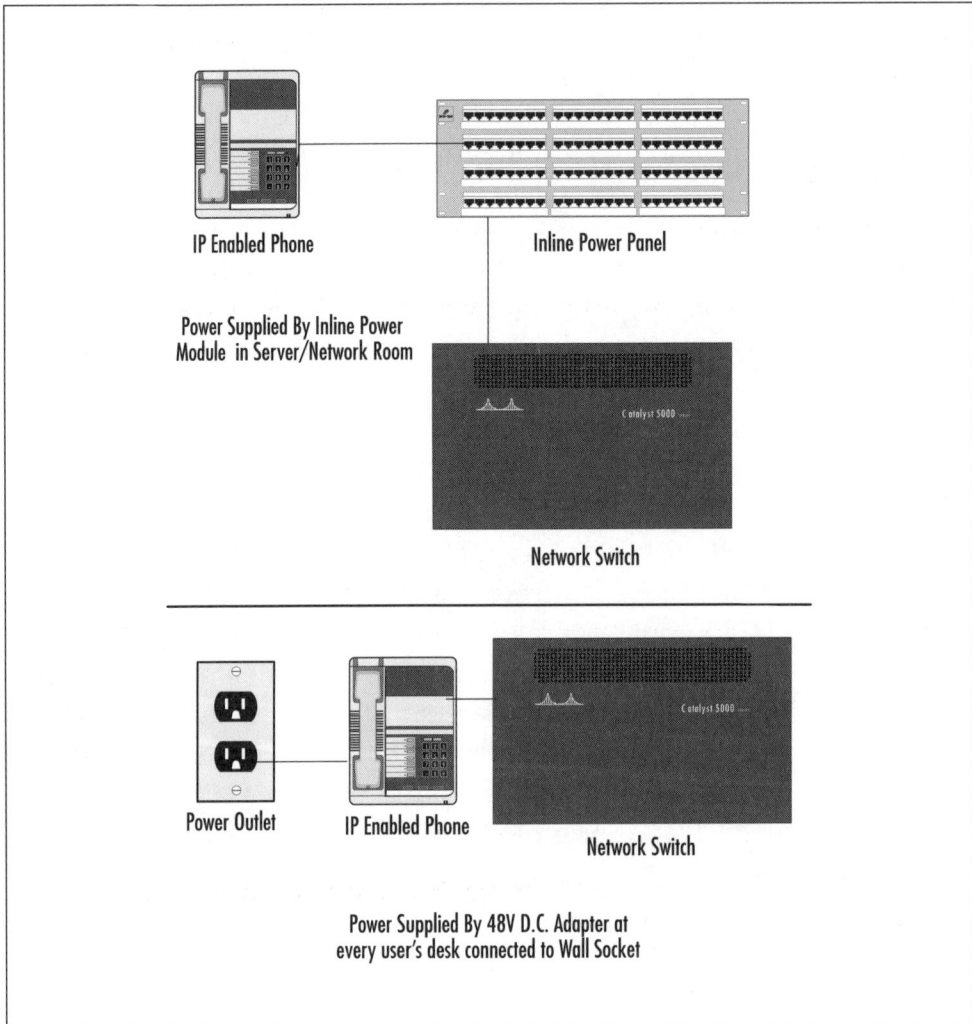

Cisco produces two types of modular options—network modules and interfaces cards. Network modules are carriers that simply adapt interface cards to the router. Interface cards, however, are the actual ports and interfaces that can be placed inside a network module. Commonly interface cards are either described as WAN Interface Cards (WICs) or Voice Interface Cards (VICs). A WIC is simply an adapter that provides support for a particular data communications technology, such as ISDN, Frame Relay, and so on. VICs, on the other hand, deal with verbal communications such as those capabilities listed in the following section on voice and video interfaces.

Utilizing Voice and Video Interfaces

Voice is divided into two categories: analog and digital. Analog interfaces are common to most homes that use a service described as POTS, or Plain Old Telephone Service. In multiline businesses where only a few phone lines are used, it is common that multiple POTS lines are used and are terminated into a customer-owned analog private branch exchange (PBX).

In analog communications, typical configurations are one telephone line to one voice call. In Cisco terms, however, analog interfaces are sold in accordance with a number of channels, where each channel can support two analog phone calls. As you might imagine at this point, given the number of phone system manufacturers—Nortel, Samsung, Lucent/AT&T, Toshiba, Rolm, and others—how can any of them ever be configured to interact with a remote system over a third-party system? The answer is simple—standardization. Currently there are three main types of analog interface ports. These standardized ports are outlined here:

- **FXS port** Foreign Exchange Station is an interface that connects to any standard phone, fax, or modem via an RJ-11 jack. This type of port supplies ring, voltage, and dial tone.

- **FXO port** Foreign Exchange Office is an interface that is used to link to the public switched telephone network (PSTN) via the telephone company's central office (CO). Like the FXS port, this interface uses an RJ-11 interface. The key difference between an FXS and an FXO port is that an FXO port can be directed to the PSTN central office or to an analog station port on a PBX.

- **E&M port** Ear and mouth (Also know as a Send and Receive or DC5) is a port configuration that allows trunking typically between switches or a switch and a network. Unlike FXO and FXS, the E&M port utilizes an RJ-48 adapter for connections to a PBX. The connection to the PBX is commonly referred to as tie lines or trunk lines. The E&M port offers availability in both analog and digital interfaces (E1 and T1 lines).

NOTE

Digital line provisions are typically handled by using tie lines or by using trunking technology, discussed later.

In practical use, if our voice solution called for phone-to-phone or fax-to-fax connectivity, we would utilize an FXS-to-FXS configuration. On the other hand, if we were looking to implement a long line PBX extension, such as a phone that is remote to a PBX, we might utilize a combination of an FXS-to-FXO setup. Suppose, however, that this same configuration were between two PBXes; the configuration would then be an FXO-to-FXO adaptation for each required channel (set of two lines). Considering the costs of utilizing an FXO port if the phone switches supported the configuration, an E&M-to-E&M configuration would provide better efficiency in that it could support trunking.

The video component is much more convoluted than the audio side in that port standardization is difficult to define and a number of compression and encoding technologies are available to convert video signal to digital transmissions and must include audio. For the most part, this interaction between systems is defined by the supported codec and compression method used. For example, two common standards that are prominent with Cisco equipment are H.320 and H.323. Simply put, H.320 is an ITU-T standard for video conferencing across circuit-switched connections, such as T1 and ISDN lines. The H323 is simply an extension ITU-T standard that builds on H.320 by enabling video conferencing across packet-switched networks, such as LANs and the Internet.

Video interfaces come in a number of form factors that can be linked to their software control counterparts. Depending of the video device used, interfaces may be propriety to the camera they support or may be a standard, such as an RCA type interface. In most implementations, video systems are typically linked by a standard interface that allows easy transitions to digital conversion. Video interfaces are commonly hosted on a PC platform system; however, if a non-PC video device can handle an interfacing to the network and its protocols, this is not a requirement. All conversions between video transmissions to network transmissions are handled by the hardware device. Once on the network wire, data can be assigned to a transport queue, as can any data.

Voice Compression

The modern telephone company provides a 56 Kbps analog line, which is used for voice communications. This line is linked throughout the public switched telephone network by digital switches that carry data on these lines from caller to receiver. The analog telephone has been designed to provide audio transmissions for signals ranging from 300 to 3000Hz. Within this audio range, only a small percentage of the actual allotted transmission range is used. Of the range that is used, only a small percentage the audio tones being sent are actually required for a clear verbal communication between people.

Using a near instantaneous lossy compression and decompression algorithm, Cisco is capable of reducing voice conversations down to 12 Kbps maximum network utilization in full duplex. Lossy compression is a method by which non-required data is thrown away so that only essential information is sent. If too much compression is used, verbal quality is lost and conversations begin to sound flat—somewhat of a digital simulation of two soup cans and some string. The broadest application of lossy compression is with music such as with WAV files, which are converted to MP3 files. Again, the quality will vary depending on the number of cycles per second that are maintained for voice transmission.

Cisco deploys two types of digital-signal-processor (DSP) voice compression modules (VCMs)—DSP VSP VCMs and DSP high=density VCMs. The DSP VSP VCM has been discontinued from Cisco's product line and supported only analog calls, while its replacement, the DSP high-sensity VPM, supports both digital and analog. Each VCM is available in a differing number of supported DSPs.

NOTE

For all Cisco VCMs, two channels per DSP are supported.

Utilizing Trunk Cards

In a common wide area network configuration, routers are linked to each other directly via CSU/DSU connected to a leased, frame, or other similar technology. This is only a partial truth, though, in dealing with telecommunications. In a number of environments, data communications can also take place indirectly by using bandwidth governed by a phone system that is perhaps linked by leased lines between PBXs. Essentially, the PBX or phone system switch defines a channel or a certain number of channels are combined into a trunk that is used for data rather than voice traffic. Under this situation, a trunk card is used to place data over a phone network originally configured for voice traffic, effectively creating a situation where the WAN connection is provided by the phone switch.

Those who are new to telephony technologies usually are not aware of this, but larger businesses with more than 20 lines (not counting extensions) typically utilize one or more T1 lines to provide communications to their in-house phone switch. Use of a T1 line provides a clean and manageable wiring assembly in the writing closet and reduces the costs. For example, suppose that we worked for a 480-person telemarketing company where up to 240 people could be on the phone at any one given time. Could you imagine running 240 lines into your switch? Ideally, the 240 lines can be consolidated into 10 T1 lines.

Before we move forward on this topic, however, it is important to note that a T1 is a generic line specification for 1.544 Mbps, and it comes with many provisions, with differing connections, dial types, cabling schemes, interface types, signal or framing types, and more. Cisco's vast hardware functionality and number of trunk interfaces are available to suit the needs of your PBX's required interface.

MCS 3810

The MCS 3810 is Cisco's all-encompassing flexible solution for media convergence. This router was Cisco's first unit to provide AVVID support, and it is tightly integrated with Cisco IGX.

While common at facilities where AVVID has been deployed in early configurations, this router is no longer very popular as it is too expensive and has little advantage over routers such as the 2600 series at its cost point and throughput (about 15,000 packets per second) or the 3600 for an equivalent cost.

The MCS 3810 combines switched voice, LAN traffic, and legacy data over Frame Relay or leased lines at speeds up to those of T1/E1. As with most of Cisco's routers, the 3810 is based on IOS and offers available support for Voice over IP, Voice over ATM, IPSec, and H.323 compatibility. The only major consideration about using this product is the fact that it does not offer security, such as a firewall or VPN support. While the MCS 3810 is positioned as a media convergence server, the IP Plus IOS software must be purchased in order to support voice, as it is required on all other Cisco products, which are used for this purpose.

In summary, the MCS 3810 provides options for redundant power supplies, up to 64 megabytes of RAM, use of a 16- or 32-megabyte flash depending on the IOS image selected, up to 6 analog voice ports, T1/E1 digital voice connectivity, up to four BRI ports, a serial digital video RS366 port, or six DSP voice compression module (no longer sold), two or six high-density voice compression module, and multiflex trunk options for T1 or E1 with RJ48 or BNC Interface with an optional BRI S/T interface.

NOTE

Interfaces to the MCS 3810 are proprietary and are physically not compatible with those of other routers.

The 26xx Router Series

The 2600 series of routers consists of eight different models fulfilling three different performance levels. All 2600 series routers include two WIC slots, a network module slot, and an advanced integrated module (AIM) slot and are available with AC, DC, and redundant power supplies. For the most part, the distinction between each model of the 2600 series is the number of integrated slots and the packets per second that the router is capable of processing, as outlined in Table 2.3.

Table 2.3 A comparistion of the 2600 Series Routers

Model	Market Position	Integrated Ports	Packets per Second
2610	Entry Level	one 10 Mbps Ethernet	15000
2611	Entry Level	two 10 Mbps Ethernet	15000
2612	Entry Level	one 10 Mbps Ethernet one Token-Ring	15000
2613	Entry Level	two Token Ring	15000
2620	Mid Level	one 10/100 Mbps Ethernet	25000
2621	Mid Level	two 10/100 Mbps Ethernet	25000
2650	High Performance	one 10/100 Mbps Ethernet	37000
2651	High Performance	one 10/100 Mbps Ethernet	37000

The 2600 series shares a compatible module design with the 1600, 1700, and 3600 series; however, only the 2600 and 3600 series are capable of voice support. Due to the high flexibility of IOS, the 2600 series routers can accommodate over 50 different types of WICs including ISDN basic rate interface/primary rate interface (BRI/PRI), ATM, IMA (multiple T1 bound together), and T1/E1 with integrated channel service unit/data service unit (CSU/DCU).

The option for modular WICs allows a common base router to be purchased and adapted to any environment or connectivity required. Effectively, a 2600 series router can be configured as a firewall, multiservice voice and data, serial, or ATM process, all from one unit.

For AVVID-specific use, the 2600 series router supports both analog and digital telephony connections. Analog ports are designed so that they are one port to one phone line; however, a two-port voice module can be used to support two VICs (voice interface cards), of which each provides two E&M, FXO, or FXS ports. Essentially, up to four analog lines can be supported on a single 2600 series router.

Environments that require more than four lines of analog support require the use of a digital interface (provided the PBX supports it). Digital connections provide T1/E1 type links in either to a telephone switch. These digital ports are available either as single or dual ports providing 24- or 48-line support for T1s and 30- or 60-line support for E1s. With the exception of the high-density voice module spare (no-T1 interface) all digital voice interfaces include compression and DSP functionality.

Many companies have in place voice communications that are established over their own dedicated T1 lines. A perfect example of this is department stores that commonly call back to headquarters or other branches through their own telephone network, but need only a few terminals for data services, such as price lookups and adjustments to their registers. For this type of environment, the 2600 series router provides multiflex trunks in one and two RJ-48 port capacities, providing a combination of both WAN and voice interface cards. A dual version of this card assists companies in the migration of data or voice-only networks to one that is fully integrated. In summary, a multiflex trunk interface provides the following:

- Fully managed CSU/DSU from data communications (WIC)
- Packet voice communications via T1 to a PBX or central office (VIC)
- Drop and insert multiplexer with integrated DSU/CSU
- Optional G.703 support

Once it has been determined which modules are to be used in the router, an IOS software image must be selected to support those interfaces. IOS software varies greatly in size and its use of resources. As such, memory and flash requirements will vary according the each router configuration. Cisco IOS for the 2600 series router includes options for the following:

- Voice support
- Firewall
- DES/triple DES encryption
- APPN (advanced peer-to-peer networking)
- IP, IPX, AppleTalk, DECnet, and SNA protocol support
- H.323 MCM

Note that voice support requires a minimum IOS software of IP + and that the Enterprise version of Cisco's IOS includes protocol support for IP, IPX, and AppleTalk.

Although the voice modules provide data compression through the DSP, the data portion of your network data will not be compressed. This has the unfortunate effect of bottlenecking WAN links and, in some cases, jeopardizing the throughput and quality of voice communications despite Quality of Service (QoS). For this dilemma, the choice is either to expand the capacity of the line or purchase a data compression AIM option. The purchase of the data compression

AIM option provides a better, more efficient use of WAN links, reducing the monthly reoccurring cost while offloading compression from the router CPU, producing up to 8 Mbps of throughput.

The 36xx Router Series

The 3600 series routers functionally are identical to the 2600 series with the exception of greater capacity and faster processing. The 2600 series router, while powerful, is not considered a core operations router. It was designed to be placed at the edge of a given network so that it can perform support functions such as those needed at a field office of an enterprise environment. In an enterprise environment, however, a core routing technology is required that has the capacity and speed to service all interlinked systems. Like the 2600, all 3600 series routers are available with AC, DC, and redundant power supplies.

The 3600 series is composed of three classes—the 3620, 3640, and 3660. The 3620 offers two expansion module slots while the 3640 provides four. Respectively, the 3620, 3640, and 3660 perform at a rate of 15,000, 40,000 and 100,000 packets per second. Unlike the WIC slots that are available on the 2600 series, the slots of the 3600 series routers take a carrier card that provides plug-in support for network modules that provide LAN, WAN, voice, and other services. More than 70 modular adapters are available for the 3600 series router. The 3620 and 3640 routers utilize modular interfaces to provide LAN connectivity for 10 Mbps Ethernet, 10/100 Mbps Fast Ethernet, and Token Ring. These LAN modules are available as single- or dual-port Ethernet and Fast Ethernet, or Mixed Ethernet/ Fast Ethernet combined with Token Ring. Additionally, all network modules come with dual WAN slots.

The 3660 class of routers is actually composed of the 3661 and 3662 units. These routers combine one or two integrated 10/100 Fast Ethernet ports (respectively speaking) and six expansion slots. Aside from the expandability of the 3660 class, this router provides all the capabilities of the 2600, 3620, and 3640 series routers, but with the added features of hot swappable module slots, a faster CPU, and optional internally redundant power supply.

Commonly the 3660 class of router is used as a primary concentration point for a collapsed (consolidated) network. To support the potential load of the multitude of WAN connectivity that the router is physically capable of handling, it also offer two AIM slots for use with data compression or encryption options.

Cisco Catalyst Switches

In early Ethernet networks, hubs were used to migrate users from coax cable to a more reliable twisted-pair media. Hubs were convenient and easy to configure but suffered great performance issues with collisions occurring over the hub's shared medium. As such, bridges and routers were used to break up broadcast and collision domains. Because a router does not forward broadcast, microsegmenting was simple but problematic with protocols, which did not support hierarchical protocols. An aftereffect was the configuration of Cisco routers as bridges. Today, these bridges still exist but in a multiport format known as a switch. Unlike hubs, switches do not have collision problems; however, they tend to suffer great performance loss with regard to large numbers of broadcasts. In an innovative move, Cisco introduced the first form of VLANs and integrated them into their routing.

VLANs define a broadcast domain for which an administrator may associate ports in one or more switches as members. As a Layer 2 topology, switches are unable to view IP information, and therefore a router is required to communicate between VLANs. Frequently a router is integrated within the switch to produce Layer 3 switching. When operating between switches, designating VLAN trunks, which carry traffic of multiple VLANS, preserves VLAN information. Depending on the destination that a trunk leads, Cisco provides the ability to prune certain VLANs to trim unnecessary traffic between switches.

While switches make large advances in performance, they also have caused issues in many broadcast and multicast technologies. To assist in resolving such issues, Cisco products are tightly integrated, such as routers that are able to process IP multicast switching through CGMP (Cisco Group Management Protocol). CGMP works as a supplement to IGMP (Internet Group Management Protocol) so that routers are made directly aware of which ports on a switch are members of a multicast conversation. Today, Cisco produces some of the most functional, high-performance switches available. While a number of Cisco's features are proprietary, such as ISL, Cisco also offers the industry standard configurations, such as 802.1q, as the review industry or standards associations (IETF, IEEE, ANSI, Etc), make their final specification known.

3500 Series Switches

The Catalyst 3500 series is designed as "scaleable" entry-level switches that provide interoperability to additional Cisco devices via fiber or copper connection. Unlike lower-end models, such as the 2900 series, the 3500 series switches provide faster forwarding of packets in addition to the ability to interlink to one another through gigabit uplinks. Each 3500 series switch utilizes 4MB of memory, used to buffer between all ports beyond the 8MB used for IOS and its 4-megabyte flash.

Independently, each Catalyst 3500 switch is capable of storing 8192 MAC addresses and can be interlinked in a cluster formation of up to 16 members. Also, with the Enterprise edition of the IOS software, as many as 250 VLANs can be recognized by a single switch, all processed by either Cisco's ISL (Inter-Switch link) or 802.1q. In a VLAN configuration, the 3500 series is capable of segregating broadcast domains. On the back end, the switching fabric is capable of forwarding at a rate of 5.4 Gbps or 10.8 Gbps actual transfers (full duplex).

For 3500 series switches, all share a common set of attributes with the exception of 10/100 ports and the forwarding rate as outlined in Table 2.4.

Table 2.4 A Comparison of the Port Attributes for the 3500 Series Routers

Model	10/100 TX Ports	GBIC Ports	Forwarding Rate
3512XL	12	2	4.8 Million PPS
3524XL	24	2	6.5 Million PPS
3524XL-PWR	24	2	6.5 Million PPS
3548XL	48	2	8.8 Million PPS
3508G	0	8	7.5 Million PPS

TIP

For AVVID purposes, only the 3524XL-PWR is a true direct benefit. Primarily, this unit has built-in capabilities to support inline power to interoperate with second-generation IP phones. All other 3500 series switches can be used as well; however, they require either a Catalyst inline power patch panel or a power adapter at the phone.

4000 Series Switches

The Catalyst 4000 series is made up of four switches: 4003, 4006, 4840G, and 4908G. Ideally, Cisco has positioned these switches as an advance modular step above the 3500 series and an answer to the significantly higher costs of the 6000 series. With a performance starting at 14.3 (C4003) to 17.9 (C4006) million packets per second, the 4000 series maintains ground as an extremely capable switch when compared to similar competitors. The mainstays of the 4000 line are the 4003 and 4006 switches, providing three and six modular slots, respectively. In a typical configuration, the 4003 utilizes a supervisor I module, while the 4006 utilizes a supervisor II.

WARNING

Neither the 4003 nor the 4006 provides any options or support for a redundant supervisor option. Those users who seek this level of functionality and require the ability to route protocols other than IP and IPX must upgrade to the 6000 series.

The modularity of the 4003 and 4006 switch lead to its flexibility; however, Cisco does offer some fixed and preconfigured port arrangements. For instance, all switches come as bundles with a supervisor module. The 4003 supports up to 96 expanded 10/100 Fast Ethernet ports while the 4006 is expandable up to 240 ports. Other options for the 4000 series include gigabyte connectivity, Layer 3 switch processing, and hybrid modules that provide mixed support. For AVVID support the 4003 and 4006 switches are capable of providing inline power; however, they require the use of an auxiliary power shelf (WS-P4603).

The 4840G switch is actually part of a differing series of switches than the 4003, 4006, and 4908G switches. Ideally, the 4840G is designed for high availability and load balancing for e-commerce Web servers. Unfortunately, this switch has little to do with AVVID, and it must be deferred from our topic of conversation.

Distributed switch networks such as the 3500 series do not offer integrated routing, and they rely on products such as the 4908G as an intermediary for Layer 3 switching. The 4908G is intended for use in environments with distributed data centers by offering connectivity of eight 1000 BaseX Gigabit Ethernet. Using a GBIC (Gigabit interface converter) data is transported to and from the 4908G's 11 Mbps internal fabric and transferred throughout a campus or corporate environment. The 4908G provides QoS with multiple queues including support for Weighted Round Robin (WWR) scheduling.

NOTE

Please see the "Gateway" section in this chapter to review the 400X series gateway module option(s).

6000 Series Switches

The Cisco 6000 series of switches is based on four entirely modular, highly available configurations—6006, 6009, 6506, and 6509. As you have probably already determined, the last number in the model number specifies the number of module switches while the 60 and 65 prefixes designate performance. All 6000 series have modular power supplies offering varying wattage and redundancy. Furthermore, this series boasts functional capabilities such as standby supervisor modules and integrated routing. Routing in the 6000 series has grown from a module that requires its own slot— MSM (multilayer switch module) that forwards at a rate of five million packets per second (pps)—to a MSFC (multilayer switch feature card) that resides directly with the supervisor module that nearly triples the forwarding rate to 15 million pps. Effectively, the routing of the 6000 series functions similar to a Cisco 4500 router.

Unlike other switches, the 6000 series offers true AVVID support by providing inline power at 48 ports per blade directly to second-generation IP phones. In many environments, where a cleaner solution is required, it is not desirable to use the Catalyst inline power patch panel or an external power adapter for the phone. The extra link in the wiring from the switch to the panel, then to the computer can easily become overwhelming. To address the needs of such customers, Cisco offers the Catalyst inline power patch panel as an integrated 48-port blade for the Catalyst 6000. The Catalyst 6000 version of the power panel offers an additional key advantage of automatically segregating IP phone sets to a separate VLAN. By virtue of being integrated into a Catalyst 6000 series switch, additional 10/100 48-port inline powered blades can be in a single unit. For example, the nine-slot Catalyst 6509 can support eight–48 port blades, totaling 384 ports in a single unit.

NOTE

With the Catalyst 6000 series, one port is used for the supervisor module, and any of the 48-port inline power modules can be hot-swapped and managed with standard tools. In order to use the inline power modules, the Cisco 2500 watt power supply upgrade must be purchased. In high-availability environments, it is highly recommended that redundant power supplies be purchased. Considering the 384 possible phones, a 2500-watt power supply averages less then 6.5 watts per phone.

In the enterprise environment, many IS managers are concerned that voice traffic combined with data will overburden the network. In looking at an infrastructure, regardless of the platform, the primary focus is locating bottlenecks and streamlining services where possible. The main concern is that telecommunications may sound choppy or distorted. Core critical and voice traffic are essential for driving the business, but yet when configured in queue they allow only for high-priority queuing. Essentially, neither type of traffic is very forgiving for delay, and queue processing on a heavy utilized switch or router still adds delay. To address this very important issue, Cisco introduced a PFC (policy feature card) option to guarantee true Quality of Service at near wire speeds. The important factor is to understand that this option adds intelligence to switching that is otherwise governed by MAC address. The PFC option is an available add-on to the supervisor IA blade.

The 6000 series switches boast one of the fastest performances of all switches in the industry. By providing 15 million packets per second of forwarding throughput in the 6000 line and as much as 150 million packets per second in the 6500, the 6000 series is a highly capable device for handling enterprise voice and data in a core configuration. The performance is due greatly in part to the 6000's 32 Gbps back plane and processing capability. The 6500 adds to the capabilities of the 6000 by adding scalability that can potentially enhance performance to as much as 256 Gbps across the back plane—in other words, these switches scale extremely well.

In addition to speed, high availability in the 6000 series is one of its key selling features. Both supervisor modules and integrated components such as MSFCs and PFCs can be duplicated with automatic failover. When configuring a 6000 series switch for fault tolerance, the only real effort involves redundant MSFCs. MSFCs are integrated routers and should be configured with Hot Standby Routing Protocol (HSRP) and must be configured separately from one another even though they will usually work in tandem. Supervisor switch configurations, however, are automatically copied from the active module to the backup when changes are added.

The 6000 series also extends the capabilities of your phone switch by providing enterprise-level support with 24 FXS ports per blade or eight T1 or eight E1 digital interfaces. In s acting as a gateway, the 6000 series switch maintains the highest-speed, most-available solution to address telephony needs. Furthermore, the 6000 series switch also provides high Quality of Service and direct network functionality by providing direct GBIC support at up to eight interfaces per blade, ATM support, and gigabit Ethernet.

NOTE

See the "Gateway" section in this chapter to review the 600X series gateway module options.

CSS 11000 Series

In addition to Cisco's Catalyst switches, it also has the CSS 11000 series designed specifically to operate with Internet-related sites. Unlike Cisco's other switches that operate on either Cisco IOS or Cisco's traditional switch operating system, the 11000 series runs on Cisco's Web Network Services, or Web NS for short.

Web NS provides for OSI Layers 5, 6, and 7 switching, which represent the topmost layer in the DOD stack. Through this technology, the CSS 11000 series switches are fully capable of identifying users according to cookies in their HTTP header, the type of transition the users are requesting, the information being sent, and how to optimize filling the clients' needs based on a distributed Web infrastructure.

Three models of this switch are available depending on the type of load that a Web site is under. These models are the 11050 (small sites), 11500 (mid-sized to large sites), and 11800 (large sites). While none of these switches specifically addresses voice functions, these switches are commonly used as frontend interfaces in a demilitarized zone (DMZ) to spearhead this type of support.

Utilizing Media Convergence Servers (MCS 78xx)

The Cisco Media Convergence servers are PC-based systems that operate on Windows 2000 operating systems to supply call management control and unified messaging services to AVVID clients. Although the systems that govern the unified messaging and Cisco's call management software functionality have enough memory and processing capacity to house both services in a single server for smaller environments, currently they operate on different operating systems and need to be placed on different units.

Media convergence servers are covered in heavy detail in Chapter 4 and as such are simply summarized for hardware in Table 2.5.

Table 2.5 The Hardware and Software Requirements for Media Convergence Servers

	MCS 7822	MCS 7835
Processor	Pentium III 550Mhz	Pentium III 733Mhz
Cache	512Kb secondary	256Kb secondary
RAM	512MB 100Mhz ECC SDRAM	512MB 133Mhz ECC SDRAM
Network Adapter	10/100 TX Fast Ethernet	10/100 TX Fast Ethernet
Storage	One 9.1G Ultra 2 SCSI	Dual 18.2G Ultra 2 SCSI Hot-Plug
Floppy Drive	1.44 Megabyte Standard PC Floppy Drive	1.44 Megabyte Standard PC Floppy Drive
CD-ROM	High Speed IDE	High Speed IDE
Power Supply	Fixed	Hot-plug redundant
Operating System	Windows 2000	Windows 2000

AVVID Video Hardware Overview

The video component of the AVVID specification is primarily hosted by Cisco's IP/VC and IP/TV systems. Cisco's IP/VC systems provide video conferencing for H323- and H320-compliant applications, such as Microsoft NetMeeting, while IP/TV serves high-grade streaming video similar to television for simplex communications, such as internal company news, training, and business TV. Together, IP/VC and IP/TV make up the major video functionality of AVVID.

IP Video Conferencing (IP/VC)

IP-based video conferencing allows face-to-face meetings in a world that has become less receptive to travel. Utilizing IP video conferencing, companies enhance relations with customers, build better workforces, and are able to communicate more clearly. IP video conferencing over the past several years has become an essential part of doing business and communicating with business associates, friends, and family.

Many home users utilize consumer versions of IP video conferencing by purchasing small, low-resolution video cameras and establishing picture and dialog over the Internet. Although it is fun, the consumer version of video conferring tends to be unstable and choppy at lower bandwidths. Corporations use similar video technology with the advantage of having higher bandwidth and quality.

Cisco IP/VC Product Overview

Cisco's IP/VC 3500 series defines the AVVID solution for video conferencing. Essentially a hardware-based solution, Cisco's video conferencing offers H.323 and H.320 compatibility for interaction with applications such as Microsoft's NetMeeting or solutions by PictureTel, Polycom, Tandberg, Sony, and others. Video conferencing allows a duplex transmission between stations as hosted by a control device. Unlike simplex technologies such as video on demand or streaming television, video conferencing provides for two-way communications and typically provides for smaller video size, resolutions, and captures cycles.

Utilizing four components, the Cisco 3500 series consists of the 3510, 3520, 3525, and 3530 units. The Cisco 3510 is at the heart of the video conferencing architecture by providing a multipoint control for all video conferencing communications. By defining a single control point, video conferencing controls can be enabled that govern establishing, joining, and terminating a meeting.

The video conferencing functionality is extended with the 3520 and 3525 gateway products, which provide protocol translation for H.323 and H.320, allowing video conferencing to extend beyond the network. Using these standard protocols, not only can network meetings be established, but also extended conferences with systems via ISDN or other connectivity can be set up. Sessions established through the 3520 or 3525 gateways can be set at rates ranging from 64 to 768 Kbps. As a gateway, calls can be placed between H.320 and H.323 end points and need not require video, such as linking a telephone conversation. Collectively, sessions established through the 3520 and 3525 can be routed though inter-active voice response (IVR), multiple subscriber number (MSN), direct inward dialing (DID), TCS4, and direct destination.

The IP/VC 3520 gateway is designed as a modular unit that pro-vides for five configuration options composed of two or four ISDN BRI ports, two or four V.35 ports, or a combination of two ISDN BRI and twp V.35 ports. As you may have surmised, lower-bandwidth links—64, 128, 256, and 384 Kbps—are established via ISDN using aggregated or bond lines, while the V.35 provides the higher-speed 768 Kbps connections. Sessions established at higher speeds through the v.35 port utilize RS-366 signaling so that a circuit-switched connection through an IMUX (inverse multiplexor) is used. On the network through the 3520's 10/100mbps Fast Ethernet interface, the IP/VC 3520 enables full end-to-end T.120 support for data conferencing.

The IP/VC 3525 is very similar to the 3520, except that it is designed for a large volume of calls through its ISDN PRI interfaces. Unlike the 3520, which can support only four simultaneous ses-sions, the 3525 can support up to eight at 128 Kbps each; however, it also supports higher quality through multilinked or bound lines yielding up to three sessions at 384 Kbps on a PRI-T1 or four on a PRI-E1.

Finally, the IP/VC 3530 video adapter allows a company to pre-serve investments in older technologies that support only H.320. Through a conversion process, legacy equipment signals are con-verted to H.323 so that they operate correctly over an IP-enabled network. Video throughput varies according to user-specified set-tings at rates as low as 112 Kbps and at a maximum of 768 Kbps.

NOTE

There are quite a few options when it comes to the "client" end of the IPVC infrastructure – Cisco doesn't sell a client (IP/VC end station/camera), but Cisco does interoperate with all standards-based clients.

The Advantages of Content Delivery Networks (CDN)

Corporations often need a means by which information can be disseminated to employees quickly, personally, and in a format that is easily understandable. Frequently, information of this nature is sent by e-mail, which is quite often misread or ignored. By implementing a CDN solution, companies are enabling instant content delivery to personnel—providing education, training, and seminar services at the viewer's convenience.

CDN is made up of two major technologies, both of which operate in simplex or uni-directional communications: streaming television and video on demand. The key difference between the two is that streaming television is scheduled while video on demand is requested.

Cisco IP/TV Video Streaming Products

Cisco's IP/TV server product line provides video broadcasting services very similar in nature to television, which provides a solution to issues such as information dissemination, poor communications, and other problems of this nature with regards to scheduling issues. Functionally controlled, streaming video films and recordings can be requested through Cisco's IP/TV management utility which establishes a system that provides video-on-demand or which allows for the scheduling of programs akin to television broadcasts that are listed in TV Guide.

IP/TV allows the training room to be pushed to the user's desktop with a solution that is right for the environment, taking note of systems speed, network capacity, and the size of the audience that the service is addressing. All of the IP/TV servers are delivered with a pre-configured software load according to their function on a Windows NT/2000 Platform. IP/TV provides scalability, integration, support of industry standards, and ease of use.

In addition to providing video services, the IP/TV servers can also provide audio services similar to those of radio technologies. Cisco currently provides support for pulse code modulation (PCM), Global System for Mobile Communication (GSM), 8- and 16-bit linear (many sampling and frequency rates), DVI, True-speech, MPEG, MPEG-1 Layer 3 (MP3), and Microsoft Audio.

Content is delivered over existing network lines to 32-bit Windows clients, Macintosh, and UNIX systems. Essentially, the sole requirement is support to interface with MPEG (Motions Pictures Experts Group) video standards (usually MPEG-2) delivered over an IP segment. Due to the wide spread of number viewers and video capabilities, Cisco provides its own MPEG software client (part number IPTV-VIEW-MP2-ADD); however, it shares compatibility with Microsoft's media player as well as Apple's QuickTime application.

Considering the content that is being deployed, faster systems operating over a streamed line network tend to perform best as bottlenecks in the network can cause choppy video and sound delivery. Ideally, the minimum client for Cisco's IP/TV should be at least an Intel Pentium II 300Mhz, 512L Layer 2 cache with 128 Mbps of RAM and a 100 Mbps NIC. This is not the type of application that you would want to use over slow links, as the minimum flow rate for IP/TV requires 128 Kbps over MPEG-2. Other, less common codec technologies, such as MPEG-4, support 14.4 Kbps to 3 Mbps with an ideal broadcasting range of 28.8 Kbps to 1 Mbps. With higher compressed codecs, such as MPEG-4, more CPU resources are consumed so that a service providing 30 frames per second at 1 Mbps streaming video would be right-sized to use at least an Intel Pentium III 500Mhz processor. For those companies that have systems than don't meet these requirements, an MPEG-2 decoder card can be purchased. As of the time of this writing, Cisco supports only the Optibase Videoplex Xpress decoder card that is sold though Optibase at www.optibase.com or its distributors.

Cisco's television series systems consist of five different specialties as summarized in Table 2.6.

Table 2.6 A Summary of Cisco's Television Series Products

Server	Primary Function
3411 Control Server	Management of broadcast services including scheduling, control of video types, access to archive servers, and more
3415 Video Starter System	All-in-one, small-scale video services including control functionality, storage, and broadcast functionality
3422 Broadcast Server	Provides streaming real-time or pre-recorded video services via MPEG-4 over low-bandwidth links
3423 Broadcast Server	Similar to the 3422 Broadcast Server offering MPEG-1, MPEG-2, MPEG-4, Indeo, and H.261 compression with more of a focus on performance over bandwidth
3431 Archive Server	Repository for prerecorded video services

All IP TV servers utilize a single 10/100 Mbps Ethernet interface and include a keyboard, mouse, CD-ROM, floppy drive, and VGA support. The hard drive in each unit varies in capacity; however, the only important detail is the amount of video storage a server can store. The video storage (expressed in megabytes) varies based the compression used, the data rate, and the size of the displayed screen. The IP/TV interface uses a standard video size that is based on the following formula:

$$\frac{\{[\text{Rate (kbps)}] \, [60(\text{seconds})][\# \text{ of Minutes}]\}/ \, [8 \, (\text{bits})]}{[1000 \, (\text{Kbytes})]}$$

For example, if you had a one-hour program that you wanted to deliver at 1 Mbps you would find that it would require 450MB, as illustrated here:

[1000kbps][60seconds][60minutes]/8bits per byte/1000kbps per megabytes = 450MB

As you can see from this equation, the key to the size of the video storage is truly based on the delivery rate. Depending on the codec (coder/decoder or compressor/decompressor) used to define compression and quality, the delivery rate will vary, thus affecting the content storage capacity of the server, which is outlined in Table 2.7.

Table 2.7 A Comparision of the Video Storage Capabilities of the Various Video Servers

	3415 Video Starter System	3422 Broadcast Server	3423 Broadcast Server	3431 Archive Server
Estimated hours of video storage	40 hours @ 1 Mbps (MPEG-1)	80 hours @ _ Mbps or 40 hours @ 1 Mbps (MPEG-4);	80 hours @ 1 Mbps (MPEG-1) or 13 hours @ 6 Mbps (MPEG-2)	160 hours @ 1Mbps (MPEG-1)
Capture card (Actual card in **bold** lettering)	**MPEG** - MPEG-2 Half D1, MPEG-1	**VFW** - MPEG-4, H.261, Indeo, MP3, WM Audio	**MPEG** - MPEG-2 Full D1, MPEG-2 Half D1, MPEG-1 **VFW** - MPEG-4, H.261, Indeo, MP3, WM Audio	None

Note that the preceding codec list is not complete as Cisco maintains the ability to add more support. For instance, Cisco currently supports the Optibase MovieMaker 200 encoder card, which provides MPEG-2 (half D1 and full D1) and MPEG-1 support.

When configured with IP/TV, your network will most likely look similar to the sample implementation shown in Figure 2.3.

Figure 2.3 IP/TV Implemented in a Network Environment

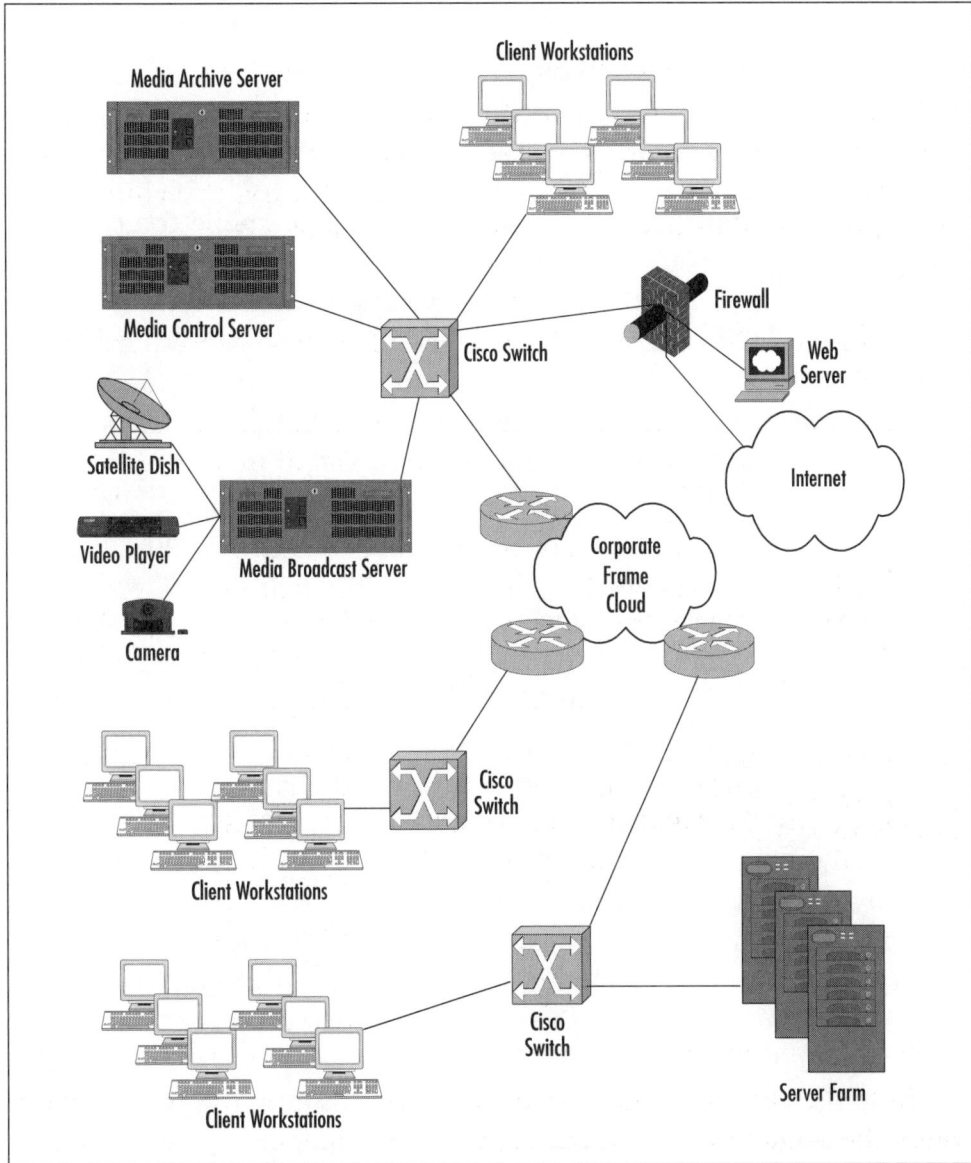

The AVVID Telephony Infrastructure

The AVVID telephony infrastructure is the framework by which Cisco has designed its network integrated voice services. In many respects, this infrastructure can be best thought of as a guide for building PBX systems piece by piece over a network and adding specialized functionality as you go.

Voice Gateways (Analog and Digital)

Products such as Cisco voice gateways host and enable the communication between voice and data networks. These voice gateways serve to provide connectivity between your private network and conventional telephone trunks, legacy voice-mail systems, and other analog devices that are not capable of direct communications. These gateways, when configured correctly and with the proper electronic support, are capable of resending an input signal to a destination at near wire speeds.

Voice gateways are available in two flavors—analog and digital. Depending on the equipment to which you are connecting, your choice will be determined by the accommodation of the available interface. As with other AVVID communications, the same restrictions apply—that is, the number of lines supported by the gateway are a direct function of the support that the legacy device can oblige. The gateway does not increase the number of supported connections beyond the capacity of the legacy switch.

Digital gateways typically provide for two types of transports. As you may have assumed, these transports are provisions for T1 and E1 circuits. In the United States, Canada, Japan, and a few other countries, T1 lines are common and use µ-law encoding. In most of Europe and part the rest of the world where E1 lines are used, a-law encoding is employed. All Cisco digital voice gateways support these standards as common functionality including the mapping of IP addresses to phone numbers and vice versa.

Cisco provides a number of features that enhance the configuration of their gateway service products that are inherent in a number of their regular analog devices. For example, Cisco produces a noise comfort level that simulates a kind of static background noise even when no communication is taking place, allowing the parties speaking to have full realization of a conversation as on a normal phone.

Cisco provides a number of products for gateway services. Some of these devices are analog only; others are purely digital, and some support both. Throughout this chapter, we have discussed a number of voice-enabled products, some of which also maintain voice gateway services. In the best interest of not repeating material, we will refrain from duplication; however, in certain instances it is a requirement. In short, voice gateways provide a cost-effective solution and alternative to Voice over IP gateways when routing functions are not used.

The Catalyst 6000 Family Voice T1/E1 and Services Module

The Catalyst 6000 series of switches can operate as voice gateways for AVVID networks and legacy PBXes or the PSTN. In this capacity, this series permits a large-capacity voice gateway, allowing up to 24 FXS analog ports or eight T1/E1 PRI ISDN interfaces per blade.

For the most part, this series has already been covered in great detail earlier in this chapter. It is worth mentioning that the 6000 series provides its voice gateway support by utilizing the same T1/E1 line card but with the DSP services card utilizing a different software configuration load, permitting gateway communications via skinny station protocol.

The Catalyst 4000 Family Access Gateway Module

As noted earlier, the 4000 series switch is a scaled-down version of the 6000 that lacks certain functionality. Of that service that had been removed, Cisco adds the 4000 access gateway module. This module provides field office support for network voice services, voice gateway functionality, and IP routing.

Through the use of the access gateway module, a 4000 series router gains the capability of direct use of many functions primarily reserved for routers. This access gateway module provide two VIC or WIC slots, a dedicated VIC slot, a high-density analog slot, and direct support for integrating with the switch itself. Configuration of the access gateway module is very similar to that of a Cisco router and offers a common console port for easy access.

The access gateway module includes its own DSP and supports both H.323 and the skinny client protocol. Conveniently, with the integration of an access module, the Catalyst 4000 can provide this device and can then be configured to operate as a standard network device, as under CiscoWorks, or as a voice resource through Cisco Call Manager.

Cisco Digital IP Telephony Gateway: DT-24+/DE-30+

The DT-24+ and DE-30+ represent Cisco's solution to interfacing a legacy PSTN- or ISDN (PRI)-based digital trunk to a Cisco AVVID telephone network whereby either solution is controlled via Cisco's Call Manager. The DT-24+ is design for United States standards where T1 is used; the D-E30+ is design to operate with the European E1 circuit. Both T1 and E1 lines are channelized within all gateway solutions as 24 and 31 channels, respectively. Because clocking for each channel of the digital line is handled out of band, one channel per T1 or E1 line is removed. As such, a T1 link that is composed of 24 channels will effectively allow for utilization of 23 for communications while an E1 permits 30.

As an ISDN PRI interface, both gateway solutions have capabilities that extend their functionality to include support for many Layer 3 protocols including NI-2 (National ISDN-2), 4ESS (Electronic Switching System), 5ESS/Custom, SL1/100, DMS100/250, DSC (digital switch) 600E, and many others. Depending on the environment, either solution will emulate user-side terminal equipment or network-side ISDN signaling equipment as required. Q.931 call management is then used to control call setup and teardown, as with any other ISDN configuration. Once communications are established, the skinny gateway protocol is then utilized though Call Manager to provide services, such as hold, transfer, conference, park, and so forth, to IP phone clients. Furthermore, flexibility is also extended by each gateway's support capabilities for H.323 support (via Call Manager for proxy signaling), G.711 (A-Law or M-law) encoding, line echo cancellation, and DTMF detection and generation. Cisco currently claims support for a variety of legacy phone switches, including all options of the Nortel Meridian, all G3 option of Lucent's Definity, the Matra 6500, the Intercom E, InterTel Product via T1 PRI, Ericsson's MD100, Siemens' HiCom, and Rolm's 9000 Series, to name a few. Once integrated, users can seamlessly communicate with the legacy phone system despite the original limitations.

The key functionality behind the DT-24+ and the DE-30+ gateways is their support for DID and caller ID. These features common to digital circuits allow outside users to directly dial an extension whereby analog systems generally lack this support and require operator intervention or a much more complex call-routing system. Combining call routing with quality support, the DT-24+ and DE-30+ gateways are ideal for gateway services where larger channel quantities are needed. Remember that analog communications are typically one to one whereas digital, as in this case, handles either 23 (T1) or 30 (E1) calls per line.

Both the DT-24+ and the DE-30+ consist solely of a PCI-based system board that is installed into any PC that has PCI architecture. Once in place, the PCI card will simply use the PC's power, but no other system resource, software, or driver. Because there is virtually no draw on the system, any number of gateway interface cards can be placed into a PC, up to the number of available slots. This PC can utilize any CPU and is best segregated to the system that is not often rebooted, such as the call manager, a server, or a standalone unit. Each gateway adapter contains a host of integrated functionality including DSPs (digital signal processors), a female RJ-48c interface to connect a T1 or E1, a RJ-45 10Base-T Ethernet port, an onboard processor for interoperating with Cisco's Call Manager, DHCP for assigning an IP address to the interface (regardless of the system's address), and a TFTP client for upgrading firmware.

When a DT-24+ or DE-30+ gateway is powered on it will automatically respond to a network configuration and indicate status through LED lights on the card. Once on the network, the gateway will then accept a DHCP address and register with Cisco's Call Manager. If required, a configuration or firmware update can automatically be downloaded to either adapter as specified through Call Manager.

VG200: Cisco IP Telephony Voice Gateway

Cisco's VG200 is an advanced Voice Gateway interface that allows communications between an IP-based phone system and analog telephony devices. In this capacity, the VG200 allows users on the IP-based system to both make and receive calls with seamless integration to an existing legacy phone system.

Like other Cisco AVVID devices, the VG200 is controlled through Cisco's Call Manager application. Like its router counterparts that utilize Cisco IOS, it also provides for a command-line interface. The command-line interface can be accessed in all the ways common to IOS devices such as Telnet, serial cable, and so forth.

As a modular unit, the VG200 shares a common architecture with the 1750, 2600, and 3600 series routers whereby other network modules and voice interface cards can be interchanged, allowing all the flexibility that is inherent to its router counterparts. For example, the VG200 can be used to provide analog and digital dial access services, in addition to PBX or PSTN connectivity, as well as other devices, such as legacy voice-mail systems.

While the VG200 has both digital and analog support, in the traditional sense, however, it is marketed for small and medium-sized offices as an analog protocol device utilizing either FXS or FXO ports. In analog configuration, the VG200 can support one to four devices; digitally it can support two T1 or E1 interfaces. Unlike other Cisco voice gateways, the VG200 does not offer "Skinny Station Protocol" but rather utilizes Media Gateway Control Protocol (MGCP) and works as an H.323 gateway with T1 ports. Utilizing a single 10/100 Ethernet port, the VG200 transports digital IP signals that are converted by onboard DSPs from analog. The VG200 includes support for many codecs, such as G.711, G.723.1, and G.729a, to name a few.

The VG200 can best be summarized as a modified 2621 router. The VG200 comes standard with 32MB of DRAM and 8MB of flash memory. Essentially, any interface that can be installed in a 2621 can be installed in the VG200 as well. Configuration via IOS shares common commands with a few adaptations for gateway specialization. Like the 2621, higher availability is an option as well as management through SNMP products.

NOTE

In the capacity of using a BRI interface, both the 2600 and the 3600 series routers can be used as a voice gateway. The 2600 series router can provide up to 4 channels of communications while the 3600 can provide up to 12. The number of channels is a quantity of two for each ISDN BRI line.

Cisco 7200 Series High-Performance Multifunction Routers

The Cisco 7200 series is the enterprise version of the 3600 series providing modular configurations. This series offers a multiprocessor configuration that produces an output of up to 300,000 routed packets per second. Key features of the 7200 series router are summarized here:

- ATM and SONET support

- Up to 256MB of RAM

- Up to 110MB of flash

- ISDN BRI and PRI

- T1, E1, E3, and T3 interface support

- IP and ATM Quality of Service

- VPN functionality

- Scalability

The primary interest, however, lies in the 7200 series multiservice interchange (MIX) functionality. Through MIX technology, the 7200 supports digital voice and offers gateway features. Currently Cisco support two options for the 7200 series—a high-capacity, two-port T1/E1 trunk interface and a medium capacity. The primary difference between the two trunk interfaces in the ability for the onboard DSPs to process calls. As of this writing, the medium capacity is no longer sold, and the large capacity interface is being offered to those customers as a trade-in upgrade.

The 7200 series router comes in two form factors, offering either 4 or 6 slots. Depending on the module and the capacity of the voice trunk card, the 7200 series has 48 to 120 channels of compress voice. Like other Cisco routers such as the 2600, the slots on this router can be used to adapt other technologies.

Voice support is provided in a number of capacities under the 7200 series. Like the 2600, analog support can be obtained through the use of a VIC option while an high-density voice (HDV) network module is used for digital. Once enabled, this series of routers is then capable of communicating with any IP telephony device that supports the H.323 (version 2) standard. In addition, an MFT (multiflex trunk) option can be integrated into the 7200 series to provide both voice and data connections emulating the segregate channelization that is common to the PRI WIC. The key difference between the MFT and PRI is that PRI uses ISDN channelization while the

MFT relies on the internal interface. Through the use of VIP (versatile interface processors), as functionality and load increase, the 7200 can scale to manage the resources it has been assigned.

NOTE

Cisco has made plans to extend voice gateway functionality in future options for the 7500 series routers.

The Cisco AS5300 Voice Gateway

The Cisco AS5300 is a high-end, high-capacity device providing for both dialup remote PC dial in access and Voice-over-IP gateway services. The original intent of the AS5200 and AS5300 series systems was to provide a simple access point for communications like an ISP. By implementing one of these devices, a company could maintain a single device and avoid using stacks upon stacks of modems combined with PC-based hardware. The AS5200 was designed around POTS lines while the AS5300 was more of a digital solution that offered support for ISDN. Currently the AS5200 series has been retired from manufacturing, and newer devices such as the AS5300 have taken its place.

Cisco's AS5300 is a robust communications server designed around a RISC processor architecture utilizing 64MB of RAM and an 8MB flash. Using IOS, the AS5300 provides superior QoS, variable frame sizing, and H.323 services. The AS5300 becomes voice enabled, by use of a VFC (voice feature card), along with an upgrade version of IOS. The VFC adds to the AS5300's MIPS 4700 CPU operating at 100 or 150Mhz (depending on when it was purchased) in combination with its own 4MB of RAM and 8MB of flash storage, which can be combined with transitional telephone interfaces or with a digital line such as a T1 or E1 to function as a gateway. Structurally, an AS5300 is composed of three slots—one for a four-port T1, E1, or PRI, and the other two for voice or modem cards.

With a full population of four lines, the AS5300 can provide up to 120 voice/fax ports with E1 and 96 with T1s. PRI line capacity will be approximately the same as the T1 counterparts, less one line (channel) for data control and timing.

When enabled, the AS5300 is well suited to handle large quantities of voice traffic with the VGFC by the use of its high-speed DSP processors, which deliver performance at 100 MIPS and high compression with lower overhead codec support for G.711, G.729, G.729a, and G.723.1. The DSPs are at the heart of the AS5300's voice support as they provide line quality services such as echo cancellation, silence suppression, jitter buffers, noise comfort generation, Group 3 Fax support, and more. It is because of Cisco's complex algorithms that support voice function that the AS5300 maintains its support levels. For instance, the silence suppression feature of the DSP prevents the AS5300 from consuming bandwidth when unnecessary and is capable of this level of detection as quickly as 200 milliseconds after a person has stopped talking.

The AS5300 when configured as a gateway retains its other functionality to interoperate as a dial (in and out) access point, fax processing server, and so forth. Faxes can be sent to a number outside the company or between two fax machines internally. One would expect that a service such as fax represents data transmission and should take up the full available bandwidth. As a detectable signal, however, data is taken in a demodulated state and forwarded across a network at rates between 9600 and 14.4 baud utilizing T.30 spoofing without damaging quality or Group 3 compatibility. Realizing that the AS5300 is a communications device, Cisco also realizes that channel reduction is a necessity regardless of the size of the link (normally 56-64 Kbps) in a PSTN.

Cisco has yet one more variety of the AS5300 called the AS5350. Essentially, this unit is a smaller-capacity server that operates faster. When the Cisco AS5300 came available, it was based on the CPU that was efficient and cost-competitive at the time. Now, several years later, Cisco has released the AS5350, which provides the same functionality but with a 250Mhz RM7000 CPU. Also, with the addition of new features, Cisco has expanded the configuration limits of the AS5300 as demonstrated in Table 2.8.

Table 2.8 The Configuration Limits of the AS5300 Communications Server

Component	AS5300	AS5350
CPU	100 or 150Mhz RM7000 RISC	250Mhz RM7000 RISC
Unit RAM	64MB expandable to 128MB	128MB expandable to 512MB
Shared IO memory	16MB (packet DRAM)	64MB expandable to 128MB
Boot flash	Up to 8MB	8MB expandable to 16MB
System flash	Up to 16MB	32MB expandable to 64MB
Cache	None	2MB Layer 3
Maximum number of calls	120 (Using E1s)	60 (Using E1s)
Rack height	2U	1U

AS5400 and 5800 Voice Gateways

You are probably aware at this point that Cisco produces two standard consumer/business modules of the AS5x00 series devices—the AS5200 and the AS 5300. Cisco also produces a commercial or industrial version of these devices that is based on the same concept but taken to a much higher level. Cisco's AS5400 and AS5800 device are known thoughout the telephone industry as some of the highest, most feature-rich products designed for regional Bell offices where super-high availability and hot swapping are requirements.

Both the AS5400 and AS5800 are based on Cisco's 7200 series router interfacing with an access server. In place of T1s, Cisco provides support for CT-3 (the T1's much bigger brother), which enables support of up to 672 voice ports and operates at speeds up to 44.736 Mbps—an equivalent of 28 T1s. Note that the C in CT-3 simply designates the line as channelized.

Like the AS5300, the AS5400 uses IOS and supports multiple protocols and flexible interfaces. The AS5400 represents a bridge point between the AS5300 and AS5800 by providing one CT-3 port or eight T1 interfaces. Ideally, you would expect to find an AS5400 in an environment such as large ISPs such as America Online (AOL) where a larger number of dialin pools would be configured. The AS5400 comes equipped with 256MB of system RAM, 64MB of share I/O, a system flash of 32MB, a boot flash of 8MB, and a non-volatile capacity of 512Kb. With the exception of the nonvolatile memory, the AS5400 can double all its default memory capacities to reaching its design maximum. In addition, depending on load, the AS5400 has the ability to scale by providing up to 20 processors for routing, signaling, and so forth to assist its RM7000 64-bit super-scalar microprocessor that operates at 250Mhz.

The AS5800 is yet a larger extension of the AS5400, based on the same idea as the AS5400, providing either 12 T1/E1s or 3 CT-3 line support and up to 2016 voice ports; however, it provides support for IP only. This device is commonly used in voice communication such as a gateway, and it supports SS7 signaling (as does the 5400), which provides regional Bell companies the ability to route calls in the PTSN, such as finding a free path to a phone number or reporting a busy signal. The AS5800 is designed to never go down by providing redundant hot-swappable power supplies, dial shelf controllers, and load balancing. By nature of the AS5800's design it is the ideal solution for ultra-large ISPs as well.

AccessPath VS3

At the ultra-high end of Cisco's gateway resource list is the AccessPath VS3. The AssessPath VS3 is a completely scalable solution for very large enterprises whereby support for up to 2520 voice lines can be obtained utilizing what amounts to 84 E1 or T1 lines. Cisco has positioned this unit to address the needs of regional Bell operating companies and mega-sized ISPs.

The AccessPath VS3 is essentially a stacked compilation of AS5300 series devices that have no single point of failure. The Access Path VS3 is a self-contained network, all within itself. In fact, the Accesspath VS3 utilizes its own Catalyst 5002 switch for backbone functionality and either 7205 or 3640s for routing capabilities, all under the controller of a Web-enabled controller. The AccessPath VS3 supports voice services at a high-availability level of 99.99998 percent uptime and hot-swappable component recovery. Because the AccessPath VS3 utilizes the AS5300 technology, it shares in the same functionality, but at a carrier level.

ICS 7750

The final product that we have to present is the Cisco integrated communications server (ICS) model 7750. Unlike other Cisco offers, this device is design specifically for e-commerce and Web site integration. The ICS 7750 uses a Web-based interface for configuration and is built on IOS. This unit most notably provides for QoS, providing the missing element required to support voice, video, and data. This flexibility allows the merging of voice and data streams, facilitating companies to reduce telecommunication expenses.

In Cisco's intended design, the ICS can be used by remote organizations and users to make IP-based phone calls and take the use of the Internet one step further. As a frontend component to the Internet, the ICS 7750 offers the availability of IOS with firewall services, in addition to the voice software that is included by default.

Like other Cisco products, the ICS 7750 uses a modular design that allows for the integration of both WIC and VIC options. WIC options are reasonably standard, providing high-speed and asynchronous serial interfaces, ISDN BRI support, and 56K and fractional T1 with integrated CSU/DSU provisions. Similarly, the VIC options are on par with the 2600, providing capabilities for digital multiflex trunks (one or two ports) and analog two ports for E&M, FXO, and FXS.

The ICS 7750 is a six-slot modular-based router that provides functionality as required by adding cards, memory, and processors.

Each of the slots can be expanded to use either Cisco's MRP (Multiservice Router Processor) or SPE (System Processing Engine) option. The MRP comes standard with 64MB of RAM and is expandable to 96MB, enabling it to support either two WICs or VICs and two PVDM (packet voice/fax DSP).

The SPE is perhaps the greatest feature of the ICS 7750. In a remote field office, it is often not feasible to utilize a Call Manager installation at the corporate office. Essentially, the SPE provides for this. Fundamentally, the SPE is a single-board computer that is capable of running Cisco Call Manager as well as voice-mail, call routing, and attendant and interactive voice-driven functions.

Toll By-Pass

A key benefit of Cisco AVVID and Voice over IP technology is a feature known as Toll By-Pass. With this technology, calls are routed within the company network to the point at which the least charge is incurred, if any charge at all. Although a router in the Cisco lineup of products may not necessarily support AVVID technology, it may provide support for call routing. Toll By-pass features are currently available on the following routers:

- Cisco 1750 Modular Access Router—Low-end router ideal for a small office of one to five users, providing three modular slots for voice and data interface cards, compatible with Cisco 1600, 1720, 2600, and 3600 routers.

- Cisco 2600 Series Modular Access Router—Midrange router, described earlier.

- Cisco 3600 Series Modular Access Router—High-end router, described earlier.

- Cisco MC3810 Multiservice Access Concentrator—First-generation proprietary-based router, described earlier.

Continued

- Cisco 7100 Series VPN Router—High-end VPN router that features one slot capable of supporting a voice or data interface.

- Cisco 7500-Advanced Router System—Enterprise-level router typically used for core functionality supports high-speed routing and Quality of Service.

- Cisco MGX 8220 Edge Concentrator—Midlevel concentrator that provides high-volume transportation of data across a Frame Relay or ATM backbone.

- Cisco IGX 8400 Voice Network Switching (VNS)—High-end PBX integration unit for providing voice and data transmission over a wide area network via Frame Relay or ATM.

- Catalyst 8540 Multiservice ATM Switch Router—The ultimate in Cisco switch routing functionality at 24 million packets per second with capabilities of supporting voice over ATM and gigabit Layer 3 switching at wire speeds over its internal 40 Gigabit fabric.

- Cisco BPX 8600 Series—A scalable solution of cost-effective interfaces for narrow and broadband wide area ATM communications, functionally capable of supporting an OC-12 interface.

Web Cache Engine Technologies

Internet-based AVVID communications requires optimization in order to ensure proper delivery of Voice over IP-enabled traffic. While many bottlenecks such as weak and oversubscribed points on an ISP's backbone will be out of our control, our link to the Internet can be optimized. The primary concern with regard to the Internet connection is the availability of bandwidth. As such, the main focus is to eliminate unauthorized traffic, perhaps at a router or firewall, and to minimize duplicate requests for common data. The primary method for reducing duplicate Internet requests is to cache the data that is returned from each site through a device known as a proxy server. Cisco's implementation of a proxy server is what it calls its Web Cache Engine.

Cisco offers four versions of its Web Cache Engine product. Accordingly, each version of the Web Cache Engine scales according to the link size to the Internet and the amount of data to be cached. These solutions are outlined in Table 2.9.

Table 2.9 The Web Cache Engine Usage and Specifications

Model	Usage	Line Type	Capacity	Storage
Content Engine 507	Entry-level unit	T1/E1	Up to 2.0 Mbps	18 to 36GB
Content Engine 560	Midsized company	IMA/T2	Up to 20 Mbps	36 to 144GB
Content Engine 590	ISPs/enterprises	T3/ATM	45+ Mbps	36 to 252GB
Content Engine 7320	Large ISP	ATM/OC3	155+ Mbps	36 to 144GB

Cisco's Web Cache Engine actually does not do anything to cache a communications stream or relay data in an AVVID configuration; however, it does assist in lowering the cost associated with accessing the Internet by lowering the requirement for higher-bandwidth lines. Essentially, the Cache Engine stores material as it is requested, as it is simply pulled from storage rather than from the Net. Using HTTP expiration and date stamps, the Web Cache Engine can determine if stored data is current or if it must be downloaded again.

Voice and video connections are time-sensitive and cannot be cached. As such, the configuration of the Web Cache Engine is exclusive of voice and video traffic. Depending on the environment, voice traffic is actually more dependent on access lists on routers, open conduits on a firewall, and VPN connections between networks.

Summary

AVVID is a loosely applied term used to describe voice, data, and multimedia services that are integrated into a network. While many of the technologies under the AVVID umbrella have been available for years, never before have they been so closely integrated. This should have a familiar ring, much like the story of Microsoft Windows and its capabilities to integrate. Like Microsoft, Cisco's AVVID structure will only grow and become a much tighter focus of future developed technologies. As companies migrate more to AVVID, new vendors will offer additional hardware solutions.

In this chapter we presented and reviewed a number of technologies defined either directly or indirectly as support equipment necessary for an AVVID environment. Putting it all together, an ideal AVVID design deploys routers with voice-enabled capabilities that are, in turn, linked to voice-enabled switches, such as the Catalyst 6000 series, that provide a separate VLAN and power to IP-enabled phones such as the 7940 and 7960. IP phones are logically assigned call functions, extended as services by Cisco's Call Manager. The Active Voice Product completes voice services by providing unified messaging, combining voice-mail and e-mail services in a single location. When legacy equipment exists, gateways are configured so that the existing network can be migrated to a pure IP system as time allows.

Video services are composed of video on demand, streaming television media services, and video conferencing. In extending voice over IP, sessions from an IP-based phone can be linked into video conferencing while preserving other conference members' ability to utilize video. Video conferencing at the professional level utilizes higher bandwidth and quality than home systems, and it enables corporate professionals to hold face-to-face meetings despite different physical location. Video on demand and streaming television media services such as IP/TV provide an open-ended configuration that also allows for the immediate dissemination of information in simplex communications.

FAQs

Q: I have a digital phone switch at my main office and analog at my remote offices. Can I use a digital interface into the router at my central office and analog at my remote sites? If so, how does this work?

A: At your central site, you would use a digital trunk card interfaced to a voice-enabled router. At the remote facilities, you would either use an FXO or FXS interface based on the type of connection that your phone system supported. The router handles all conversions and transportation of conversations.

Q: Suppose that I had a voice-enabled router that was connected to the Internet via high-speed DSL utilizing a single voice line. Could I use this line to connect multiple phone calls though my PBX even though I have only a single line? If so, how does it work?

A: Once a voice conversation is converted by a DSP, it is data. Regardless of the number of voice lines, the real test is bandwidth capacity. The key to the number of calls is the amount of constant data that can be maintained, so, effectively, this limit is then based on how good your compression is and the DSL service. At some point, however, if communicating to a PTSN, a gateway must be used that is one channel per conversation.

Q: When utilizing multiple gateway adapters, do multiple network T1 or E1 lines need to be used?

A: Each gateway is independent of the other even if in the same system, even though they can be combined in an aggregated configuration at a logical level. Effectively, each gateway requires its own network and ISDN PRI (T1 or E1) interface.

Q: I'm looking at implementing a voice-mail service for my AVVID phone system. All my phones are IP enabled. What type of interface do I need for the voice-mail to function?

A: The voice-mail component operates just as another IP device operates a computer, phone, printer, and so forth. When you connect to a voice-mail system such as Active Voice, the connection should be done by Ethernet.

Q: I have been tasked with deploying an IP/TV system, and I wanted to know if I should go with a single starter system or components. How do I make this determination?

A: This question is amazingly simple to answer. If you have more than 40 hours of total video storage, you will need to work with components or have an array of independent Cisco 3415 systems so that multiples are used to get around the hourly limitation.

Q: What is the difference between an E1 and a T1?

A: This question is a bit on the vague side, but let me give you the short answer. First, a T1 is used basically in the United States and provides 1.544 Mbps while an E1 is primarily used in Europe and provides 2048 Mbps. Both circuits come in different provisions and standards, such as Robbed Bit, ISDN PRI, and so on. You must use the type supported by the device you are interfacing with or the telecommunications vendors that is providing your service. T1, E1, and PRI circuit support can be manipulated on a Cisco router so that framing and configuration variation can be adapted.

Q: I have existing switches and would like to implement second-generation IP telephones. Does this require me to replace my existing switches?

A: No. While the newer switches (the Cisco Catalyst 3500XL, 4000, and 6000 series) provide better functionality and options like inline power, it is not a requirement. You have two options here—you will either connect your phones to a power patch panel, or each phone will need its own standard power pack and power cord.

Q: Why is it that Cisco offers so many different products that all appear to do the same thing. Is this just to confuse the market?

A: Cisco offers many similar products because they share a common modular structure and use IOS. In Cisco's view, it is a positive option to purchase only the components that are required for an existing network, thereby preserving investments rather than doing forklift replacements. Additionally, various products define differing capacities so that consumer companies need not purchase all expensive products when they need only a fraction of their capabilities.

Chapter 3

Migrating Your Network to AVVID Technologies

Solutions in this chapter:

- Planning and Executing a PBX Migration

- Legacy-Based PBX Migration Strategies

- Planning and Executing a Voice Mail Migration

- Voice Mail Migration Strategies

Introduction

Migration from legacy private branch exchanges (PBXs) and voice messaging systems to IP telephony systems is a challenge for many organizations. It would be unrealistic to expect any organization looking to deploy IP-based voice systems to immediately replace all of its installed legacy voice systems when the decision is made to implement an AVVID solution. Therefore, we can expect that we will face the challenge of integrating legacy systems with the respective AVVID components.

NOTE

Standard protocols are available in the industry for the integration of legacy systems with current hardware and software, including AVVID; however, these standards have not been universally adopted by all vendors.

In addition to making the proper physical connections, system applications and user features must also be preserved. This preservation can be achieved with different levels of compatibility, depending on the method of integration that is available. Selecting the best migration strategy involves understanding the capabilities of the existing equipment and the AVVID components, as well as understanding what features and applications are most important to users. Some features may be unavailable during migration, while others may not be possible even after the migration is complete. Most organizations consider their phone system as a whole to be mission-critical, and they will not tolerate any loss of functionality during a system migration. Therefore, it is important for system designers to be aware of any caveats up front and set user expectations accordingly. In this chapter, we will investigate the possible options and evaluate the trade-offs of using several different approaches for integration during a system migration.

Several device interconnections must be considered. First, connections between PBXs (IP or legacy) and the Public Switched Telephone Network (PSTN) must be considered to preserve connectivity to the outside world during the migration. Second, connections between PBXs and voice messaging systems must be preserved so that users can continue using voice mail services. Last, the connections between multiple voice mail systems for networking systems between separate locations must also be taken into account.

Planning and Executing a PBX Migration

In addition to the physical connectivity, the associated communications protocols, including an analysis of both open standards and proprietary ones, are critical elements to consider in the planning process. We will discuss some of these important factors in performing a PBX migration.

Analyzing the Protocols

One of the first steps in understanding the potential migration strategies is to analyze the options for physical connectivity and the associated communications protocols between all devices in the system. Essentially, a common denominator must be found between the installed PBX(s), voice messaging systems, CallManager, and any required gateways. The communications protocols that are used between these devices can be divided into two general categories: open standards or proprietary. Possible choices for open standards include ISDN (Integrated Services Digital Network) PRI (Primary Rate Interface), QSIG (Q is derived from the fact that it is an extension of the ITU-T Q.93x series of SIGnaling standards), and channel associated signaling (CAS). Each of these open standard choices may be supported in some fashion by legacy telephony vendors; however, they are by no means universally available on all vendors' equipment. Many vendors have proprietary protocols of their own such as Lucent's DCS/DCS+, Nortel's MCDN, and Siemens' Cornet. The obvious issue with these protocols is that because they are not open industry standards, none of them is supported by Cisco AVVID devices. If we are looking for a common denominator among all devices, proprietary protocols will obviously not meet that requirement.

Because user features and message waiting indications are passed between systems using these protocols, they are important for preserving feature transparency between new and old systems. Some of the more common features that many organizations rely on that will need to be preserved throughout the migration phase include the following:

Calling number Presented on called party's handset display and also used for billing and voice mail routing.

Called number Required by receiving switch to route a call directly to a subscriber without the need for an attendant; may also be used for voice mail.

Calling name Is similar to calling number; can be presented to called party's handset phone.

Diversion reason Used by voice mail systems to present different greetings to callers for busy or ring-no-answer events.

Message waiting indicator (MWI) Voice mail systems can inform a switch to set an MWI on when a user has a new voice mail message. This may be required for switches that are both local and remote to the voice messaging system.

Both-ways origination The ability to initiate and receive a call on the same trunk facility.

One last consideration when determining which protocol will be used for interconnection to legacy devices includes cost. As always, there is a trade-off between the cost of the required facilities and the feature functionality that is derived from the connection. An early part of the design process must include determining which protocol will be used for each of the device interconnections in order to preserve the required feature functionality at an acceptable cost.

Standard Protocols for Integrating with PBXs

Several standard protocols are available for integrating IP telephony networks with legacy PBX systems. In the sections to follow, we will describe some of the standard protocols that can be used in an AVVID environment for integrating with legacy systems.

Foreign Exchange Office (FXO)/ Foreign Exchange Station (FXS)

The primary advantages of integrating with analog facilities are the low cost and the common availability of such interfaces on legacy equipment. There is a significant trade-off, though, in feature functionality. Of the features listed previously, only called number information can be passed using FXO/FXS facilities. These connections are supported on a number of Cisco voice gateways. As of this writing, FXS/FXO connectivity is available on the VG-200 analog gateway, 1750, 3810, 2600, and 3600 series routers, and the Catalyst 4000 LAN switch with analog gateway modules. The Catalyst 6000 provides only FXS connectivity by way of an analog gateway module.

ISDN Basic Rate Interface (BRI) and Primary Rate Interface (PRI)

ISDN BRI and PRI are both good choices for connecting between a legacy PBX and the IP voice network via the appropriate gateway. All of the features listed previously can be maintained with the exception of diversion reason and MWI. The costs associated with ISDN services will vary depending on whether BRI or PRI services are used; they will also depend on local tariffs. PBXs may also require software upgrades for ISDN support.

Both of these protocols are widely supported by many PBX vendors as well as Cisco gateways and CallManager. Currently, all Cisco voice gateways support ISDN PRI facilities, with the exception of the 1750 and VG-200 voice gateways. BRI facilities are currently supported on the 3810, 2600, and 3600 voice gateways.

QSIG

The major benefit of the QSIG protocol is that it provides the most robust set of features. Even though many vendors provide support for QSIG, it is a relatively new protocol, and many installed systems do not have the proper hardware and software to support QSIG. For this reason, a substantial cost may be incurred when upgrading existing equipment to support QSIG. It is also important to note that as of this writing, CallManager 3.0 does not provide any support for QSIG; Cisco is expected to add support for QSIG to CallManager in a future release. Cisco voice gateways that support QSIG include the MC3810, 2600, 3600, and 7200 series routers with IOS 12.0(7)XK or later IOS releases.

Legacy-Based PBX Migration Strategies

Migrating to a converged AVVID network will mean different things to different organizations based on the number and types of legacy equipment currently installed and the network size. Some generalizations can be made, however, that will help identify a few strategies that can be used when an organization is faced with migrating to an AVVID network.

New Installations

The migration to a CallManager PBX system will be simplest for those organizations that do not yet have any voice network equipment installed. This may include new startup businesses, small businesses previously using Centrex services, or any other organization that has not yet invested in a phone system. Because there will be no existing equipment on hand, the only real integration that will be required is to the PSTN for calls to outside users.

Immediate Migration

Some organizations may choose to do an immediate migration ("flash cut") of all users from the legacy system to a new AVVID system. The advantage of this approach is that it will minimize integration issues with legacy equipment because the cutover to the new system will be immediate. For example, if an organization will be implementing a CallManager system to replace a legacy PBX (as indicated in Figure 3.1), there will be no need for the legacy components to coexist. This will eliminate any interoperability issues when preserving calling features and messaging waiting indications.

Figure 3.1 An Immediate "Flash Cut" Migration from an Existing PBX to CallManager

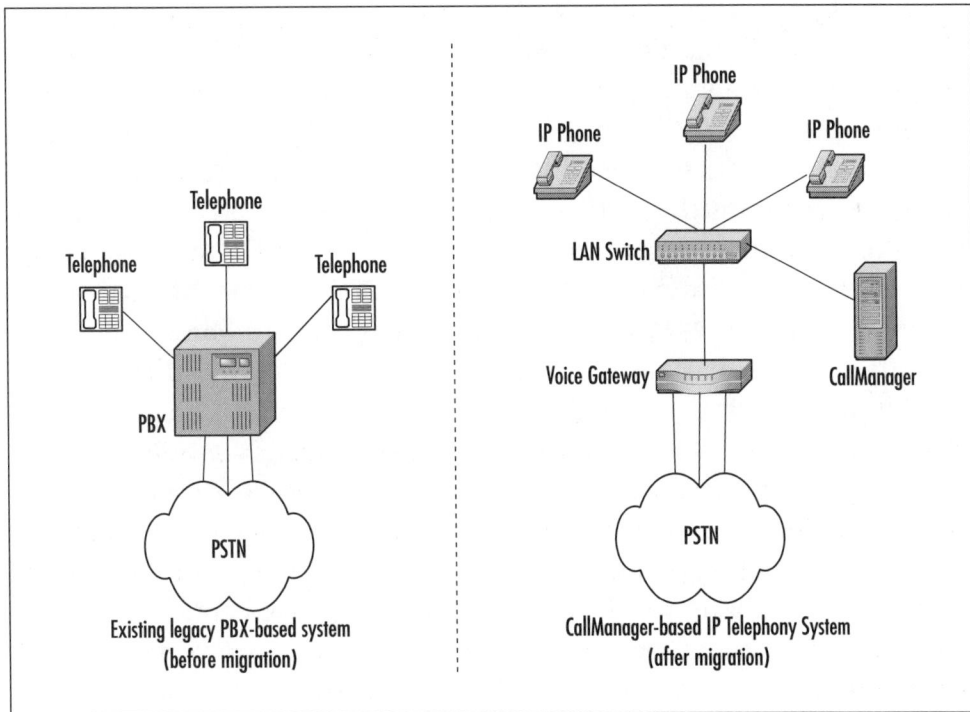

Phased Migration

The most challenging strategy in terms of preserving interoperability will be the phased migration. A phased migration assumes that an organization will implement an AVVID solution and gradually migrate users from the old system to the new AVVID system. This approach may also include a partial AVVID implementation while relying on legacy components for some functions. For example, a large organization may choose to implement CallManager as a replacement for its legacy PBXs while continuing to use a legacy voice messaging system.

There are typically three distinct phases for this migration strategy. First, a pilot system is deployed with a limited number of users. A common location where this begins within the organization is in the IT department. The pilot phase allows for all major components to be included and tested so that any issues can be worked out at this time. Once a successful pilot phase has been completed, the first group of users can be migrated, and the system is now in production mode. This initial migration may be carried out over a weekend to minimize service interruptions to system users. Finally, when all remaining users have been moved, the system is considered in full production, and the legacy equipment can be decommissioned. There are two variations for carrying out a phased migration. The first option assumes that users will retain their existing directory numbers (DNs) after the migration for use in the new IP telephony system. This would be the most desirable for systems with Direct Inward Dialing (DID) services because users would not be willing to change DNs in order to migrate to an AVVID system. This strategy requires that migrated extensions be deleted from the PBX, then added into the CallManager system.

The second variation of the phased migration is to run both systems in parallel. This approach requires that IP phones be configured for each user with new, unique phone numbers. Although this approach offers lower risk and greater fault tolerance, it would require users to have two working phones on their desktop during the migration phase. The obvious drawback to this approach is that users would not be too accepting of the fact that they now have two phone numbers. This also raises the issue of which phone numbers would be used in the long term.

Another consideration of a phased migration is that PSTN trunk facilities must be available for both systems during the migration because each system will be handling active users. There are two ways to handle this issue. First, all WAN facilities could remain on the existing PBX, requiring all PSTN calls to be routed through the existing PBX (see Figure 3.2). This may be desirable so that billing could be done at one location; however, billing for calls from an IP telephone in this configuration would be possible only if the connection method to the PBX supports calling number information. Once all users have been migrated from the existing PBX, WAN facilities can be moved to the appropriate AVVID PSTN gateway. The other approach is to make PSTN facilities available for both systems (see Figure 3.2). This approach would most likely involve extra costs during the migration phase due to the extra PSTN facilities that would be required. This approach would also mean that billing information would have to be captured at two different points. Once all users have been fully migrated to the AVVID system, the PSTN trunks on the existing PBX could be terminated or moved to the AVVID system.

Tromboning

Regardless of the exact approach taken for a phased migration, it is inherent that multiple systems will be in use simultaneously. This will invariably lead to the potential for a call to be transferred between systems. Transferring calls from the existing PBX to an IP telephone can lead to a situation known as tromboning. This situation results when a call originates on one system, gets transferred to the other system, then gets transferred back. Two channels will be consumed on a T1 facility when tromboning occurs and will remain in use until the call is completed. In the extreme case where this happens multiple times, a T1 facility could handle only 11 such calls.

Figure 3.2 Phased Migration Strategies

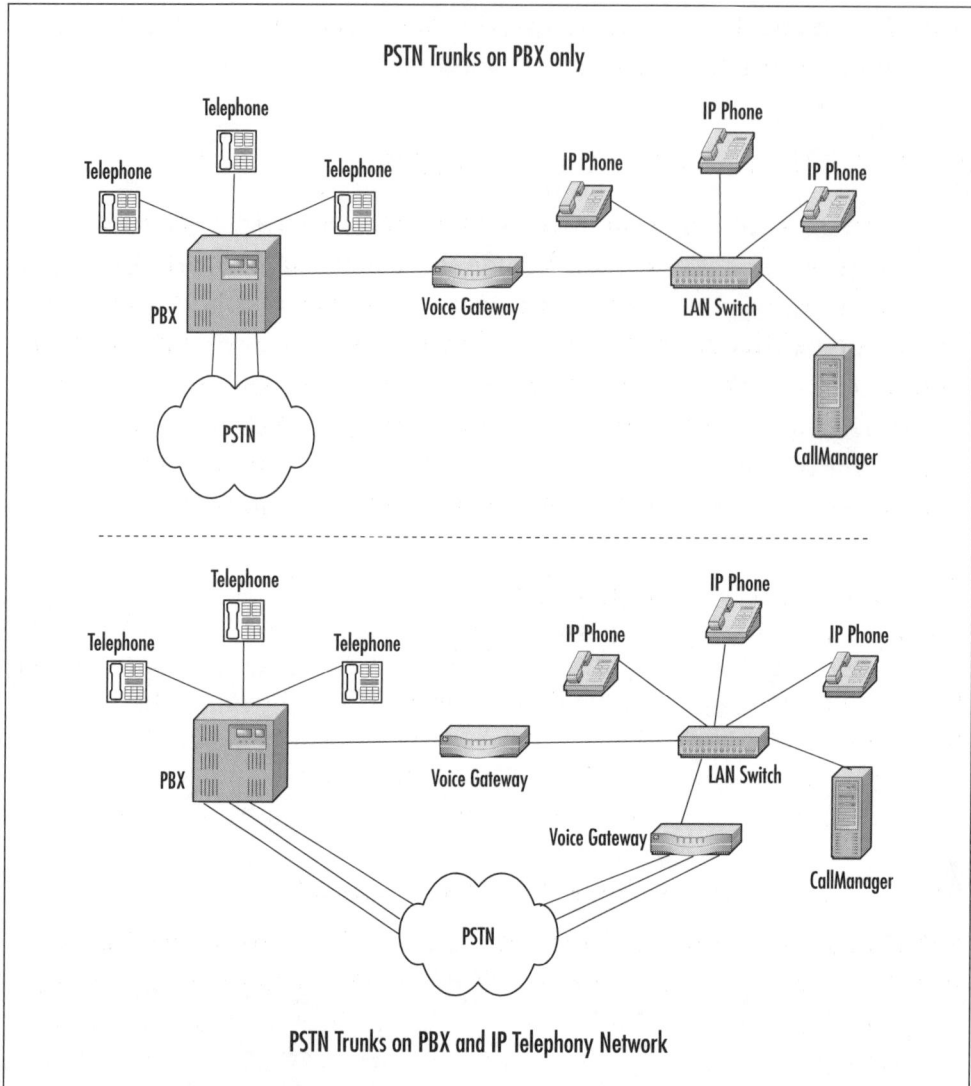

Planning and Executing a Voice Mail Migration

There was a time when voice mail was considered an optional component of an organization's telephony system. In today's business environment, however, it is very rare that an organization does not use voice mail. For this reason, we must consider how voice mail functionality will be preserved during the migration from a legacy system to an AVVID voice network.

Physical Interfaces and Protocols

There are essentially three communications paths that must be considered when migrating from legacy voice mail platforms to an AVVID system. The first consideration is the actual voice path between systems. Second, when messages are left for users, there must be a signaling path between systems in order to light or extinguish an MWI. Third, it may be necessary to network multiple voice messages together in order to pass messages between separate physical locations or between systems from different vendors.

Standard Protocols for Integrating with Voice Mail

In this section, we will discuss the standard protocols available for integrating and networking voice mail systems, including Simplified Message Desk Interface (SMDI), Audio Messaging Interchange Specification (AMIS), and Voice Profile for Internet Mail (VPIM).

Simplified Message Desk Interface (SMDI)

SMDI provides an open standard interface that can be used in an AVVID network for integrating a CallManager system with a legacy voice mail system. Originally defined in 1985 by Bellcore in document TR TSY-000283 for use with Centrex services, it has emerged as the de facto standard for integrating voice mail systems to PBXs or Central-Office (CO) switches.

The purpose of SMDI is to pass information between a switch and VM system for several different functions when calls are forwarded. First, SMDI can pass information about the calling party to the voice mail system such as called-station number, calling-station number, type of call forwarding situation, and more. Passing caller-ID information along with calls that are forwarded to voice mail eliminates the need for the VM system to prompt the caller for the desired extension. Similarly, when a local user calls through the PBX to retrieve voice messages, SMDI passes the calling extension to the VM system, avoiding the need to prompt the user for their extension. Another important function of SMDI is to pass information back from the VM system to the PBX in order to provide a message waiting indication). The actual MWI may take the form of a stutter dial tone, a flashing light, or a message displayed at the station. SMDI would also enable the MWI to be cleared when messages have been retrieved.

SMDI provides a dedicated signaling interface between a voice switch and a voice messaging system. For example, SMDI may be used between a PBX and voice messaging system that are co-located. Another possible use of SMDI is between a CO switch and a voice mail system that exists at a customer's site. The physical connection for an SMDI link is typically over an RS-232 interface. SMDI interfaces are provided via the standard COM ports of the MCS 7800 platforms for CallManager systems. SMDI interfaces are also available on many PBXs, including systems from Lucent, Nortel, Siemens, NEC, Mitel, Ericsson, and others. Figure 3.3 illustrates the use of SMDI in a legacy network between a voice mail system and a PBX and in an AVVID network between a CallManager and a legacy voice mail system.

Audio Messaging Interchange Specification (AMIS)

AMIS is a multi-vendor international standard for forwarding and transferring messages between voice messaging systems over analog facilities. This standard may be used in an AVVID network for networking a unified messaging server application to a legacy voice mail system. While it could also be used between multiple unified messaging servers, there are better alternatives for this type of connectivity such as Voice Profile for Internet Mail (VPIM), as described in the next section.

Figure 3.3 Voice Mail Integration Using SMDI

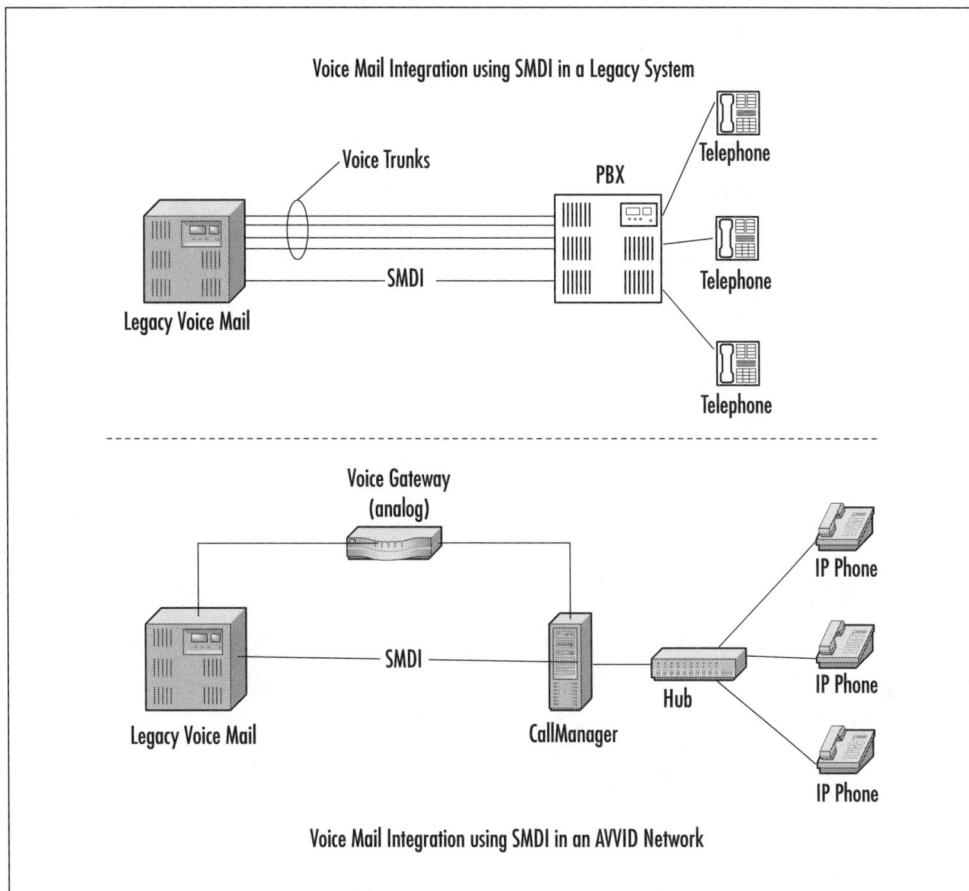

The AMIS standard emerged from a group of voice mail vendors and system users that initially met in 1988 to define a single standard for interoperability. There are actually two separate AMIS protocols defined: AMIS-A (analog) and AMIS-D (digital). The formal standard was issued in February of 1990. Prior to AMIS, there was no way for messaging systems from different vendors to exchange messages.

Using AMIS, multiple messaging systems located in the same building, on the same campus, in different cities, or even in different countries can be interconnected via the PSTN. A voice mail system that needs to send a message to another simply places a phone call to the receiving system and passes the message as analog voice data. DTMF tones can be used by the sending system to indicate the recipient's mailbox. AMIS is a relatively easy method of networking VM systems because it simply requires analog voice facilities. As a result, it is has become widely supported by most legacy voice mail system vendors.

Voice Profile for Internet Mail (VPIM)

VPIM is an international standard for transferring voice and fax messages between different voice mail systems using standard e-mail systems within an intranet or the public Internet. It is based on the Internet e-mail standards, Simple Mail Transfer Protocol (SMTP) and Multipurpose Internet Mail Extensions (MIME). Different voice mail systems can exchange messages if they can send and receive e-mail with audio attachments. VPIM can be used in an AVVID network for integrating a voice messaging (VM) or unified messaging (UM) server with a legacy voice mail system, or for networking multiple VM/UM servers together as a single system.

VPIM was developed by a consortium of messaging vendors including AVT, Centigram, Lucent, Nortel, Siemens, and others in conjunction with the Electronic Messaging Association. VPIM version 1 was formally approved by the IETF and published as RFC 1911 in February 1996. Version 2 was subsequently approved as a proposed standard and was published as RFC 2421 in September 1998. Work is currently underway on version 3, which has been renamed as Internet Voice Mail. The entire history and specifications for VPIM are available from the Electronic Messaging Association at www.ema.org/vpim.

There are major benefits of using VPIM for voice message networking over earlier alternatives such as AMIS. First, VPIM supports digital message formats, which means that it can be used in unified messaging environments that require support for fax messages. AMIS does not provide any support for routing faxes between messaging systems. Second, VPIM utilizes an IP network as the transmission facility between systems. This is a powerful capability because it would obviously include the possibility of using the public Internet as a communication path between messaging systems, thus eliminating the need for dedicated digital transmission facilities for networking multiple systems in the WAN. Figure 3.4 illustrates the use of VPIM to pass messages between systems across an IP WAN between multiple locations, and the use of VPIM to connect systems from different vendors at the same location. Third, the quality of the original message is maintained because there is no need to convert the message to analog for transmission because VPIM supports direct transfer of digital message formats. Fourth, most major messaging vendors will be providing support for VPIM, including Lucent, Nortel, Siemens, Centigram, Active Voice, and, of course, Cisco (currently, a limited number of vendors are actually shipping VPIM-capable products). For this reason, VPIM will enable the coexistence of multiple messaging systems during a system migration.

Figure 3.4 Voice Mail Networking Using VPIM

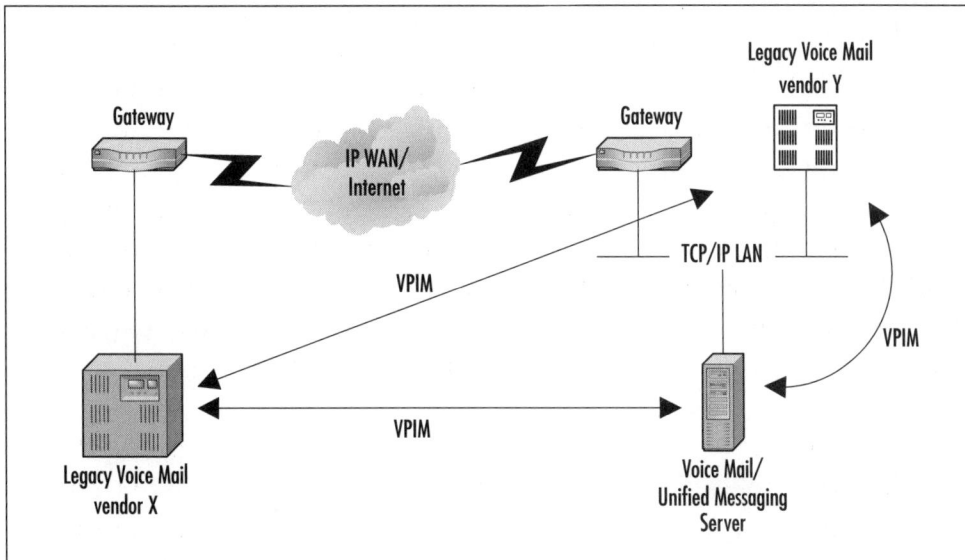

Like many of the industry standard protocols used in the Internet, the VPIM standard leverages work that has already been completed in other standards efforts. In the case of VPIM, this includes SMTP [RFC 821] and MIME [RFCs 20452049], which are currently used within many organizations today. In addition to these existing Internet standards, VPIM also specifies that voice messages being forwarded between systems from different vendors will be encoded using G.726 (32 Kbps ADPCM). Using these existing and widely adopted standards as a foundation will help to ensure the acceptance and stability of VPIM and guarantee that it will run on virtually all existing data networks. In short, VPIM formats compressed voice or fax messages using the MIME protocol and uses SMTP to send these messages between servers over an IP network.

VPIM provides support for basic message transfer functions such as sending, replying, and forwarding of messages between systems. In addition, it also includes the ability to send a message to multiple subscribers (the number of recipients for a single message is actually unlimited), non-delivery notification, and sending priority indications. VPIM actually provides 14 new functions that are not supported by AMIS-A. Below is a summary of the features supported by VPIM:

- Send/receive/reply/forward voice and fax messages

- Delivery/non-delivery notification

- Full-duplex message flow

- Message privacy

- Message sending priority

- Separate originator's voice name, text subject, spoken subject

- Service notification

- Unlimited number of messages/recipients per call

- Unlimited message length

Voice Mail Migration Strategies

Voice mail has become a necessary business tool for most organizations in today's world. This means that designing an AVVID voice network will require planning for voice messaging services in some fashion. Voice messaging in an AVVID network may be provided from a legacy voice mail system by an AVVID voice mail or unified messaging system. In either case, there are important considerations for providing this fundamental service in a converged network environment.

Voice mail users have come to expect a certain level of functionality based on the capabilities of most voice mail systems in place today. Most users will expect that call answer and message retrieval functions are generally automated so that users are faced with a minimum number of prompts when performing these functions. These user expectations lead to several important requirements when implementing voice mail solutions.

Call Answer When a calling party dials an IP telephone extension and the call is eventually forwarded to voice mail, the caller should automatically hear the user's greeting without responding to additional prompts from the system. This can be done only if the called number is made available to the voice mail system when the call is forwarded.

Message Retrieval When IP telephone users retrieve their messages by pressing the voice mail speed dial button, they should be automatically prompted for their password without first being prompted for an extension. This can be done only if the calling number is passed to the voice mail system in some fashion to automatically identify the calling user's voice mail box.

Message Waiting Indication (MWI) An IP telephone user's MWI should be switched on or off based on the status of the user's voice mail box.

As we will see in the scenarios that follow, these requirements are not always simple to implement in an IP telephony environment.

New Installations

As with a new installation of a CallManager PBX, a new installation of an AVVID voice messaging system is the simplest case. Assuming that an organization does not have any existing voice mail systems, an AVVID voice messaging system can be added to provide voice messaging for CallManager users. Normal call answering and message retrieval functions between CallManager IP telephone users and the voice messaging system are easily provided if CallManager and the voice messaging system may both support Cisco's Skinny Station Protocol (SSP). SSP is the call control signaling protocol used by Cisco's CallManager to set up calls between the CallManager and other devices, such as IP telephones and voice messaging servers.

Immediate Migration

The immediate migration ("flash cut") to an AVVID voice messaging system from a legacy voice messaging platform is also a relatively simple migration strategy that minimizes integration issues. Call answering and message retrieval functions are provided as in the previous scenario when Skinny Station Protocol is used. A "flash cut" strategy is depicted in Figure 3.5.

Phased Migration

The phased migration strategy is the most challenging of the three possible options. It is inherent in this approach that multiple systems will be active simultaneously; therefore this approach presents the greatest integration challenges of the three possible migration strategies.

There are three variations of the phased migration strategy. The first option assumes that voice messaging will continue to be provided for all users by an existing legacy system connected behind the PBX, as depicted in Figure 3.6. Call answer and message retrieval functions for PBX users will remain the same because

Figure 3.5 A "Flash Cut" Voice Mail Migration Strategy

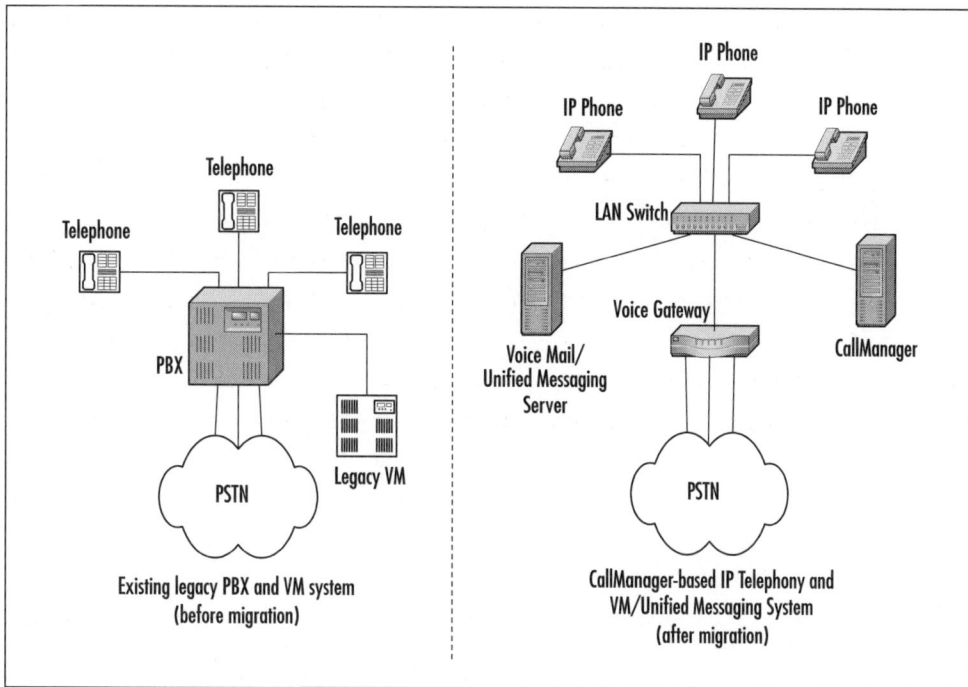

nothing will change for those users in the way that they are connected to the system. The capabilities of the actual voice message system being used will determine the level of answer/retrieval functions available to IP telephone users during the migration. If the existing voice mail system does not have any standard method for integrating with CallManager (namely SMDI), none of the minimum required features described previously will be available to IP telephone users. While there are workarounds for passing the called/calling party information, they involve additional complexity in PBX administration and the need for users to manage multiple DNs. There are no workarounds in this scenario for passing MWI to the IP telephone users.

Figure 3.6 Legacy Voice Messaging: Limited Integration

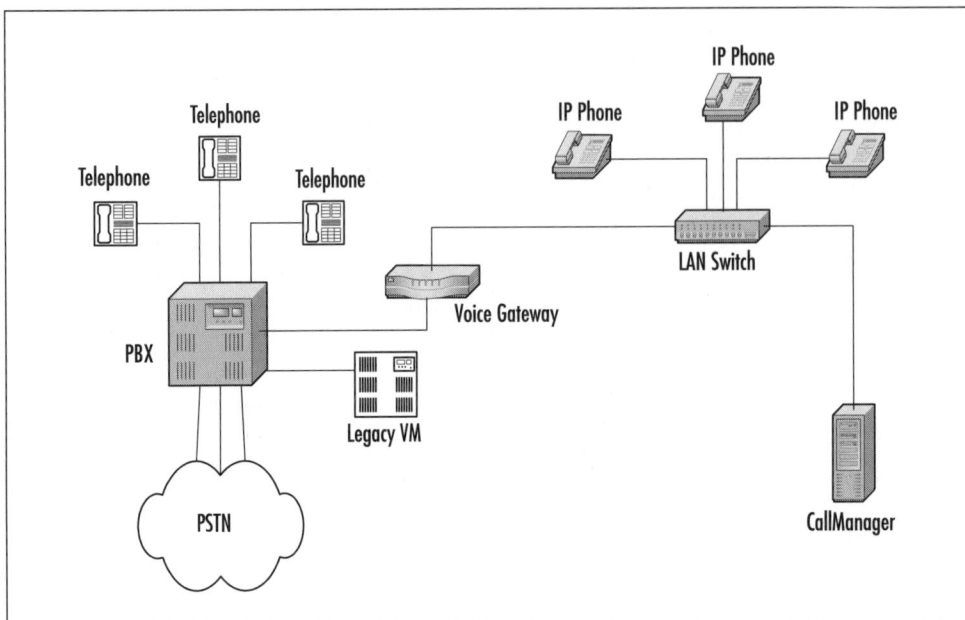

The second option for a phased migration also assumes that the existing voice messaging system will provide services for all users. The key difference in this option is that normal call answer and message retrieval functions will be available to IP telephone users. Tighter integration will be achieved by using an SMDI link and an analog gateway between the voice mail system and the CallManager IP network, as depicted in Figure 3.7. This option overcomes the limitations of the scenario described previously.

With separate paths to each system, the voice mail system can treat the PBX and CallManager as individual systems. This means that calls to IP telephones that are forwarded to voice mail can go directly to the voice mail system via a gateway without being routed through the PBX. As long as the selected gateway can pass the required called/calling party information to the voice mail system, normal call answer and message retrieval functions can be provided. Assuming that an SMDI link is available on the legacy voice mail system, MWI information can be passed to the CallManager, which can then be forwarded to individual handsets.

Figure 3.7 Legacy Voice Messaging: SMDI Integration

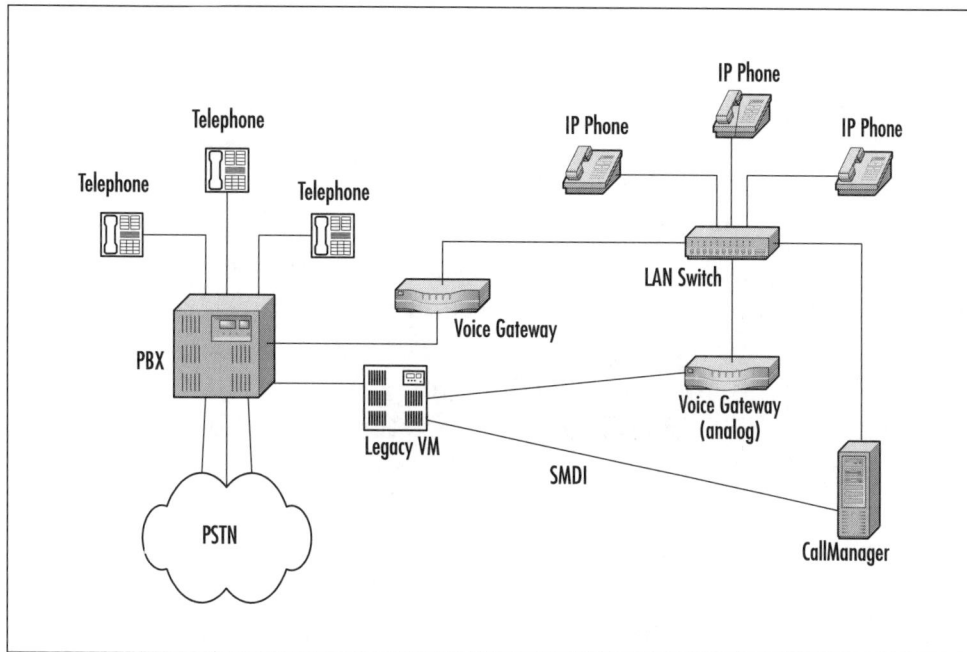

In order to provide this level of functionality, there are certain requirements for the voice messaging system. First, it must be capable of supporting multiple simultaneous PBXs in its configuration database. This would allow an individual extension to be associated with a particular PBX, and MWI information could be passed over the correct link. Second, the existing voice messaging system must have sufficient capacity to support simultaneous physical connections to the existing PBX and the gateway to the CallManager IP network. Third, the voice message system must have an SMDI interface. It is important to note that not all voice messaging systems will meet these requirements and that some may need hardware and software upgrades to meet these requirements. It is beyond the scope of this text to provide a list of such systems that meet these requirements, but note that Cisco has verified and officially supports this configuration with the Octel Aria 250 and 350 systems. A detailed description of the exact configuration for integrating with these systems is available on Cisco's Web site at www.cisco.com.

Another important restriction worth noting in this scenario is that when an SMDI link is used between the voice messaging system and CallManager, this limits the gateway selection of the voice gateway to the CallManager IP network. Only analog trunks can be used between the gateway and the voice messaging system if an SMDI link is used. Another way to view this restriction is that this scenario will not work for large organizations that have only digital trunk cards available on their voice messaging system. For such an organization to utilize SMDI to pass MWI information from the VMS to CallManager, it would require retrofitting the VMS with analog trunk cards. In many cases, this would be cost-prohibitive.

The third option for a phased migration is to deploy a Unified Messaging server for messaging services for IP telephony users, while PBX users continue to utilize the legacy voice mail system. This option is depicted in Figure 3.8. With this migration option, the answer/retrieval features available to IP telephone users will have the same restrictions as the first option discussed for a phased migration. That is, normal answer/retrieval and MWI functions would most likely not be available with this option.

Figure 3.8 Legacy Voice Messaging: Phased Migration

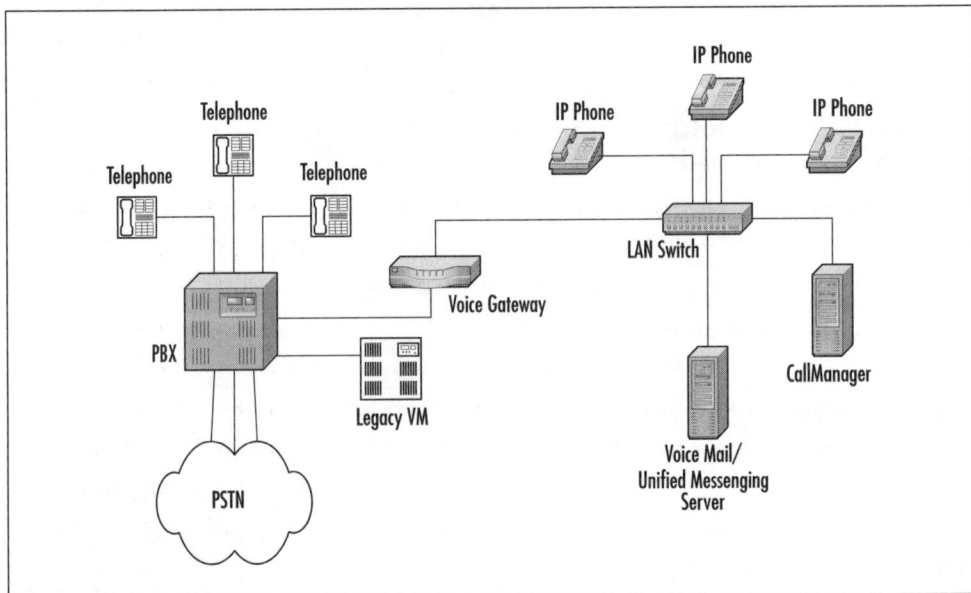

Another point to consider in this option is that there are now multiple separate voice mail systems. This could lead to some restrictions for users of both systems if the new voice messaging system does not support a VMS networking solution such as AMIS-A or VPIM. Without networking support, users from either system cannot interact with VMS features such as distribution lists, message reply/forwarding, and more. For example, if a user of the existing system wanted to set up a distribution list, IP telephone users could not be part of the list because the systems cannot directly interact. While these restrictions may be significant for some users, keep in mind that this is only a temporary situation until the migration is complete.

Multiple SMDI Links

There may be cases when integrating a legacy VMS to an AVVID system that will require multiple SMDI links. For example, if a legacy VMS will provide messaging services for both PBX and IP telephone users, it is desirable to provide MWI information to the PBX and to the CallManager. Because most VMS systems were originally designed to integrate with only a single PBX at any one time, it is very common for these systems to support only a single SMDI link. While some VMS systems will provide direct support for multiple SMDI links (e.g., Octel 200/300 series systems), this is not an easily implemented solution. If the VMS being used supports only a single SMDI link, this presents a challenge.

The good news is that there is a possible solution that may provide the required functionality. Using a combination of a PC-based software application and a hardware adapter, a single SMDI link can be adapted to serve multiple PBX systems. The required hardware adapter is a PC/X Non-Intelligent Host Adapter from DigiBoard (www.digi.com), which simply provides additional COM ports for

Continued

> the host PC. The required software is a DOS-based application
> called VoiceBridge/Mux from Voice Technologies Group, Inc.
> (www.vtg.com), which can support SMDI signaling on up to 9 COM
> ports. Using this solution, a VMS can be configured as if it were
> using Centrex SMDI services on a single link, which is then connected
> to a COM port on the VB/Mux PC. Additional COM ports on the PC
> are then connected to the PBX and the CallManager's COM port.

NOTE

VTG was recently acquired by Intel and merged into its Dialogic unit.

Summary

Migrating toward an AVVID solution involves important design considerations for all components including existing PBXs, voice mail systems, CallManager, Unified Messaging servers, and gateways. Most system migrations will require some level of integration between these devices.

The first step toward migration involves gaining an understanding of the physical connections and protocols that will be used for integrating system components. This will essentially require selection of a "common denominator" between devices that must interoperate. Standards protocols are available for this task including ISDN PRI, QSIG, and analog facilities for integrating with existing PBXs. Protocols for integrating with voice messaging systems include SMDI, AMIS-A, and VPIM.

After gaining an understanding of the possible connection methods, it is important to select a migration strategy that will preserve user features and minimize system interruptions. There are many restrictions and trade-offs to consider when choosing an option for migrating toward an AVVID solution. Possible migration strategies include an immediate migration or a phased approach. For organizations installing new AVVID systems, integration issues will not be an issue because there are no installed components that must be integrated into the AVVID solution.

FAQs

Q: Can QSIG be used to integrate a legacy PBX with a CallManager IP PBX?

A: While QSIG offers the greatest potential for robust feature support between systems, Cisco's CallManager 3.x does not currently provide support for the QSIG protocol. Designers wishing to use QSIG should consider ISDN PRI as an alternative.

Q: How can voice mail systems from different vendors be networked together as a single system?

A: There are two open standard protocols available for networking voice mail systems. The first is AMIS-A, which is a simple protocol that operates over dial-up POTS lines. The second is the VPIM standard, which utilizes existing e-mail standards (SMTP and MIME) to pass encoded voice messages between systems as e-mail attachments over an IP network connection. VPIM is a more robust protocol and offers greater feature functionality; however, AMIS-A is very easy to implement.

Q: Cisco Systems has been in the "data" market for the past several years. Is the voice market (PBX-like systems) something that is new to Cisco?

A: When we look at the AVVID solution we realize that it's divided into two parts: an "infrastructure" and a "system." The infrastructure piece, although "voice/IP Telephony," is still transmitting "data." Who else but Cisco can guarantee a reliable, efficient, scalable data infrastructure? On the system side of the solution we will notice that Cisco has acquired a number of companies that have led the market in their respective technologies, thereby giving Cisco the market leading "system" solution for IP telephony.

Q: What industry standard protocols are available for integrating legacy voice systems with IP telephony systems?

A: Several industry standards have been defined for integrating between legacy systems and IP telephony systems, including SMDI, AMIS, and VPIM. However, vendor support for these protocols must be verified for all system components as they have not yet been universally adopted.

Q: It seems that there are still a lot of features and functions that are not supported by Cisco's CallManager and Active Voice. Is it fair to say that implementing an IP telephony solution now is a bit premature?

A: IP telephony, in general, is in a developmental state. A year ago many legacy PBX vendors did not believe in an IP telephony future. Cisco, on the other hand, has said all along that this is the wave of the future. Cisco is the first company to market with a complete IP telephony architecture, and although some of the features are currently not supported, it is the only "complete" solution available.

Chapter 4

Configuring Cisco CallManager

Solutions in this chapter:

- CallManager Hardware Platforms

- CallManager Software Overview: Features and Functionality

- CallManager Deployment Models

- Configuring and Deploying IP Handsets

- An Overview of VoIP Gateways

- Monitoring CallManager Activity

- Understanding the Packages, Licensing, and Upgrades

- What to Expect in the Next Version of Cisco CallManager

Introduction

Cisco's CallManager software provides the necessary functions of call-processing, signaling, and connection services for an AVVID IP telephony solution. Call processing involves the set-up and tear-down of calls, supplementary services, and other required functions for the entire telephony system. In a legacy telephony system, this function is normally provided by a PBX. CallManager provides this function via a software application on one or more PC-based hardware platforms running the Windows NT or Windows 2000 operating system.

The CallManager software communicates with devices such as IP telephones, voice gateways, legacy telephony devices, and multimedia applications such as conferencing and voice messaging in a distributed network environment. Communications with these devices is enabled with support for such protocols as the Skinny Station Protocol, H.323, MGCP, and SMDI.

CallManager also serves as a platform for extending the functionality of the telephony system. Additional voice applications are available separately from Cisco that can add voice messaging, softphone, voice conferencing, manual attendant console, and other functions. Other data, voice, and video services can also be added to a CallManager-based system by integrating with third-party software applications from a growing list of application developers. This extensibility is enabled via the Telephony Application Programming Interface (TAPI) and Java Telephony Application Programming Interface (JTAPI) standards supported on the CallManager platform. Examples of such applications include interactive voice response (IVR) systems, automated attendant, unified messaging, and multimedia conferencing.

How Reliable Is a CallManager-Based Telephony System?

This is a question that frequently arises for organizations that are considering an IP PBX telephony system as a replacement or an alternative to a traditional key system or PBX-based telephony system. There are also certain expectations about the answer to this question, such as "five nines" (99.999 percent) reliability. At first glance, it seems that this should be an easy comparison to make; however, there are some fundamental differences to consider between traditional telephony systems and IP PBX systems such as an AVVID solution.

The first key difference to understand is that a CallManager-based AVVID solution is a distributed system, whereas most legacy telephony systems rely on a single, centralized PBX to provide most of the system functions. An AVVID solution consists of the CallManager, as well as LAN switches and cabling, routers, VoIP gateways, and IP telephones. The reliability of the entire system can be quantified only when considering the associated reliability of all of the components. On the other hand, it is relatively straightforward to quantify the reliability of a legacy system since there is essentially only one device, the PBX. Although some may argue that PBXs are inherently more reliable than any of the components in a distributed system, it is important to remember that redundancy can also be provided for any of the devices in an AVVID network.

A second consideration is that reliability is like all other things in life—you get as much as you plan for and are willing to pay for. A reliable AVVID network can only be realized through proper planning and design; the entire system will be only as reliable as the foundation upon which it is built. It is possible to build VoIP networks with reliability on par with legacy business-class telephony systems. Redundancy at the hardware level for components such as LAN switches, routers, and gateways is only the beginning. It is only through proper design and implementation that these devices will actually provide a reliable foundation for a reliable VoIP network.

CallManager Hardware Platforms

CallManager software is available only as a preloaded application on a Cisco Media Convergence Server (MCS) hardware platform. The MCS servers available from Cisco are actually PC-based, server-class, high availability platforms manufactured by Compaq exclusively for Cisco. At the time of this writing, Compaq's Prosignia 720 series servers are the foundation of the Cisco MCS-782x series servers and the ProLiant 1600R servers are the foundation for the MCS-783x series servers. Additional models and upgrades to the MCS platforms will certainly be available over time as PC technology continues to advance. The requirement for CallManager to be loaded on one of the MCS platforms began with the release of version 2.4. Although it is technically possible to install CallManager on third-party hardware platforms, Cisco does not support these configurations.

At the time of this writing, four MCS platforms are available for selection as a CallManager platform. There are obvious differences between the platforms, such as the basic hardware package that is offered. There are also differences in the operating systems and additional software applications that are included with each of the server platforms. Table 4.1 summarizes the key features of each.

Table 4.1 A Media Convergence Server Comparison

	7822	7825-800	7835	7835-1000
Hardware Features				
Processor	500MHz Intel PIII	800MHz Intel PIII	733MHz Intel PIII	1GHz Intel PIII
RAM	512MB	512MB	1GB	1GB
Hard Drive	Single 9.1GB SCSI, non-hot-plug	Single 20GB Fast ATA	Dual 18.2GB Ultra2 SCSI	Dual 18.2GB Ultra3 SCSI
Hot-swap HD	No	No	Yes	Yes
Redundant PS	No	No	Yes	Yes

Continued

Table 4.1 Continued

	7822	7825-800	7835	7835-1000
Hardware Features				
Hardware RAID controller	No	No	Yes	Yes
Size	3U	1U	3U	3U
Software Features				
Operating System	Windows 2000	Windows 2000	Windows NT or Windows 2000	Windows 2000
CallManager	Yes	Yes	Yes	Yes
uOne Corporate Edition	No	No	Yes	No
IP IVR/Auto Attendant	No	Yes	Yes	Yes

One of the important differences to note between the CallManager platforms is the operating system that each platform supports. All CallManager versions 2.x required Windows NT 4.0 as the operating system. To improve the scalability and reliability of the CallManager application, Cisco chose to migrate to the Windows 2000 Server edition as the operating system beginning with version 3.0. Because of the different operating system requirements between CallManager versions, there are some important limitations to consider in conjunction with the uOne messaging software application. With the initial release of CallManager 2.4 on the MCS-7830 platforms, the uOne v4.1 Entry Edition was included with the suite of software applications. It is possible to host both of these applications on the same server since both applications run on the Windows NT 4.0 operating system. With the requirement of CallManager 3.x to run on Windows 2000 Server edition, this means that the uOne messaging application must now be hosted on a separate server since it still requires Windows NT 4.0 as the operating system. In short, Cisco CallManager and the uOne messaging application can only be deployed as an "all-in-one" solution with CallManager 2.4 on the MCS-7830 platform.

An important consideration when selecting between the MCS hardware platforms is the number of required devices that will be registering with the CallManager. Devices that must register with the CallManager include IP phones, voice mail ports, TAPI/JTAPI devices, gateways, and DSP resources. Each device that registers with the CallManager is assigned a different weighting factor according to the amount of CallManager memory and CPU resources required for support of that device. Table 4.2 summarizes these device weights for various platforms.

Table 4.2 AVVID Device Weights

Device	Weight per session/voice channel
IP phone	1
Analog/digital gateway	3
Transcoding/conferencing DSP, MTP	3
TAPI/JTAPI port	20
uOne	3

These weighting factors must then be applied to all of the devices that will be registering with a given CallManager to determine the total number of device units. Another consideration is that many device types will support multiple sessions/channel on a single device, so this must be factored in as well. For example, a 24-port digital gateway would actually consume 72 total device units per gateway ([3 device units per session] x [24 sessions maximum] = 72). For each of the MCS platforms, there is a maximum number of supported device units, of which, there is a maximum number that can be allocated to IP telephones. Table 4.3 provides a summary of these limits for each platform.

Table 4.3 Maximum Device Weights for MCS Platforms

Server Platform	Maximum Device Units	Maximum IP Phones
MCS-7835-1000	5000	2500
MCS-7835	5000	2500
MCS-7825-800	1000	500
MCS-7822	1000	500

Scalability/Redundancy

The CallManager application is responsible for the call control functionality within an AVVID IP Telephony system. Call control is obviously a very critical function; therefore, the CallManager platform must provide both scalability and reliability.

CallManager 2.x

Version 2.3 was the first release of CallManager that provided any level of redundancy. The redundancy feature available in the 2.3 and 2.4 releases provided for a simple hot-standby capability in the event that the primary CallManager server should fail. Although this provided a basic level of fault tolerance for the CallManager server, there were some important limitations to consider. First, the hot-standby CallManager could not be used to host any devices; it sat waiting in an idle state to take over in the event that the primary server failed. Also, it was necessary to make sure that the CallManager databases were maintained identically between the primary and backup servers. This involved making manual changes to both servers or using scripts to copy the necessary database files between the servers when any configuration changes were made. CallManager 2.x releases utilized Microsoft Access for the primary database.

Another limitation of the redundancy services available in the 2.x releases of CallManager was that they were available only for IP phones and gateways. Redundancy services were not supported for H.323 devices or plug-in applications such as the conference bridge, media termination point, attendant console, unified messaging interface, directory services, and TAPI ports. In addition, when the primary CallManager was restored, devices using the CallManager server needed to be re-homed manually to the primary server, and plug-in applications needed to be restarted so that they could register once again with the primary CallManager.

As for scalability, CallManager 2.x releases could officially support up to 200 users per system. The system was actually capable of supporting significantly more users—however, Cisco imposed these artificial limits in order to ensure that the early system deployments were supportable by their Technical Assistance Center. System deployments requiring more than 200 users required special authorization from Cisco prior to deployment.

CallManager 3.x

Dramatic improvements have been made with regard to both CallManager reliability and scalability with the introduction of CallManager version 3.0. With this release, Cisco has introduced clustering technology that can be deployed between multiple CallManager servers. A CallManager cluster is a collection of multiple CallManager servers that share the same common database in a distributed environment. The clustering technology overcomes the limitations of the single redundant server supported in 2.x releases and also provides significant increases in the number of simultaneous users per system. The redundancy scheme utilized in CallManager 3.0 and higher provides redundancy of the call processing function as well as the configuration database. One server in a cluster is the publisher of the master configuration database; all other servers are subscribers to the master database and also maintain their own backup copies of the master database. All database operations are handled by the database publisher during normal system operations. Clustering provides higher reliability and availability since individual members of the cluster can continue functioning using their local database if the master database becomes unavailable for any reason.

NOTE

In addition to changing the underlying operating system for CallManager, the configuration database was also changed with the release of CallManager 3.0. Prior versions of CallManager utilized Microsoft's Access database. CallManager release 3.0 and higher utilize Microsoft's SQL Server database, which improves the scalability and reliability features of the CallManager platform.

Call processing redundancy within a cluster requires the creation of groups. A group is a logical collection of CallManager servers and their associated devices, such as IP telephones and gateways, consisting of one primary CallManager server and one or two backup CallManagers. When groups are created, CallManager servers are listed in order of priority for controlling the group in the event that the primary CallManager fails. The first backup CallManager will take control of the groups devices if the primary CallManager fails. If a second backup has been defined, it will take over if the primary and first backups have failed.

A single CallManager 3.0 server can handle up to 2500 IP telephone users per system. A cluster of CallManagers can consist of a maximum of eight servers, of which up to six are capable of providing call processing functions. In large systems, the other two servers can be configured as a dedicated database publisher and a dedicated TFTP server. The database publisher is responsible for all configuration changes throughout the system and also maintaining the database of call detail records (CDRs). The TFTP server is responsible for providing the required files for devices (such as phones, gateways, etc.) as they are initialized on the network. Downloaded files would include such things as configuration files, device code images, and audio files for custom ring tones. For larger systems, it is recommended that the database publisher and TFTP server be dedicated systems. Smaller systems can combine these functions on a single server.

The optimum number of CallManager servers within a cluster is a function of the number of users that will be supported by the entire CallManager cluster. Cisco's recommended design guidelines for determining the number of servers required per cluster are summarized in Table 4.4 and further information can be found on Cisco's Web site at the following URL: www.cisco.com/univercd/cc/td/doc/product/voice/ip_tele/network/dgclustr.htm

Table 4.4 Cisco Guidelines for CallManager Capacity Planning

Required Number of IP Phones within a Cluster	Recommended Number of CallManager Servers	Maximum Number of IP Phones per CallManager Server
200	Two servers total: (1) primary CallManager (1) combined publisher/TFTP/ backup CallManager	2500
2500	Three servers total: (1) combined publisher/TFTP (1) primary CallManager (1) backup CallManager	2500
5000	Four servers total: (1) combined publisher/TFTP (2) primary CallManagers (1) backup CallManager	2500
10,000	Eight servers total: (1) Database publisher (1) TFTP server (4) Primary CallManagers (2) backup CallManagers	2500

The maximum number of users currently supported in a single cluster is 10,000. For additional scalability, multiple clusters can be interconnected. Initially, this is limited to a maximum of ten clusters;

however, it is expected that this number will be increased over time as future releases of CallManager become available.

Redundancy of the CallManager server function is provided by the clustering of multiple CallManager servers as described previously. Unlike the hot-standby server that was used in CallManager release 3.x, CallManagers that are members of a cluster can all be used to handle active calls in the system; there is no requirement to have an idle CallManager within the cluster. The only requirement is that there is enough idle capacity within the entire CallManager cluster to support the users of a single server in the event that any member of the cluster should fail. For this reason, there is a maximum of only 2000 users per system when deploying a cluster of five servers (idle capacity of 500 users on each of four systems will support the maximum 2000 users if the fifth server should fail).

The improved reliability within the cluster comes from the fact that a device such as an IP telephone or a VoIP gateway can automatically fail-over to an alternate CallManager within the cluster. Each device has a limit of up to three CallManagers that can be listed in priority as primary, secondary, and tertiary. An IP phone maintains an active TCP session with both the primary and secondary assigned CallManager. The fail-over to a redundant server typically will occur within only five seconds. When the primary CallManager is restored, the IP phone will revert back to its listed primary CallManager. This redundancy scheme also applies to gateway devices that support the Skinny Gateway Protocol.

From both the user's and administrator's point of view, a cluster of CallManagers appears as a single system. For example, when a user places a call from an IP telephone to another IP telephone that is homed to a different CallManager within the cluster, the user has no way to know that multiple CallManager's are in use. This is also true when calls are forwarded or transferred to extensions across multiple CallManagers in a cluster. To simplify operations for the system administrator, management tools can function across an entire cluster as a single system. For example, CDRs for the entire cluster are maintained on the primary CallManager database and records are synchronized for calls placed from all members of the cluster. Also, the health of an entire cluster can be monitored with common event logs and performance monitoring capabilities.

TIP

An important consideration to keep in mind when deploying CallManager clusters is that no member of a cluster may exist across a WAN link. In order to ensure proper Quality of Service (QoS) within a cluster, all members of the cluster must be co-located on the local area network, with a minimum bandwidth of 10 Mbps. It is also required that the LAN infrastructure be switched, not shared media. Besides ensuring QoS, this will also ensure proper connectivity for intracluster communications.

Communications within the cluster include replication of the configuration database that is maintained on the publisher and replicated to the subscriber nodes. This process ensures that configuration information is consistent among all members of the cluster and also provides redundancy of the database. The other type of intracluster communication is the resulting traffic from propagation and replication of runtime data that occurs during registration of IP phones, gateways, and other devices.

A CallManager Software Overview: Features and Functionality

The features provided by the CallManager software can be broken down into three main groups: user features, administrative features, and system capabilities. User features include the basic telephony services provided to IP telephone users on the system, such as call forward, call park, calling line ID (CLID), and so on. Administrative features and system capabilities refer to features of concern mostly to system managers and system designers. Although Cisco's CallManager doesn't yet support a long list of user features as compared to a traditional PBX, the basic telephony requirements of most business environments can be satisfied with the features available today. It is also worth noting that since CallManager is a software application, additional feature functionality can be provided in the future simply via software upgrades. We will list some of the current features and capabilities in the sections to follow. Realize that the CallManager product evolves and new releases roll out there will likely be added and enhanced features and capabilities.

User Features

The following is a list of CallManager's user features. It is best to visit Cisco's Web site at www.cisco.com for the most current user features available for current releases.

- Answer/answer release
- Auto-answer
- Call connection
- Call Forward-All/Busy/No Answer
- Call hold/retrieve
- Call park/pickup
- Call pickup group-directed/universal
- Call status per line (state, duration, number)
- Call waiting/retrieve
- Calling Line ID (CLID)
- Calling Party Name ID (CNID)
- Click-to-dial from Web browser
- Direct Inward Dial (DID)
- Direct Outward Dial (DOD)
- Directory dial from phone
- Distinctive ring per phone

- Hands-free, full-duplex speakerphone
- HTML help access from phone
- Last number redial
- Message waiting indication
- Multiparty conferencing (ad-hoc and meet-me)
- Multiple line appearances per phone
- Mute for speakerphone and handset
- Off-hook dialing
- Operator attendant via Web-based console
- QoS statistics at phone
- Recent dial list
- Single button data collaboration on SoftPhone
- Single directory number, multiple phones (bridged line appearances)
- Speed dial (user configured)
- Station volume controls
- Transfer-with consultation
- Web services access from phone

Administrative Features

The following is a list of CallManager's administrative features. A detailed list of CallManager administrative features in current releases can be found in the CallManager datasheets on Cisco's Web site.

- Application discovery and registration to SNMP manager
- Call Detail Records
- Centralized, replicated configuration database, distributed web-based management consoles

- Configurable and default ringer .WAV file per phone

- Database automated change notification

- Date/time display format configurable per phone

- Debug information to common syslog file

- Device addition through wizards

- Device downloadable feature upgrades

- Device groups and pools for large system management

- Device mapping tool (IP address to MAC addresses)

- DHCP block IP assignment

- Dialed number translation table (inbound/outbound)

- Dialed Number Identification Service (DNIS)

- Enhanced 911 service

- H.323 compliant interface to H.323 clients gateways, and gatekeepers

- JTAPI v1.3 CTI

- LDAP v3 directory interface

- MGCP support to VG-200 & AS2600 gateways

- Native supplementary services support to Cisco H.323 v2 gateways

- Paperless phones—no paper templates required

- Performance monitoring via SNMP

- QoS statistics per call/device

- Redirected DNIS, outbound

- Select specified line appearance to ring

- Select specified phone to ring

- Single CDR per cluster

- Single point system/device configuration

- Sortable component list be device and directory

- System event reporting
- TAPI v2.1 CTI
- Time zone configurable per phone
- Zero-cost automated phone moves/adds/changes

System Capabilities

The following is a list of CallManager's system capabilities. A detailed list of CallManager system capabilities in current releases can be found in the CallManager datasheets on Cisco's Web site.

- Alternate automatic routing
- Attenuation/gain adjustment per device
- Automated bandwidth selection per call
- Automatic route selection
- Call admission control
- Comfort noise generation
- Dial plan partitioning (multi-site and multi-tenant)
- Digit analysis and call treatment
- Distributed call processing
- FAX over IP
- H.323 interface to selected third-party devices
- Hot-line/PLAR
- Interface to H.323 gateway
- Multiple ISDN protocol support
- Multiple remote CallManager administration and debug utilities
- Off-premise station (OPX)
- Outbound call blocking (system-wide)

- Out-of-band DTMF signaling over IP

- PSTN failover

- Redundancy

- Third-party application support

- Shared resource/application management and configuration (conferencing and transcoder)

- Silence suppression and voice activity detection

- Simplified North American Numbering Plan (NANP)/Non-NANP numbering plan support

- SMDI interface (for message waiting indication)

- Toll restriction

- Unified device and system configuration

- Unified dial plan

Enhanced 911 Support

For CallManager deployments in North America, an important consideration is support for Enhanced 911 (E911) services. E911 is an important health and safety issue that must be addressed prior to system deployment as it requires careful planning of equipment and service selection. Most cities in North America handle calls for emergency services when users dial the well-known number 911 for emergency situations. Enhanced 911 service is an advanced form of 911 service that can provide additional information to the 911 dispatch center automatically at the time of the call in the event that the caller is unable to provide this information. In the United States, regulations for E911 compliance vary by city or state since currently there are no national regulations in place. Some states have very strict requirements that must be followed for any multiline telephone system (MLTS). A CallManager telephony system is considered an MLTS and therefore must provide support for E911 services.

Cisco's CallManager 2.4 and higher can provide E911 support on par with legacy telephony systems. Automatic Number Identification (ANI) information can be delivered to the public safety answering point (PSAP) via H.323 gateways using either analog or digital trunking methods. PSAP is simply the term that is used to refer to the agency that answers the 911 emergency calls. Analog trunking requires a third-party gateway with support for centralized automatic message accounting (CAMA); digital trunking requires use of ISDN PRI services in order to pass the proper information to the PSAP. Since Cisco does not yet directly support CLID on analog gateways, Cisco partners with Netergy Networks (www.netergynet.com) for this piece. Similarly, Cisco partners with Telident (www.telident.com) for support of CAMA trunking interfaces in order to provide a complete solution for E911 support in a CallManager system.

When a user places a 911 call from an IP Telephone, the CallManager is responsible for passing the calling number ID to the CO switch. At this point, the CO switch then must pass the automatic number identification (ANI) information to an E911 selective router, which then forwards the information to the correct PSAP. Once the PSAP has received the ANI information, a query is sent to an automatic location information (ALI) database to determine information about the caller. An ALI database can contain address, sub-address, nearest cross-street, and other information that may be useful to emergency services crews. This information can then be displayed for the dispatcher on a workstation in order to dispatch the appropriate emergency services personnel and resources for the emergency. The ALI database may be maintained by the local phone company or an independent agency and may be located on site or at a remote location. Figure 4.1 provides an illustration of the E911 call flow process when using CallManager.

Figure 4.1 E911 Call Flow

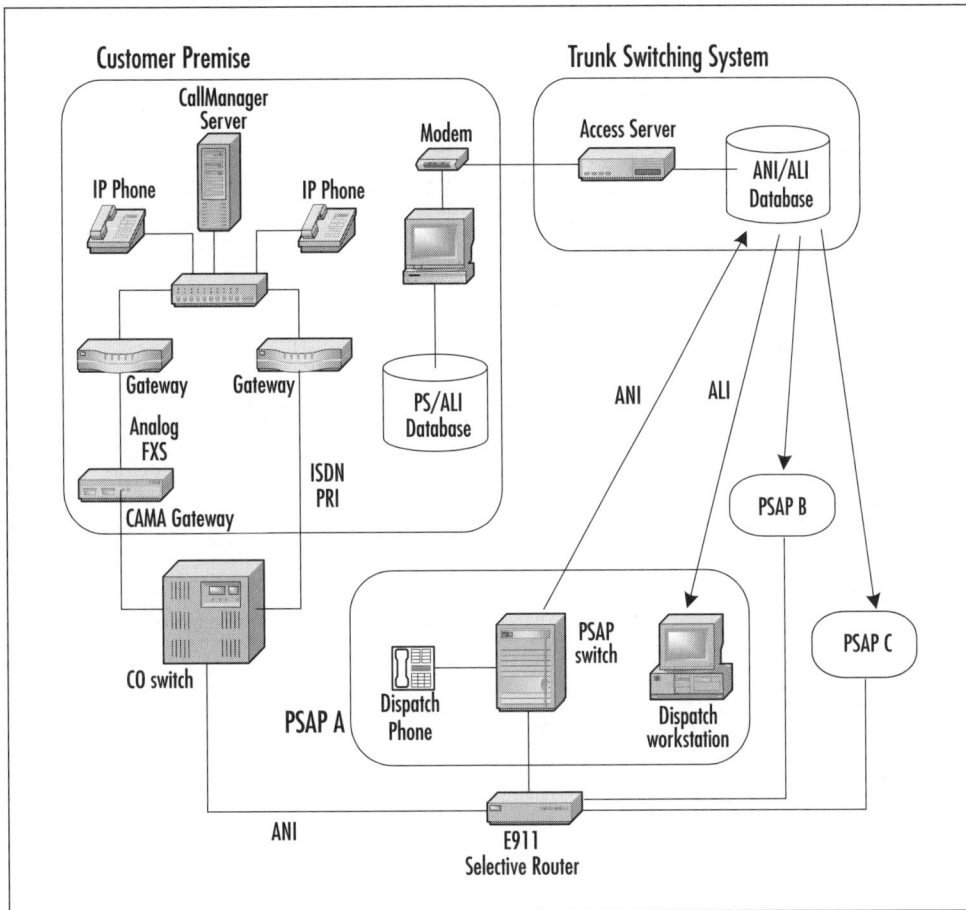

CallManager Integrated Applications

Cisco's AVVID architecture allows additional software applications to be easily integrated with CallManager. In addition to the applications that are available from third-party developers, Cisco has developed several applications that will extend the functionality of the CallManager platform. Some of these applications are included with the CallManager software distribution CD-ROM that accompanies the MCS Server; others are packaged separately and may require purchase of additional software licenses.

Understanding Media Termination Point

The Media Termination Point (MTP) was developed by Cisco in order to provide supplementary services (call hold, transfer, park, etc.) for calls from H.323 endpoints to IP telephones. H.323 endpoints might include PSTN gateways or NetMeeting terminals. Early releases of CallManager supported only H.323 version 1, which does not provide any support for supplementary services. For example, it would not be possible to transfer a call coming in from the PSTN via an H.323 gateway from one IP telephone to another since H.323 v1 does not provide any means for moving a media stream. The workaround for this is to use the MTP, which can serve to "anchor" the call leg from the H.323 v1 node and use skinny station protocol to communicate with IP telephones. CallManager can insert the MTP into the call automatically when it detects that it is required.

The MTP sounds like an attractive workaround to providing supplementary services to H.323 endpoints, but there are some important limitations to consider. First, the MTP supports G.711 coding only. This means that calls originating across the WAN that will eventually require service from the MTP must be set up using G.711. In other words, these WAN calls will consume 80 Kbps (64 Kbps G.711 payload + VoIP overhead) per call! Another consideration when using the MTP is that it is a software-based application. Coding and compression of the calls going through the MTP will be performed by the main CPU of the CallManager platform. When the MTP is coresident on the CallManager server, it is limited to a maximum of 24 simultaneous calls; to go beyond this limit requires that the MTP be installed on a separate server. If all MTP resources have been consumed, any additional calls will not have access to supplementary services for the duration of those calls.

Fortunately, there are now better alternatives for providing supplementary services in these situations. The latest releases of CallManager now provide support for H.323 version 2, which is capable of providing supplementary services. Cisco has also incorporated support for H.323 v2 in their IOS-based VoIP gateways. Alternatively, the Media Gateway Control Protocol (MGCP) is now supported by CallManager and some of the IOS-based VoIP gate-ways. Cisco VoIP gateways supporting either H.323 v2 or MGCP do not require the services of the MTP when used with CallManager 3.0 or higher.

In addition, transcoders are an alternative to using the software-based MTP. Transcoders are hardware-based DSPs available in Catalyst 4000 or 6000 series LAN switches.

The MTP application is included with the CallManager distribution CD-ROM and does not require any additional licensing fees. The MTP application is installed on the MCS server during the CallManager installation process. Although the MTP application can be loaded co-resident with the CallManager server, Cisco recommends using a separate PC in order to avoid any performance issues on the CallManager server.

Utilizing Cisco Conference Bridge

The Conference Bridge software application for Cisco CallManager is a software application designed to allow both ad-hoc and meet-me voice conferencing. Meet-me conferences allow users to dial into a conference. Ad-hoc conferences allow the conference controller to let only certain participants into the conference. The conferencing bridge is capable of hosting several simultaneous, multi-party conferences. When the conference bridge software has been installed, CallManager treats it as a conference device. In CallManager versions prior to 3.0, only software-based conference devices were available. In CallManager version 3.0 and higher, both software- and hardware-based conference devices are supported.

Meet-me conferences require that a range of directory numbers be allocated for their exclusive use. When a meet-me conference is set up, the conference controller selects a directory number and advertises it to members of the group. Participants call the directory number to join the conference. Anyone who calls the directory number while the conference is active joins the conference. Users can join the conference as long as the maximum number of participants specified for that conference type has not been exceeded, and sufficient streams are available on the conference device.

Ad-hoc conferences are controlled by the conference controller. The conference controller individually calls and adds each participant to the conference. Any number of parties can be added to the conference up to the maximum number of participants specified for ad-hoc conferences, and provided that sufficient streams are available on the conference device.

Conference devices can be one of two types: unicast or multicast. For conferencing, you must determine the total number of concurrent users, or audio streams, required at any time. Then you create and configure a device to support the calculated number of streams. These audio streams can be used for one large conference, or several small conferences. For example, assuming a conference device has been configured to support a maximum of 20 streams, this device could support a single conference with 20 participants or four conferences with five participants each. For CallManager 2.4, conferences are limited to 48 participants in the Windows NT registry. The total number of conferences supported by each conference device is calculated by taking the total number of streams and dividing by three. Therefore, in this example, you can have six conferences supported by the conference device (20/3 = 6).

Unicast conference devices can be installed on the same PC as the CallManager, or on a different PC. The available system resources will determine the location of the conference bridge application. For unicast, a conference bridge must be running for the conference feature to work. For multicast, CallManager must be running for the conference feature to work. Each conference device, whether unicast or multicast, can be configured as an ad-hoc conference bridge or a meet-me conference bridge.

There are three significant differences between unicast and multicast conference devices. First, unicast devices must physically reside on a PC and register with CallManager when started. Second, multicast devices are virtual devices, and don't actually register with CallManager. Third, multicast conferences cannot include calls that join the conference through a voice gateway, because the analog and digital gateways do not support multicast.

Multicast conference streams are actually mixed at the phone. Cisco IP telephones mix the three most recent talkers as perceived by the phone. Any number of participants can be in this multicast conference, but only the last three talkers are heard. This means that there can be a total of four talkers: the local phone and three others. If one party should stop talking, then another talker is added.

Since the conference bridge supports only G.711 calls, any call across the WAN that will be joining a conference must be set up using the G.711 coder. This means that these calls will be consuming 80 Kbps per call across the WAN.

For CallManager release 3.0, the IP Voice Streaming Application (Media Application) combines the Conference Bridge and the Media Termination Point (MTP) components that were in the previous versions of the Cisco CallManager. The Media Application consists of two parts: a Windows NT service and Windows NT kernel mode driver. The Windows NT service is responsible for registering with the Cisco CallManager and handling Device Recovery. The kernel driver processes and controls the voice data packets.

Similar to the MTP application, the Conference Bridge application is included with the CallManager distribution CD-ROM and does not require any additional licensing fees. Cisco also recommends installing the Conference Bridge on a separate PC in order to avoid any performance impacts on the CallManager server.

WARNING

You cannot have both hardware and software conference-bridge or MTP devices on the same Cisco CallManager. If both exist, the Cisco CallManager will disable the software version.

The Cisco WebAttendant Console

The Cisco WebAttendant Console serves as an alternative to a hardware-based console telephone that is typically used by a receptionist or central operator. The WebAttendant software application enables one or more central operators to answer and handle inbound and outbound calls that are not serviced by direct inward dialing (DID), direct outward dialing (DOD), or automated attendant functions. The WebAttendant requires a Web browser on a PC with an associated IP telephone, which provides voice stream termination. User functions are signaled to the CallManager using the TAPI interface. The WebAttendant is dependent upon an associated IP telephone's keypad template for operation. Use the default WebAttendant template that is provided for you, or be sure any custom keypad template you create has a maximum number of lines and buttons for hold, transfer, and answer/release.

The WebAttendant uses information in the CallManager database to direct calls. This requires that all system users be entered in the User area of Cisco CallManager Administration, as well as any other devices where calls may be dispatched, such as conference rooms with phones. The WebAttendant can be used by an operator to handle call traffic for multiple IP telephones, or by an individual to handle call traffic for a single IP telephone. In addition, the WebAttendant requires four- or five-digit extensions for all destination devices.

NOTE

The WebAttendant application is not available in all versions of CallManager. Early releases of CallManager included support for the WebAttendant up to version 2.4. With the initial release of CallManager 3.0, the WebAttendant was not available. CallManager 3.0(3) and subsequent releases will support the WebAttendant console.

To understand the functionality of the WebAttendant, it is best thought of as a client/server application. The client components consist of the actual WebAttendant client application and the Attendant Console Administration application. All Cisco IP phone features are available with browser-based WebAttendant client application, including answering calls, dialing outbound calls, transferring calls, disconnecting calls, call hold, retrieving calls from hold, and conferencing. The Attendant Console Administration application is a Web-based interface that allows a CallManager administrator to establish the hunt groups that are used by the Telephony Call Dispatcher (TCD) to send calls to the appropriate destination.

The server components include the Line State Server and the Telephony Call Dispatcher (TCD). The Line State Server provides real-time statistical data about line activity for all four- or five-digit directory numbers in the system. TCD provides statistical information about the number of redirected calls and the number of WebAttendants that are online. The TCD dispatches calls that have arrived at pilot point numbers to the appropriate destination based on hunt groups, which are configured in the Attendant Console Administration application. The TCD must be installed on the CallManager server. The Line State Server is a prerequisite for the TCD.

Utilizing IP IVR and AutoAttendant

Cisco's IP IVR (interactive voice response) software application is provided as an alternative to a traditional hardware-based IVR solution. The IVR can be used to automate incoming call handling and to collect data from a caller, such as account numbers or passwords. The IVR application is written completely in Java, which allows customers to build a customized IVR solution by adding custom-built extensions. Custom call-handling routines can be built using the IVR application engine, or existing applications can be used. The AutoAttendant is an example of a Cisco-provided routine that executes with the IVR application engine.

There are actually five components to the IVR application. The primary component is the Application Engine; other components are complimentary and add functionality.

Application Engine This is the heart of the IP IVR application. It is a runtime environment that executes Cisco-provided or custom-developed IVR flows (flows are analogous to "scripts" on legacy IVR equipment). This component executes on an MCS server or a separate Windows 2000 server.

Application Editor Flows are created using this Windows-based drag-and-drop application development tool. The editor can be used to create new flows or modify existing flows. A flow is simply the series of steps that will be followed to handle calls to the IVR.

Step Libraries Steps are referred to as "blocks of logic" that are connected to create flows. The Application Editor organizes related steps into one of four folders called Step Libraries.

Flow Repository The IP IVR uses the same LDAP directory as the CallManager to store the flows; flows are not stored with the application engine. Tools for uploading and downloading flows are also included.

Reporting Tool Reports on statistics for individual flow execution and total system activity are available in real time using the Reporting Tool. This is a Java plug-in applet that communicates with the application server in real time. Available reports include overall application engine activity, activity by application, and activity by task.

As a key component in the AVVID architecture, the IP IVR is designed to work in several different environments. The IVR application can be used in CallCenter environments, or in standard business telephony environments with stand-alone or clustered CallManagers. The IP IVR is currently available in three different packages.

The first option is referred to as the CallManager AutoAttendant and is included with CallManager at no additional charge beginning with release 3.0(5). This package will not include all of the components listed previously. This basic offering will include only the Application Engine along with the AutoAttendant flow and can coexist on the CallManager server. The Application Editor is not included; therefore, the AutoAttendant flow is the only one that can be used. The CallManager AutoAttendant will support up to four ports; additional ports will require an upgrade to a dedicated IVR package.

The first of the dedicated IVR packages is referred to as the base system and can support between four to 30 ports. This package will include all of the IVR components listed earlier and will require a dedicated MCS server. A dedicated IP IVR solution is shown in Figure 4.2.

Figure 4.2 Dedicated IP IVR

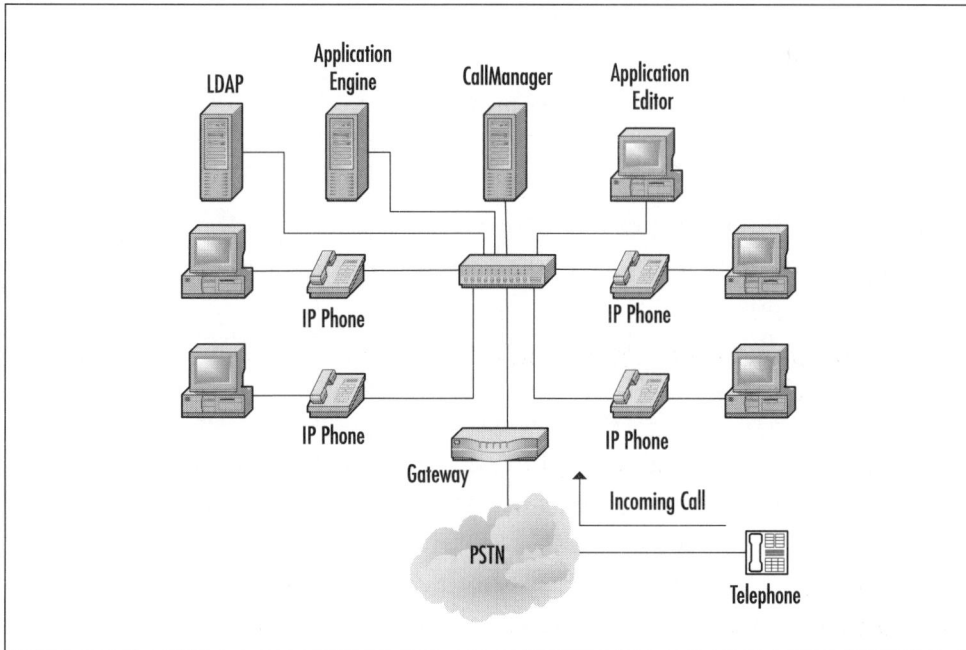

A higher port density package for larger environments will support up to 48 ports. Similar to the base package, this package also includes all components and requires a dedicated MCS server.

The dedicated IVR packages will include a license for a limited number of ports. Additional port capacity will require the purchase of additional port licenses.

Using IP SoftPhone

The IP SoftPhone is a PC-based application that enables a Windows-based PC to be used as a stand-alone telephony client or to be used in conjunction with a regular Cisco IP Telephone. When used as a standalone application, it is particularly useful to telecommuters or traveling users since it enables them to receive calls anywhere that they can connect to the corporate network. For example, if a user dials in to the main campus network from a remote location, he or she would be able to retrieve voice mail or even place calls. Using the SoftPhone to control an IP phone, users can set up individual calls or conference calls using the drag-and-drop capabilities within Windows instead of dialing from the IP phone.

One of the more interesting aspects of the SoftPhone is the multimedia collaboration capability by way of integration with NetMeeting. Leveraging the capabilities of NetMeeting (which must be installed on the PC along with SoftPhone), the SoftPhone allows users to share files from their desktops with other participants in a virtual conference room.

With both hardware-based IP phones and the SoftPhone application, users can choose which device they prefer depending on their individual needs. Users that are frequently traveling or telecommuting may require only the SoftPhone application. On the other hand, users that primarily work in the office and do not travel frequently may need only a desktop IP phone. Some users may want the best of both worlds, the SoftPhone application along with the 7900 series desktop phones. It is important to consider which users will benefit from the SoftPhone as it is not practical to deploy SoftPhones for all users.

The IP SoftPhone application relies on TAPI to integrate with the AVVID network. For example, when a user dials an extension from the SoftPhone, the SoftPhone communicates the request to the CallManager and the call is actually set up by the CallManager server. Since CallManager is providing these services to the SoftPhone application, the SoftPhone must first register with the CallManager, similar to a standard IP phone. Adding a SoftPhone device to the CallManager database is similar to the procedure for a standard IP phone. When the SoftPhone will be used as an end-station, it must be added as a *CTI port* in CallManager. A CTI port is a virtual device that exists only in the CallManager database. If the SoftPhone will only be used to control an IP phone, it is not necessary to add a CTI port.

There are some important design considerations when deploying the SoftPhone application in an AVVID network. Since the SoftPhone application integrates with CallManager by way of the TAPI interface, it is much more resource intensive on the CallManager than on a standard IP Telephone. It is important to consider the number of SoftPhone clients that each CallManager server will handle. Currently, Cisco recommends limiting the maximum number of SoftPhones on a CallManager to approximately 200 clients to limit potential performance impacts on the CallManager server. Supporting additional SoftPhone users beyond the recommended maximum will require additional CallManager servers.

Another design consideration for the SoftPhone is in regard to availability. Early releases of the SoftPhone application do not provide the automatic fail-over feature similar to hardware phones when connected to a CallManager cluster. If the CallManager on which the SoftPhone registered were to fail, the user must recognize this and manually select an alternate CallManager, or wait for the failed CallManager to return to service. For this reason, it is best to plan on deploying a hardware-based phone for users requiring the high availability feature that IP phones can offer today.

The SoftPhone is a separately priced application and not included with the CallManager distribution software. A user license must be purchased for each SoftPhone user. User licenses for hardware-based

IP phones and SoftPhone clients are completely separate; a license must be purchased for each device. Licenses can be purchased individually, or can be purchased in discounted bundles for a large number of users. The SoftPhone application works in conjunction with CallManager release 3.0(6) and later.

CallManager Deployment Models

One of the more important aspects of designing an AVVID network is determining the quantity and location of the CallManager servers. At the same time, if remote users are required, it must also be determined how service will be provided to both local and remote IP telephone users. This section will evaluate the possible alternatives and weigh the pros and cons of each deployment model. In general, there are four recommended models to choose from: single site, multiple sites with independent call processing, multiple sites with centralized call processing, and multiple sites with distributed call processing.

Single-Site Deployment

The single-site deployment model is characterized by a single CallManager or a cluster of CallManager servers. All users are colocated within a single campus or building so there is no requirement for IP telephony traffic to cross the WAN. The limitations of this model are 10,000 users maximum on a single cluster of up to eight CallManager servers based on currently available CallManager releases. To scale beyond the 10,000-user limit per cluster, multiple clusters can be interconnected using H.323 between the clusters.

It is assumed that connectivity to remote sites and all external calls in this model will be provided via the PSTN. Voice messaging services may be provided by a legacy voice mail system or by an AVVID unified messaging system. If there will be a requirement for a significant amount of conferencing traffic, hardware-based conferencing resources can be added to improve performance and scalability.

One advantage of this deployment model is that it presents the fewest QoS issues to be solved since all users and AVVID devices will be interconnected within the local area. No calls will be traversing the IP WAN; therefore, there will be no WAN QoS issues to address. Solving QoS issues in the campus LAN begins by using LAN switches that provide multiple queues per interface. This allows for traffic classification and prioritization on each user port of the switch. Since all calls will originate and terminate in the LAN, compressed voice will not be required so the G.711 CODEC will be used by the IP phones for all calls; this will require 80 Kbps per call.

Figure 4.3 illustrates sample CallManager deployments using the single-site deployment model.

Multiple-Site Deployment with Independent Call Processing

When considering deployment of CallManager servers at multiple sites, there are three deployment models that can be considered. The simplest of the multisite models is the independent call processing model; this may also be referred to as isolated deployment. The key characteristic of this model is that there are, of course, CallManagers at multiple sites, but the IP WAN is not used for connectivity between them. Each site will have its own CallManager or cluster of CallManagers to provide call control for the site. Connectivity between sites is provided by the PSTN only, thus, the CallManagers are essentially isolated. This also means that the number of sites that can be interconnected in this manner is essentially unlimited. All of the characteristics and limitations previously described for the single-site model will also apply to the independent call processing model.

The primary advantage to this model is that reliability and QoS issues in the WAN are completely avoided since the IP WAN is not being used for voice traffic between sites. Of course, this also leads to the primary disadvantage of this model. Since the PSTN is being used between sites, this model does not give you the full advantage of toll bypass—using IP telephony to reduce costs associated with the PSTN traffic.

Figure 4.3 Single-Site Deployment Models

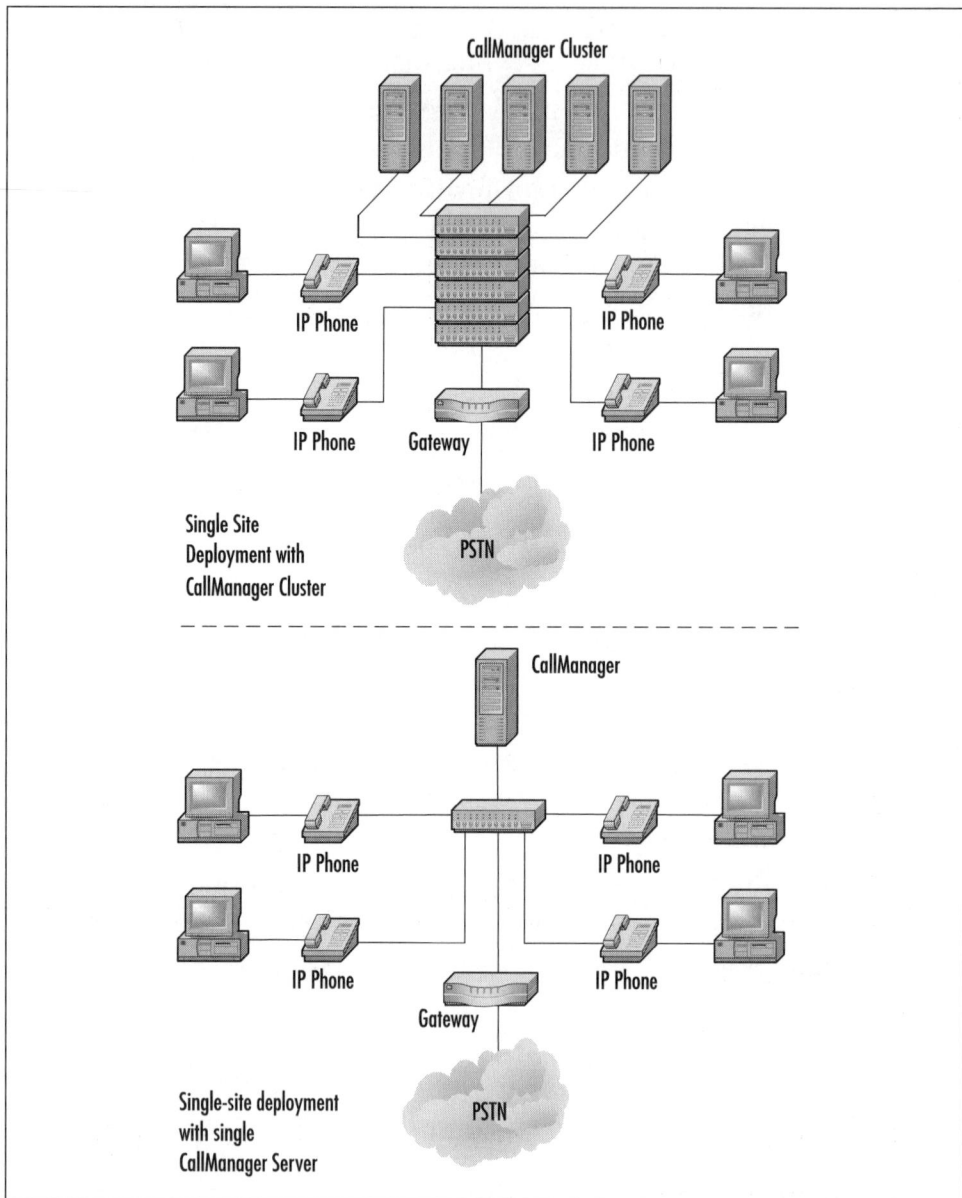

Figure 4.4 illustrates a sample deployment model for multiple, isolated sites that are not connected by an IP WAN.

Figure 4.4 Multiple Sites with Independent Call Processing

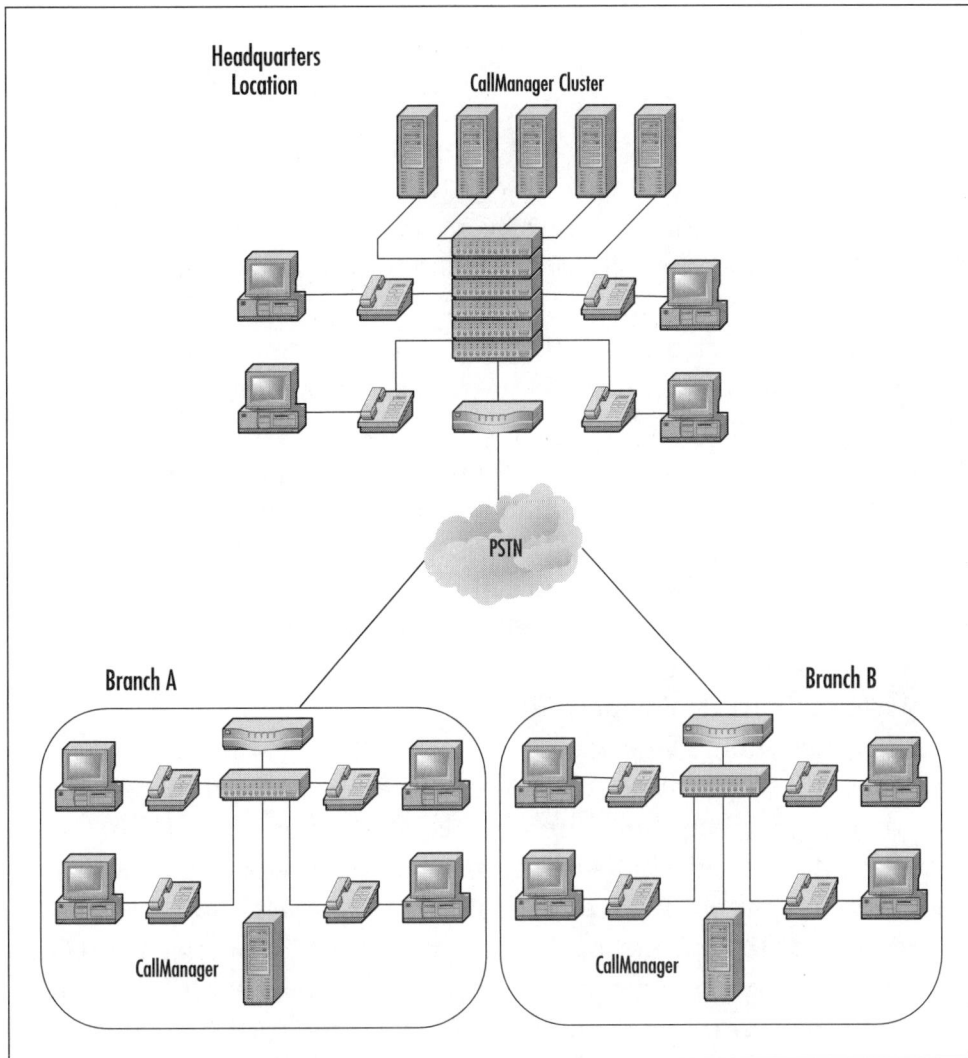

Multiple Sites with Centralized Call Processing

Organizations with multiple small remote sites may consider the centralized call processing model. The primary characteristic of this deployment model is the use of a single CallManager or cluster of CallManagers at the main location to handle call processing for all sites. CallManagers will not be deployed at the small remote sites, so IP telephone users at remote sites will be served by the central CallManager or cluster.

An important distinction between this model and the previous models is that the IP WAN will be used as the primary path for voice traffic between sites. This leads to important considerations for managing reliability and QoS across the WAN, such as ensuring proper bandwidth guarantees for voice, implementing call admission control (CAC), and ensuring that remote phones can communicate with the central CallManager server.

Ensuring proper bandwidth for WAN calls must be done using CAC. In addition, there must be provisions for using the PSTN in the event that the IP WAN fails between sites. If CallManager is used for CAC, fail-over to the PSTN will not be automatic. This means that users will be required to hang-up in the event that the call fails over the IP WAN and then redial using a different prefix to force the call manually over the PSTN. Although this is a possible workaround, it is by no means elegant. With the IP WAN as the primary path between sites, compressed calls will be desirable and are supported in this deployment model.

Since the phones at remote sites will not have a local CallManager, they will not be able to place any calls in the event that they cannot communicate with a CallManager server. This means that even local calls within the remote branch office will not be possible between IP telephones if the IP WAN should go down. To guard against this scenario, it will be necessary to provision ISDN dial-backup services (or a similar mechanism) between the remote sites and the central site. Another consideration in this scenario would be to plan for a minimum number of "life-line" phones using dedicated POTS connections in the event that all WAN services are lost.

Previous versions of CallManager restricted the use of gateways at remote sites to those supporting the Skinny Station Protocol only. With additional protocol support in both gateways and CallManager 3.0, the choice of gateways for remote sites is no longer so restrictive. Cisco IOS-based gateways can now be used at remote sites in

addition to the gateways that support Skinny Station Protocol.
Figure 4.5 illustrates multiple sites with centralized call processing.

Figure 4.5 Multiple Sites with Centralized Call Processing

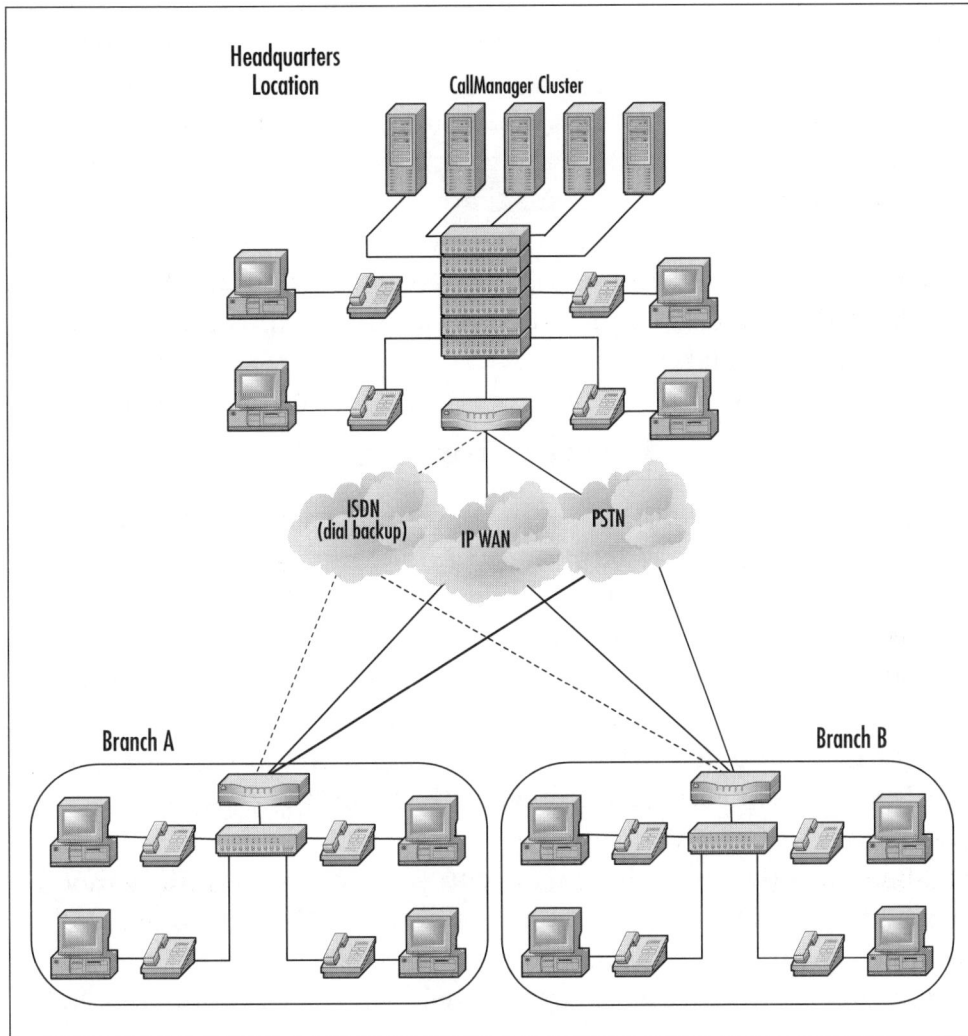

Services such as voice mail, unified messaging, and DSP
resources would be provided at the central site. In using voice mail
in this model, be careful not to overlap directory number (DN)
ranges between sites when developing a dial plan. Each site must

have a unique range of DNs. If hardware-based conferencing or transcoder resources are not available at the central site, calls between sites that utilize voice mail or conferencing will require 80 Kbps per call. This is because the software-based conference bridge and voice mail application support G.711 coding only. The workaround for this limitation is to deploy DSP resources (hardware-based transcoders and conferencing resources) in the Catalyst LAN switches so that calls may originate using low-bit rate coders.

The primary advantage of the centralized call processing model is that all CallManager servers are centrally located. This reduces equipment costs and administrative overhead for the small remote sites. The main disadvantage of this model is the potential for the remote sites to become isolated with no services in the event that all IP WAN service is lost.

Multiple Sites with Distributed Call Processing

Organizations with multiple large sites may consider the distributed call processing model. The primary characteristic of this deployment model is the use of a CallManager or cluster of CallManagers at each location to handle call processing for all sites. CallManagers will be deployed at remote sites, so IP telephone users at remote sites will be served by a local CallManager or cluster. There is a maximum limit of ten sites that can be interconnected across the IP WAN using this deployment model with the current available CallManager releases.

Similar to the centralized call processing model, the IP WAN will be used as the primary path between sites. CAC will also be required in this model as a result. Using a Cisco IOS-based gatekeeper to implement CAC in this model can provide automatic failover to the PSTN in the event that the PSTN is congested or unavailable. Note that the gatekeeper functionality can be provided by a dedicated router or by a router that is also functioning as a voice gateway. Figure 4.6 illustrates multiple sites with distributed call processing.

Figure 4.6 Multiple Sites with Distributed Call Processing

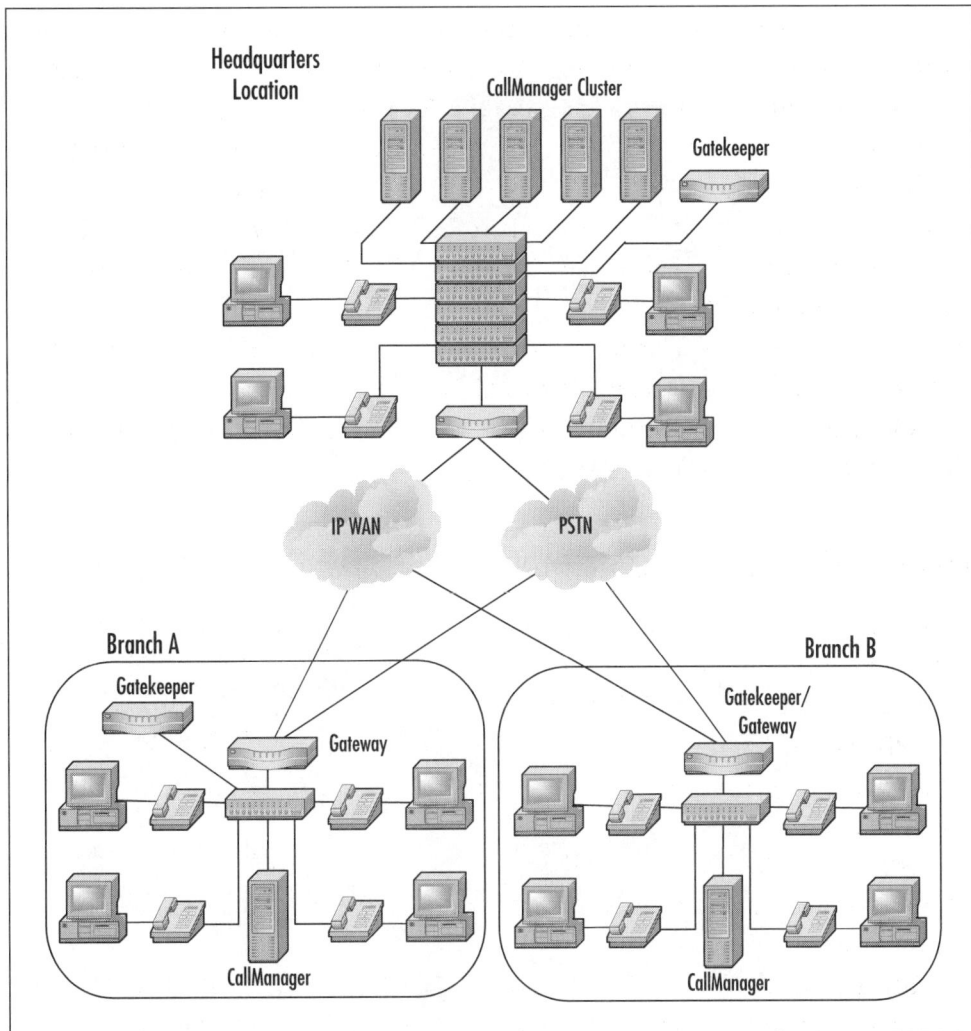

Unlike the centralized call processing model, services such as voice mail, unified messaging, and DSP resources could be provided at each site. With DSP resources at each site, low bit-rate calls across the WAN would be supported in this model.

The primary advantage of the distributed call processing model is that it eliminates the reliance on the IP WAN for services at the remote sites, as in the centralized call processing model. All features and capabilities will be available for the local sites, even if the IP WAN should fail.

Configuring and Deploying IP Handsets

If you are new to the world if IP Telephony, it just doesn't seem right to plug a telephone into the Ethernet LAN. In fact, once you plug your new IP phone into the data network, it somehow seems magical that there is even dial tone. Data networks aren't supposed to provide dial tones, are they? Well, in this section we'll take a look at Cisco's IP telephone handsets and see how all of it works.

An IP Handset Overview

There are currently two generations of telephone handsets available for use in a Cisco AVVID network. The original telephones available from Cisco were the 30 VIP and 12 SP+ models. These two models were essentially the same offering as the original telephones offered by Selsius prior to being acquired by Cisco. These models are no longer produced by Cisco; however, you may still run into a number of them, which were deployed along with early CallManager systems. Although these phones provide the necessary functionality of a business-quality handset, there are some important limitations to consider. First, the physical connectivity on both of these models is limited to an integrated 10 Mbps Ethernet hub. This allows daisy-chaining of a co-located PC, but it limits the PC to only a 10 Mbps connection.

Second, IP telephones require a 48-volt DC power source; the only option for power on these two models is an external local power connection to an AC wall outlet for the AC-to-DC converter. The 12 SP+ and 30 VIP do not support in-line power. The requirement for local power means that installation of a phone in a given location requires an AC outlet as well as an Ethernet connection. This may be an inconvenience in some cases if an AC outlet is not located near the desired installation location. Another limitation of local power is that phone service will be interrupted in the event of a power outage unless all AC outlets where phones are serviced have backup power. Of course, this would also affect connectivity for any PCs that are daisy-chained from one of these handsets.

With the introduction of the 7900 series telephones, Cisco has made significant improvements to the handsets. In addition to overcoming the limitations of the first-generation handsets, many other new features have been added. For starters, the physical connectivity has been upgraded to integrated 10/100Mb switch Ethernet ports rather than 10 Mbps hub ports. The advantage of this upgrade is that it no longer limits the throughput for daisy-chained devices and also enables VLAN support (802.1Q) for separation of the phone and PC traffic when they are sharing a single switch port. Another significant improvement is support for in-line power, which eliminates the restrictions of local power as described earlier. This means, simply, that there is no need for a power supply to be physically connected to the IP telephone handset. The handset will receive its power from the network port it plugs into. Other new features include a completely new user interface by way of an LCD display and soft-keys rather than the multi-button approach on the first-generation handsets; LDAP-based directory services for enabling personal, local, or corporate directories at the handset; and XML support for delivering custom content to the handset display.

For conference applications, Cisco has collaborated with Polycom to produce an IP version of Polycom's popular Soundstation conference phones. The IP Conference Station has the familiar triangular shape of Polycom's analog Soundstation with full-duplex, hands-free operation for use in a desktop or conference room environment. Similar to the other Cisco desktop IP phones, it supports DHCP for automatic IP address assignment and it will register automatically with the CallManager when connected to the network. One important difference to note, however, is that the IP Conference Station does not support in-line power, and requires an external power supply.

For compressed voice calls in the wide area, the first generation telephones support the G.723 voice coder; the new generation of handsets supports G.729a. All handsets support the G.711 voice coder for full 64 Kbps PCM voice coding.

Utilizing Skinny Station Protocol

Cisco's IP telephones use the Skinny Station Protocol (SSP) to communicate with CallManager and other devices in the network. SSP is used for registration of handsets and gateways with the CallManager, and for call processing functions such as call set-up, tear-down, and supplementary services. SSP was selected as a "lightweight" alternative to using H.323 to handle the call processing functions required in an IP telephony system. The logic behind the SSP-based call processing model used by Cisco's AVVID solution is that the CallManager is a high-powered server device and can handle the proxy services much more efficiently than implementing a robust protocol such as H.323 at the handset. Also, limiting the resource requirements of the handset should eventually lead to much lower cost handsets in the long term. Implementing H.323 terminal capabilities in a handset requires a significant amount of memory and CPU resources since it defines a fully functional terminal device using H.225 and H.245 for call processing functions.

The advantage of using SSP for the handsets instead of H.323 is that the phones will require less intelligence and processing resources (thus the term "skinny station"). Of course, this means that the handsets will always need a CallManager to serve as a proxy for call processing functions in order to speak with other non-SSP devices in the network. Also, SSP is not yet as ubiquitous as the H.323 standard, so this will limit choices in terms of interoperability. In combination with the CallManager's proxy services, however, the IP telephones can communicate with other non-SSP devices such as H.323 terminals and gateways. In practice, this means that CallManager will be terminating the H.225 and H.245 signaling from terminals and gateways and redirecting the media streams to the IP telephones via SSP.

Performing Phone Registration with Skinny Station Protocol

The process of adding an IP handset to the network can be completely automatic or can be done manually. Once a phone has been connected to the network and power is supplied, IP address parameters must be obtained and a configuration file must be downloaded from the CallManager database. The IP address parameters (host address, mask, default gateway, and TFTP server) can be entered into the phone manually or can be obtained automatically through DHCP; DNS queries can also be used to automatically obtain the address of the TFTP server. Once the proper IP parameters have been obtained, the phone can proceed through the initialization process by obtaining its configuration (CNF) file from the TFTP server. Each handset in the network should have a unique CNF file associated with it by way of its MAC address; the CNF filenames are actually constructed using the phones MAC address. If a unique CNF file is not available, a default configuration file will be used.

The configuration file provides the phone with information such as the list of available CallManager servers (in order of group preference). Once a configuration file has been obtained, the phone must also obtain the proper code image; this download only occurs the first time the phone registers with the CallManager. From this point on, the code image will be downloaded only if a newer version is available. The phone will check the code image version each time it registers on the network (due to a forced reset, loss of power, phone move, etc.). If a new code image must be downloaded, the phone will request it from the TFTP server and will then reset and begin the initialization procedure again. A nice feature here is the ability for an individual to unplug his or her phone, move to another office (possibly in a shared office environment), and receive his or her telephone configuration (including a preassigned telephone extension) over the converged network infrastructure. Figure 4.7 shows a summary of the phone initialization process.

Figure 4.7 IP Phone Startup Process

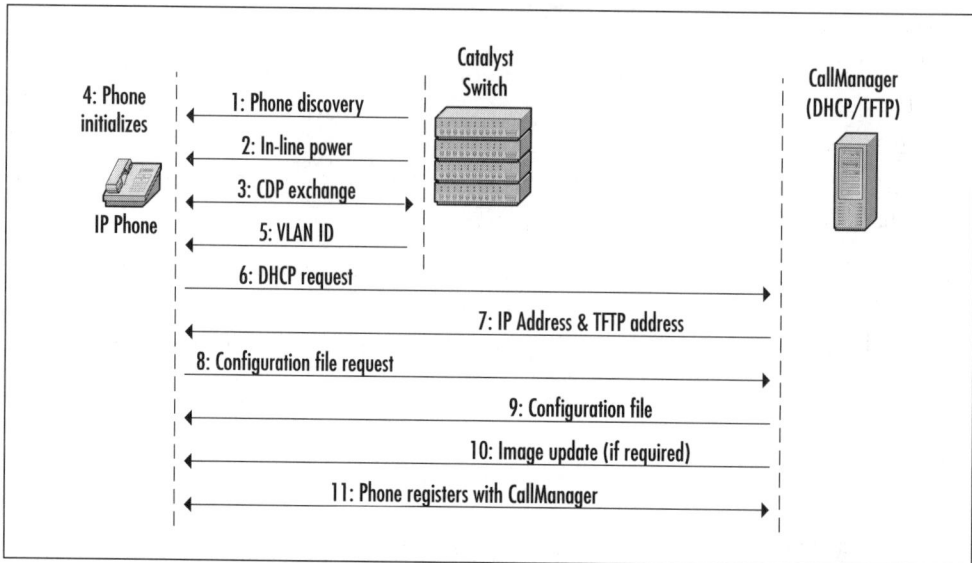

Assigning Directory Numbers

Registration of a handset with the CallManager can occur only if the device has been added to the CallManager database and has been assigned a directory number (DN). Assigning DNs to handsets can be done automatically or manually as they are added to the network. In either case, all assignment of phone numbers is handled centrally through the CallManager administration application. When manually assigning DNs, handsets are added to CallManager by providing the MAC address of the handset and associating the appropriate DN with this device. For automatic assignment, CallManager supports a feature known as auto-registration. This feature is enabled in the CallManager simply by assigning a range of available DNs for auto-registration purposes. Once a phone has been assigned a DN and has successfully registered with the CallManager, it is then ready to place or receive calls on the network.

Other Phone Configuration Tasks

User features available on handsets, such as call park, forward, redial, voice mail, etc., are configured by way of keypad or phone button templates. Administrators can use templates to simplify the assignment of common configurations for a large number of users. A default template is provided in CallManager for each of the available handset models; the CallManager administrator can then modify these templates. Optionally, users can create a unique template to assign a custom configuration for their own handsets. Other settings that can be customized by users include ring sounds, ringing volume, display settings, and speed dials.

Creating Custom Ring Tones

An unsupported, but great feature of CallManager 3.0, is the ability to create custom ring tones for your IP phones. It is a very simple process that involves two basic steps: creating the custom ring tone audio file, and telling CallManager about the new file.

To create the audio file for the ring tone, a sound editor/converter program that can create raw PCM files will be required. Two popular sound editors that you may consider for this task are Cool Edit from Syntrillium Software or Sound Forge from Sonic Foundry. A list of sound conversion and editing tools can be found at the following URL:

www.hitsquad.com/smm/win95/FORMAT_CONVERTERS/?ng

Any digital sound that can be imported into one of these editors can be used as a ring tone. First, import the desired sound into the editor, then export it as a raw PCM file using the following sampling parameters: mono, 8000 samples/sec, 8-bit sample, uLaw companding. Be sure to save the file with a .RAW extension. Once the file has been created, it must be saved on the CallManager server in the \Program Files\Cisco\TFTPPath directory. You should notice other

Continued

.RAW files in this directory, which are the default ring tones supplied with CallManager.

Another important file in this same directory is RingList.DAT, a plain ASCII text file that contains a list of all available ring tone files. The new ring tone file that you just created needs to be added to the list in this file. The only tricky part is to make sure that the file ends with a carriage return.

The new ring tone should now be selectable from the Ring Type settings menu on the handset, which is accessed on the 7900 series phones by pressing the settings soft-key. Detailed instructions for selecting ring sounds is provided in the Cisco document "Using Your Cisco IP Phone."

An Overview of VoIP Gateways

Integration of a CallManager system to legacy systems such as a PBX or the PSTN will require selection of one or more VoIP gateways. Selecting the proper gateway based on a given set of requirements is one of the more challenging issues to tackle when designing a Cisco AVVID voice network. First, there are many requirements to sort through when determining which gateway will provide the best fit. Also, there are many choices available from Cisco. In this section, we will attempt to sort through all of these issues.

Utilizing Cisco's VoIP Gateways

The possible gateway choices from Cisco can be broken down into three broad categories: standalone gateways, router-based integrated gateways, and LAN switch-based integrated gateways (see Table 4.5). The standalone gateways are application-specific devices and provide only voice gateway services. The router-based gateways can provide full-featured routing services in addition to the voice gateway services since they run Cisco's IOS software. The Catalyst 4000 and Catalyst 6000 series LAN switches now have optional modules that can add voice gateway services to these existing modular LAN switch platforms. As Cisco continues to develop their AVVID solution set over time, we can certainly expect even more choices in the future.

Table 4.5 A Summary of AVVID Gateway Options

Gateway Types	Specific Cisco Hardware
Standalone gateways	AT/AS-2, -4, -8; DT-24; DE-30; VG-200
Router-based gateways	Cisco 800, 1700, 2600, 3600, 7200 7500 series routers; AS5300 access server
LAN switch-based gateways	Catalyst 4000 and 6000 gateway modules

Understanding Legacy Telephony Interfaces and Signaling

One of the first issues to address when selecting a VoIP gateway is to understand how the interconnection will be made from the VoIP network to the legacy PBX or PSTN services—in other words, what physical connectivity will be required and what signaling protocols will be used. The two choices for physical connectivity will, of course, be analog or digital facilities.

The VoIP gateway is only one side of the connection between a VoIP network and a legacy system. When designing an AVVID solution, it is also important to understand the constraints imposed by the incumbent legacy equipment and the available interfaces. For example, a fixed-configuration PBX will most likely have limited choices for connecting to a VoIP gateway. If there are no available facilities, no additional line or trunk cards can be added to a fixed configuration system. Alternatively, a modular PBX system does provide more flexibility; however, there will certainly be costs incurred if additional line or trunk cards are required (and any required system software upgrades to support the cards).

Analog Connectivity

Analog facilities are generally used to interconnect telephony systems when low port densities are required. When analog connectivity is required, there are three primary connection types

Foreign exchange station (FXS) Required when connecting handsets, FAX machines, modems or other end station devices to the network. FXS interfaces will provide dial tone and battery voltage to the connected device.

Foreign exchange office (FXO) Required when connecting to the PBX or PSTN via analog facilities. FXO interfaces will connect to a facility that provides dial tone and battery voltage.

Ear and Mouth (E&M) Required when connecting PBXs over dedicated analog facilities between sites.

Another important consideration for many organizations will be support for direct inward dial (DID) and calling line ID (CLID) over analog facilities. DID is a feature that permits outside callers to reach a telephone user on a PBX or Centrex system by dialing a direct number, eliminating the need for an operator to switch the call manually. CLID is a commonly known and used feature in both business and residential telephony environments that provides the phone number and other information about the calling party. Currently, support for these features on analog facilities is limited to Cisco 3810, 2600, and 3600 IOS-based gateways and the Catalyst 4000 gateway module. These features will require the proper hardware interfaces and IOS releases 12.1(4)T/12.1(2)Xx or later.

Table 4.6 outlines the analog VoIP gateways signaling support on AVVID gateways and further information can be found on Cisco's Web site at the following URL: www.cisco.com/univercd/cc/td/doc/product/voice/ip_tele/network/dggatewy.htm.

Table 4.6 Analog VoIP Gateway Signaling Support on AVVID Gateways

Gateway	FXS	FXO	E & M	Analog DID/CLID
VG-200	Yes	Yes	H.323v2 mode	Future
Cisco 1750	Yes	Yes	Yes	Future
Cisco 3810 v3	Yes	Yes	Yes	Yes *
Cisco 2600	Yes	Yes	Yes	Yes *
Cisco 3600	Yes	Yes	Yes	Yes *
Catalyst 4000 gateway module	Yes	Yes	Yes	Yes *
Catalyst 6000 gateway module	Yes	No	No	No/Yes

* Requires IOS version 12.1(4)T/12.1(2)XH

Digital Connectivity

To provide scalability for larger voice networking systems, digital facilities can provide much higher port densities. The digital facilities supported by CallManager include T1/E1 CAS, E1 R2, ISDN PRI, and ISDN BRI.

T1/E1 CAS Channel associated signaling is a commonly used form of digital signaling for both T1 and E1 digital facilities. Many legacy PBX systems in use today provide support for T1 or E1 CAS signaling interfaces. CAS signaling is also commonly known as "robbed bit" signaling.

ISDN Primary Rate Interface (PRI) ISDN PRI facilities provide 23 voice channels (T1) or 30 voice channels (E1) on a single physical port. ISDN PRI is commonly supported on many PBX systems. ISDN PRI services can be further subdivided into user-side or network-side support.

ISDN Basic Rate Interface (BRI) A lower-density implementation of ISDN services that provides two digital voice channels on a single physical connection. Similar to ISDN PRI services, ISDN

BRI services can be further subdivided into user-side or net-work-side support.

Table 4.7 outlines the digital VoIP gateways signaling support on AVVID gateways and further information can be found on Cisco's Web site at the following URL: www.cisco.com/univercd/cc/td/doc/product/voice/ip_tele/network/dggatewy.htm.

Table 4.7 Digital VoIP Gateway Signaling Support on AVVID Gateways

Gateway	T1 CAS	E1/R2	E1 CAS	PRI-U	PRI-N	BRI-U	BRI-N	DID/CLID
VG200	H.323 v2 mode	No	H.323 v2 mode	No	No	No	No	N/A
DT-24/DE30	No	No	No	Yes	Yes	No	No	Yes
Cisco 1750	No	No	No	No	No	Future	Future	N/A
Cisco 3810 v3	Yes	No	Yes	No	No	Yes	No	Yes
Cisco 2600	Yes	Yes*	Yes*	Yes*	Yes*	Yes	Future	Yes
Cisco 3600	Yes	Yes*	Yes*	Yes*	Yes*	Yes	Future	Yes
Cisco 7200	Yes	Yes*	Yes*	Yes*	Yes*	No	No	Yes
Cisco 7500	Yes	Yes*	Yes*	Yes*	Yes*	No	No	Yes
Cisco AS5300	Yes	Yes	Yes	Yes	Yes **	No	No	Yes
Catalyst 4000	Yes	Yes	Yes	Yes	Yes	Future	Future	Yes
Catalyst 6000	No	No	No	Yes	Yes	No	No	Yes

* Requires IOS 12.1(3)T

** Requires IOS 12.0(7)T

Gateway Protocol Support

One of the primary considerations when selecting a VoIP gateway is the gateway protocol that each of the available models supports. Today, there are three primary gateway protocols of interest, including the Skinny Gateway Protocol, the Media Gateway Control Protocol, and H.323 v2.

Skinny Gateway Protocol is supported on the DT-24, DE-30, and Catalyst 6000 voice gateway modules. Skinny Gateway Protocol is also supported on the original AT/AS-2, -4, -8 analog trunk/station gateways based on the original Selsius products. Support for Skinny Gateway Protocol is included in both CallManager 2.x and 3.x releases. This protocol is based on the industry standard SGCP protocol; however, it is unique to Cisco's gateway products today.

Media Gateway Control Protocol is supported on the VG-200 standalone voice gateway with analog modules (FXS and FXO) to communicate with CallManager v3.0 and later. Cisco is also committed to supporting this protocol in the future on other IOS-based router gateways.

H.323 v2 is supported on IOS-based router gateways beginning with IOS release 12.0(7)T to communicate with CallManager v3.0 and later. Cisco is also committed to supporting H.323 v2 on the VG-200 gateway in the future. Support for H.323 v2 on the IOS-based gateways is an important feature since it eliminates the need for a software-based MTP in order to provide supplementary services. H.323 is an ITU-T developed standard that provides peer-to-peer multimedia conferencing capabilities between terminals.

Table 4.8 outlines supported gateway protocols and further information can be found on Cisco's Web site at the following URL: www.cisco.com/univercd/cc/td/doc/product/voice/ip_tele/network/dggatewy.htm.

Table 4.8 Supported Gateway Protocols

Gateway	Skinny Gateway Protocol	H.323	MGCP
VG200	No	Yes	Yes
DT-24/DE-30	Yes	No	No
Cisco 1750	No	Yes	No
Cisco 3810 v3	No	Yes	Future
Cisco 2600	No	Yes	Future
Cisco 3600	No	Yes	Future
Cisco 7200	No	Yes	No
Cisco 7500	No	Future	No
Cisco AS5300	No	Yes	No
Catalyst 4000	Yes*	Yes**	Future
Catalyst 6000	Yes	No	Future

* For conferencing and MTP transcoding services

** For PSTN interfaces

Monitoring CallManager Activity

Monitoring an AVVID network requires a set of tools that can view activity on all components of the network, including routers, voice gateways, LAN switches, IP telephones, and CallManager servers. Cisco's solution for managing all of these components is the CiscoWorks 2000 suite of management applications. Cisco has enhanced the CiscoWorks components to provide better support for managing AVVID networks so that customers can use a single set of tools to manage the entire network. In addition, CallManager 3.0 provides new management capabilities for tighter integration with CiscoWorks Applications. The CallManager server also has a set of tools that can be used for managing certain components of an AVVID network.

CiscoWorks 2000

CiscoWorks 2000 provides a common GUI interface and database across a set of network management applications with a Web-based application called the Common Management Framework (CMF). CiscoWorks applications, such as Campus Manager and Resource Manager Essentials, can be accessed through the CMF desktop. CiscoWorks 2000 is a separate suite of network management applications that must be purchased separately; it is not included on the MCS server or with any other AVVID component. Since there are several applications within the CiscoWorks family, it must be decided which components are required.

The Campus Manager

The Campus Manager component of CiscoWorks is responsible for discovery of network devices and maintenance of the network topology map. This is accomplished with the User Tracking (UT) service module within the Campus Manager. With the addition of Cisco Discovery Protocol (CDP) to CallManager release 3.0 and the 7900 series IP telephones, Campus Manager can now discover CallManager servers and IP phones in the network. The Campus Manager can also discover routers, voice gateways, and LAN switches in the network that support CDP.

Based on information captured by the UT discovery process, Campus Manager can be used to produce a phone table report that displays information such as the extension, MAC address, IP address, status, and model number of IP telephones in the network.

Another useful application within the Campus Manager is the Path Analysis Tool for tracing IP connectivity between network nodes. The output of the Path Analysis Tool is a graphical display of the layer 3 path between phones or between a phone and the CallManager server. The output may also include information about layer 2 devices if those devices are also managed by the Campus Manager.

Resource Manager Essentials (RME)

The RME component of CiscoWorks is primarily responsible for maintaining device inventories, configuration management, and collection and analysis of system log information for network devices. RME has an extensive list of functions available for routers and LAN switches, and also has some functions that are specific to AVVID network components. Separate groups are created for CallManagers in the RME device selector and custom reports for the CallManager can be created. Custom reports are also available for Catalyst 4000 and 6000 series LAN switches that support in-line power.

RME also contains the Syslog Analyzer, a logging management tool that can collect syslog messages from network devices. The Syslog Analyzer can then filter the log messages and highlight potential problems and suggested fixes using standard or custom filters. CallManager 3.0 is capable of sending log messages in syslog format to a central RME server in the network. If CallManagers are deployed in clusters, all members of the cluster can send syslog messages to the same RME server in order to centralize the log analysis function. The Syslog Analyzer can also be configured to watch for specific log messages and generate an e-mail notification.

Call Detail Records

Call detail records (CDRs) are used in telephony networks to enable an analysis of system call activity, typically for the purposes of billing, fraud detection, and capacity planning. The approach that Cisco takes with CDR information is to make it available for use by third-party applications. For example, the CallManager suite of software does not contain any application software that can be used for generating billing reports. If this function is desired, a third-party application such as IntegraTrack may be used to generate the required reports from the information captured in the CallManager database.

CallManager servers maintain CDR entries for calls placed through the system in the SQL server 7.0 database for CallManager version 3.0 and later. In the event that a cluster of CallManagers is being used, the CDR database is maintained on the primary CallManager in the cluster. The CDR database maintained by the CallManager provides read-only access to all database tables in order to facilitate post-processing. Access to the database can be made via SQL calls or via open database connectivity (ODBC). In addition to the CDR database, it may also be necessary to access other database tables to correlate the information in the CDR database correctly with the appropriate device. Cisco provides a complete definition of the database schema in the document titled "Cisco IP Telephony Troubleshooting Guide for Cisco CallManager."

Using Remote Administration Tools

CallManager 3.0 provides a set of tools for remotely managing the CallManager server and IP telephony devices in an AVVID network system. The primary tools for remote management include bridged Telnet, a command line interface (CLI) for executing show commands, and the Windows 2000 Performance Console.

Bridged Telnet This application may be useful when Telnet access is required to a remote CallManager server that is behind a firewall. Using the bridged Telnet application can provide secure access to the CallManager server without the need to modify firewall configuration. This functionality may be desired when CallManagers are deployed at remote locations or when third-party organizations are allowed to access a CallManager for support services.

Show commands Similar to Cisco's IOS software command line interface, the CallManager can display a number of important system characteristics by way of show commands. The show commands can be accessed locally by way of a DOS shell or by way of the show.exe application, which can be accessed from a Telnet session.

Windows 2000 Performance console CallManager allows local or remote monitoring of system performance by way of the Windows 2000 Performance console application that is provided with the Windows 2000 Server operating system upon which CallManager is built. A number of system performance characteristics can be monitored in real-time with this application, including the number of active calls, call attempts, calls completed, and more. Data can be displayed in graphic or tabular format.

Understanding the Packages, Licensing, and Upgrades

The AVVID architecture is designed to be modular in order to accommodate the requirements for many different sizes and types of organizations using a common set of hardware and software. With such an architecture, the number and types of devices required for each solution will obviously vary. In the past, Cisco has offered Starter kit bundles that contained the necessary hardware and software components for a basic AVVID setup with a limited number of IP telephone users. As the AVVID components have been upgraded and expanded over time, the individual components within the starter kits have changed. In this section we will look at the licensing and ordering issues for each of the separate components in an AVVID network.

CallManager Software

CallManager software is available only as a preloaded application on a Cisco Media Convergence Server (MCS). It is not possible to purchase an individual copy of the CallManager software without also ordering an MCS. There are multiple choices for MCS platforms, and the packaging of CallManager and the associated applications varies depending on the selected MCS platform. Purchase of a Cisco

MCS server includes all of the required software licenses and distribution CD-ROMs for the base operating system and the CallManager application.

Media Convergence Servers

The MCS platforms offered by Cisco have changed over time as PC technology has advanced. For example, as newer, faster CPUs become available, Cisco updates the available MCS offerings. There are also choices in terms of the actual form factor of the server. Currently, Cisco offers a stand-alone MCS server and two rack-mount platforms. Other options for the MCS servers include DAT tape backup drives, redundant power supplies, and additional RAM and hard drives.

IP Telephones

Several models of IP telephones are currently available from Cisco, as previously discussed. IP telephones can be ordered with or without a user license. In most cases, IP telephones should be ordered with the user license included. The intent of offering IP telephones without a user license is to make spares available to customers at a lower cost.

One other choice when ordering handsets is whether or not a power supply will be required. If in-line power will be used, an external power supply is optional. In addition, there are several models of power supplies available for use in different parts of the world. There is also a locking wall-mount kit available for 7900 series phones.

Voice Gateways

Selecting the appropriate voice gateway from the many choices is quite a task in itself. There are no specific licensing issues to worry about for the gateways, but there are some issues to be aware of when selecting software versions and feature sets for the IOS-based gateways. First, make sure the proper version of IOS is ordered to obtain the required voice and QoS related features. Second, make sure a plus feature set is ordered, which is required for all IOS-based voice gateways. If a plus feature set is not ordered, the voice-specific hardware will not be recognized and the IOS image will not contain the required voice features. Lastly, if the gateway will also be used as a gatekeeper, this can be achieved only with the Enterprise plus and MCM feature set; currently, there is only a single IOS image for each platform that combines both of these functions.

What to Expect in the Next Version of Cisco CallManager

As with any new software application, we can expect a flurry of maintenance and new feature releases for CallManager. Although Cisco does not provide details of these future releases publicly, it is possible to speculate on future enhancements simply by looking at key features that are missing today on CallManager and also looking at recent VoIP enhancements on IOS-based products.

In terms of protocol support, one that is gaining popularity in the industry and noticeably absent from CallManager 2.4 and 3.0 is the Session Initiation Protocol (SIP). This protocol can be used as an alternative to Cisco's Skinny Station Protocol or H.323 for setting up media streams between devices. Although the IP telephones can participate in a SIP-initiated call, it is not possible for such a call to be set up using SIP by way of the CallManager as a proxy device. Cisco has introduced support for SIP on some of their IOS-based platforms.

With many business organizations implementing telecommuting programs, including Cisco, the phone systems used by these organizations must be capable of telecommuting features such as *hotelling* or *hot-desking*. These terms are references to the practice of employees no longer having their own dedicated cubicle or desk once an organization implements a telecommuting program. Since telecommuting employees are frequently out of the office or working from home, they will use an available desk or cubicle from a shared pool. This requires that the phone system be capable of dynamically routing calls to users' desktops depending upon their location in the office on any given day. In an office environment like this, users must typically "log in" to the phone system when arriving at the office to notify the system where to route their calls. With CallManager lacking this capability today, AVVID could not be used by telecommuting organizations if they desire this capability. With Cisco itself being a heavy user of telecommuting, it seems logical to expect this feature in future releases.

Another key capability that limits the use of CallManager in certain environments is the ability to record IP phone conversations. CallManager currently does not support this capability, which limits its use in environments where this is a requirement, such as financial institutions or call centers. This is a common feature that can be added to many legacy telephone systems. In order for CallManager to be considered on par with legacy systems in this regard, Cisco must add this capability in a future release.

The open standards-based architecture that Cisco has implemented with AVVID leads to another broad category of future capabilities for CallManager that is virtually limitless. By way of CallManager's support for the TAPI and JTAPI standards, functionality can be added to CallManager by way of third-party applications. This means that in addition to any new capabilities that Cisco adds directly to CallManager, we can also expect to see a wide range of TAPI/JTAPI-based applications that will also add new functionality. To foster such third-party development, Cisco has developed a formal program for developers of TAPI/JTAPI applications to become official partners with Cisco.

In addition to software enhancements, we can also expect on-going enhancements to the MCS platforms that are required for the CallManager software and associated applications. We have already seen the introduction of several new models of the MCS hardware platforms, as well as new processors and increased memory capacity. As PC platforms continue to advance in the industry, we can certainly expect these "technology refreshes" on the MCS platforms as well.

Summary

CallManager provides the call processing function in a Cisco AVVID IP telephony system. Along with other included software applications and operating system utilities, it provides support for a robust set of user, administrator, and system features. Functionality can also be added to this IP PBX by way of open standards-based protocols. Cisco's CallManager software is available as a preloaded application on a Cisco Media Convergence Server.

There are currently two generations of IP telephone handsets from Cisco. The first generation of handsets consisted of the 12 SP+ and 30 VIP models. The latest handsets available for use with CallManager include the 7900 series models. Cisco's IP telephones support the Skinny Station Protocol, which requires the CallManager to proxy all call processing functions.

Selecting the appropriate VoIP gateway can be a challenging task when considering all of the possible options. Cisco offers standalone, router-based, and LAN switch-based gateways for use in AVVID systems. Consideration must be given to physical connectivity and required protocol support when determining the proper gateway selection.

Monitoring system and call activity on a CallManager system is possible with a combination of Cisco-provided utilities as well as tools provided in the Windows 2000 Server operating system. Many of these applications can be used locally by way of the CallManager Administration interface. There is also a collection of administrative utilities and applications for providing remote support.

As with any software application, organizations deploying CallManager must ensure that the proper licensing is arranged for all system users. The CallManager software is available in several different system configurations, depending on user requirements.

FAQs

Q: How difficult is it to perform moves/adds/changes for IP telephones in a Cisco AVVID voice network?

A: Since telephone extensions are actually mapped to the media access control (MAC) address of the IP telephone, the moves/adds/changes process is very simple. When a phone is connected to the network, an IP address is acquired using DHCP, regardless of where the phone is plugged into the network. Once the IP address is assigned, the phone's configuration file is downloaded. The configuration file contains all of the information the phone needs to operate, including the local extension. This dynamic and automated process for initializing a phone means that the phones are completely mobile anywhere on the local area network.

Q: Can a firewall be used between IP telephones and a CallManager server?

A: Firewalls can be present in an IP telephony network; however, the firewalls cannot be used to implement network address translation (NAT) on IP telephony traffic. During the registration process between a phone and the CallManager server, the IP address is passed in the payload of the IP packet. Since NAT only translates header addresses and cannot look inside of the IP packet to translate those addresses, the registration process will fail.

Q: Is it possible to run Cisco's CallManager software on a clone PC?

A: The official answer is no. The only way that Cisco provides CallManager software is as a preloaded application on a Cisco Media Convergence Server (MCS) hardware platform. The MCS platforms are the only ones officially supported by Cisco.

The unofficial answer is yes. CallManager software will run on the standard-issue Windows 2000 Server operating system from Microsoft. If you have access to the software (such as an existing MCS platform with CallManager software), it is possible to load it on any hardware that will support the Windows 2000 Server operating system. This may be desired for setting up a lab or other non-production system for testing or training purposes. Of course, this is not supported by Cisco.

Q: What protocols are supported by Cisco's IP telephones?

A: As the client devices in a client/server architecture, the IP telephones are completely dependent on a server device for call processing functionality. This means that the IP telephones rely on the CallManager to serve as a proxy for call processing functions. As of version 3.0, CallManager provides support for Skinny Station Protocol, MGCP, and H.323 v2. In short, this means that IP telephones can communicate with any of these device types, assuming that CallManager is serving to proxy the call processing functions.

Chapter 5

Utilizing AVVID Applications and Software Solutions

Solutions in this chapter:

- **What Is Call Processing?**
- **The Development of CallManager**
- **An Introduction to Active Voice**
- **Internet Communications Software (ICS)**
- **The Video Component of AVVID**
- **Utilizing WebAttendant**
- **Soft Phone**

Introduction

In this chapter we will take a comprehensive look at CallManager call processing and how it works. We will cover how to configure components of call processing and discuss some of the special features it has to offer.

In discussing the development of CallManager, from its original release to the current version 3.05 (at the time of this writing), we will cover CallManager 2.4 and 3.x in detail. It is important that you know how to configure such features as the Bulk Administration Tool (BAT) and how to use the Cisco SC2200 to add the Signaling System #7 (SS7) feature set to utilize CallManager in your network environment.

In introducing you to Cisco's newest Unified Messaging component, Active Voice's Unity, we will also discuss Unity's basic features including ViewMail and ActiveFax.

Another product, Internet Communications Software (ICS), includes helpful features such as Automatic Call Distribution (ACD), Cisco IP Contact Solutions, Intelligent Contact Management (ICM), Customer Interaction Suite, and Network Application Manager (NAM).

In addition, we cover the AVVID video components, which are IP video conferencing (IP/VC) and CDN Content Delivery Services (CDN). IP/TV is currently being incorporated into the CDN and is discussed only briefly in this chapter. Also, you may find the most current information at Cisco's IP/TV Website at the following URL: www.cisco.com/warp/public/cc/pd/mxsv/iptv3400/index.shtml.

WebAttendant is Cisco's Web-enabled replacement of the hardware-based line monitoring devices used by PBXs. We will talk about WebAttendant's features and how it improves the ability to monitor your devices in any network setting.

Finally, we will discuss the utilization of SoftPhone. Cisco's SoftPhone is a Windows-based PC application that can be used as either a standalone or in conjunction with a Cisco IP phone. We will talk about the mobility benefits SoftPhone provides—how it integrates with LDAP for transferring calls and how it can be used with NetMeeting for virtual conferencing.

Due to the ever-changing technology in the IP Telephony field, it is difficult to keep up with the latest updates. Feature upgrades and add-ons to CallManager have been and will continue to be added frequently. Be sure to check out the Cisco's Web site at www.cisco.com for the latest up-to-date product versions.

What Is Call Processing?

Call processing is provided by Cisco's CallManager, which is a software application installed on a reliable Windows NT- or Windows 2000-based server. Call Processing provides call control services for Cisco and third-party applications.

CallManager's call processing is configured through a Web Browser interface. The Call Manager software relies on Internet Information Systems (IIS) to publish a series of Active Server Pages (ASPs), accessing SQL databases. These database entries provide for the processing of calls and their passage through gateways (for example, a VG200 or 3640 with voice interface cards (VICs) and Voice Network Modules) and between end-points (IP phones). Figure 5.1 illustrates an example of the browser interface. Note the menu options at the top of the figure—these are the general category configurations of the CallManager system.

Utilizing Call Processing

As discussed in Chapter 4, CallManagers can be distributed in many ways. The most basic variations consist of either a single-site model or the multi-site model. Multi-site deployments can vary depending on whether you use the distributed call-processing model or the centralized call-processing model.

Call processing through CallManagers can be distributed across the campus to provide spatial diversity. IP phones can be configured with a primary and multiple backup CallManagers. If an individual CallManager goes down, only phones using that CallManager as their primary are affected. They will automatically fail over to another

CallManager. Cisco IP phones currently have the ability to store up to five CallManagers to which they may connect too.

Figure 5.1 The Configuration View of CallManager 3.0

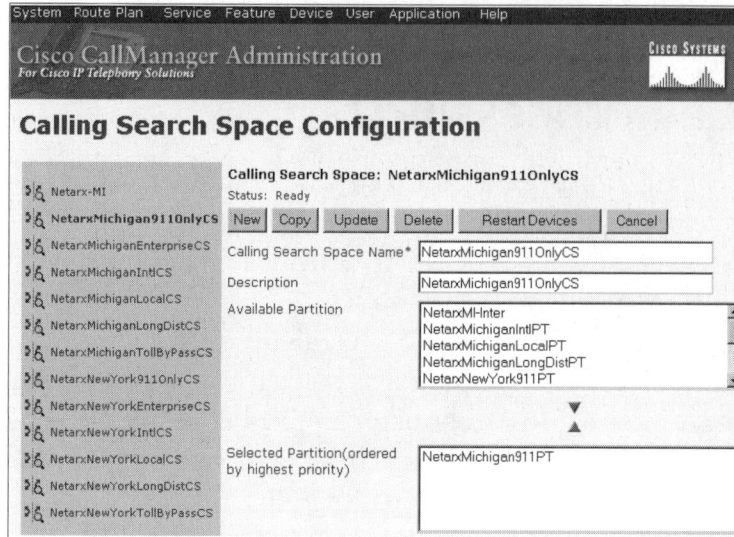

When implementing a single-site model of call processing, you are allowed up to 10,000 users per campus. You can have CallManager and voice messaging services running at each site, and you may run up to six distributed CallManagers in a cluster. This allows for your redundancy and equipment to vary with your campus size.

NOTE

The maximum number of users per campus and the number of CallManagers in a cluster are both expected to increase in the near future as the AVVID technology is further developed.

When using distributed call processing, CallManagers and Voice Messaging resources are present at each site. Each of these sites can support up to 10,000 users. There is a ten-site maximum that can be networked through the WAN. The admission control for distributed call processing is through H.323 v.2 gatekeepers and distributed call processing allows for transparent alternate routing should a WAN link fail.

When using centralized call processing, the CallManager and voice messaging services are located at a central site. Centralized call-processing supports up to 2500 users total and a maximum of three CallManagers. All IP phones must be registered to the same CallManager. The downside to a centralized call processing model is that there is no service if the WAN goes down unless there is a dial backup. However, this drawback can be accounted for by a "thin" CallManager that will be able to reside on many Cisco routers. This thin CallManager will be part of Cisco's IOS and will provide rudimentary routing functionality should the WAN (and, thus, the primary centralized CallManagers) become unavailable.

The Development of CallManager

The CallManager was developed as a software-based call-processing component of Cisco's IP Telephony solution. Cisco's CallManager is central to the AVVID distributed architecture. Cisco's CallManager versions 2.0 and 2.4 have had been deployed on a limited basis as the support for the product was minimal and did not have a wide breath of integration with the rest of Cisco's product line. The IP phones at the time, the SP 12+ and the VIP 30, were not at all elegant as are current models and gateway support was limited to a DT-24 card installed in a server or analog gateway devices.

With the release of CallManager 3.0, we see a newly designed Web browser interface. Moreover, the new CallManager is installed on a Windows 2000 Media Convergence Server (MCS) and is no longer sold as a separate software product. In fact, the current Cisco CallManager software release checks the Basic Input Output System (BIOS) of the MCS to confirm it is truly on the intended platform. Also, concurrent with the release of 3.0, Cisco has provided

IOS integration with many of its existing routers and core switches (the 2600, the 3600, and the 6500 to name a few), and it has released new IP phones models such as the 7960, the 7940, the 7910, and the conference room speaker phone the 7935. The current version of CallManager, version 3.06, was released in December of 2000 and came with the ability to manage a cluster of Call Managers in addition to support for Media Gateway Control Protocol (MGCP).

CallManager 2.4

Cisco developed CallManager 2.4 as a software-only application that enabled a telephony network made up of IP terminals, gateways, and voice applications. Released in fall of 1999, CallManager 2.4 runs on a Windows NT platform. Microsoft Internet Information Server (IIS) is installed to the Cisco CallManager server to provide a Web interface for the Cisco CallManager configuration database.

CallManager 3.0

Installed on an MCS, Cisco CallManager 3.0 improves the scalability, and availability of the enterprise IP telephony solution. CallManager 3.0 servers can be clustered and administered as one entity, which greatly improve administration. The current release of Call Manager 3.06 supports MGCP, Web Attendant, and a host of gateways not previously supported (the 2600, the 3600, and so on). The MCS-7835 is used to run CallManager 3.0 or uOne 4.1E Corporate Edition. The MCS-7835 supports up to 2500 IP Phones, and a cluster can support up to 10,000 IP Phones (2000 phones on each of five servers). The MCS-7822, is best suited to small and medium-scale organizations with up to 500 phones. It can run CallManager 3.0 and will be able to run additional AVVID applications in the future.

The MCS-7835

An MCS 7835 is a high-availability server providing server-grade components and redundant hard drives (RAID though mirroring). It is generally the platform of choice for larger installations with one to many CallManagers where Information Technology Staff wish to keep the call processing separate from the gateways. An example of a combination gateway and call-processing device is an ICS-7750. It is a chassis-based solution that has six blades; the CallManager resides on one and the remaining blades can be used for Unified Messaging or MRPs. The blades hold the digital signaling processor (DSP) resources and the gateway interface cards—examples include Foreign Exchange Office (FXO), Foreign Exchange Station (FXS), E&M (recEive and transMit or ear and mouth), Master File Table Voice/WAN interface cards MFT VWICs. Some managers are not comfortable with a single point of failure on their systems. Therefore, the MCSs are often an excellent choice, since it is easy to cluster CallManagers and provide redundancy with routers (e.g., Hot Standby Routing Protocol (HSRP)) acting as gateways. The following is a list of some of the hardware specifications of the MCS-7835:

- Pentium III 733MHz

- 1GB Error Correcting SDRAM

- Maximum of 2500 IP Phones per server

- Dual 18.2GB Hot Swap SCSI Hard Drives

- Hardware RAID Controller

- Optional 12/24GB DAT Tape Drive

- Able to run CallManager 3.0 or uOne 4.1E Corporate Edition

The MCS-7822

The MCS-7822 does not provide redundancy and is obviously not capable of handling as many callers since its resources are less than that of the MCS-7835. It is an excellent choice for designers wishing to provide cost-effective solutions in a distributed call processing environment. The MCS-7822 would be located in branch offices while the MCS-7835 and ICS-7750 product lines would exist at head-end locations. The following is a list of some of the hardware specifications of the MCS-7822:

- Pentium III 550MHz
- 512MB Error Correcting RAM
- Single 9.1GB SCSI Hard Drive
- Single power supply
- Able to run CallManager 3.0(1)
- Will support additional AVVID Applications in the future

IOS CallManager

Cisco also has a "skinny" CallManager that can be installed on many gateways, such as the Cisco 3640 Modular Router, to provide minimal functionality should an MCS or an ICS (with the full-fledged CallManager 3.X installed) be unavailable. This is helpful in branch offices where there are not enough users to justify the purchase of a full CallManager, even though the users still need to make calls to the PSTN should the primary communications through the corporate WAN fail.

Utilizing CallManager

CallManager was designed to offer an end-to-end IP Telephony solution. Its distributed deployment offers a spatial redundancy to manage locations as one entity. In other words, in a large company, a cluster of CallManagers (each at a separate location) can easily be administered from any single location.

Call Manager Features

CallManager can best be described as an integrated suite of voice applications. This collection of applications includes conferencing, manual attendant, WebAttendent, Interactive Voice Response (IVR), Auto Attendant, uOne, and Unity. CallManager comes with an extensive array of user and administrator features as well. Many of these features were highlighted in Chapter 4 already, but Table 5.1 offers you a comparison of user features provided in CallManager 2.4 and CallManager 3.0. In addition, Table 5.2 provides a listing of the administrative features offered in CallManager 2.4 and 3.0. For each table, the left-hand columns denote version 2.4 features and the right-hand columns denote the additional features included in version 3.0.

For a current listing of Call Manager versions and their user and administrative features visit the following URL: www.cisco.com/warp/public/cc/pd/nemnsw/callmn/prodlit/callm_ds.htm

Table 5.1 A Listing of User Features in CallManager 2.4 and 3.0

CallManager 2.4 User Features	CallManager 3.0 User Features
Call pickup group-directed	Call Detail Records
Call pickup group-universal	Date/time display format config-urable per phone
Calling Line Identification (CLID)	
Calling Party Name Identification CNID	Device addition through wizards
	Device downloadable feature
Click to dial from Web browser	Upgrades–Phones, hardware
Direct Inward Dial (DID)	Transcoder resource, hardware
Direct Outward Dial (DOD)	Conference bridge resource, VoIP gateway resource
Distinctive ring (internal versus external)	Device groups and pools for large DHCP block IP assignment–phones and gateways
Loop key notification,	
Message Waiting Indication	Dialed Number
Multi-party conference–Ad-hoc with add-on, Meet-me features	Identification Service (DNIS)

Continued

Table 5.1 Continued

CallManager 2.4 User Features	CallManager 3.0 User Features
Single directory number, multiple Phones - bridged line appearances	Emergency 911 service
User configured speed dial, call for-ward-all by web-access	H.323 compliant interface to H.323 clients, gateways, and gatekeepers
Web browser interface	Single point system/device configuration
	Time zone configurable per phone

Table 5.2 Listing of Administrator Features in CallManager 2.4 and 3.0

CallManager 2.4 Admin Features	CallManager 3.0 Admin Features
Call status per line (state, duration, number)	Application discovery and registration to SNMP manager
Directory dial from phone (3.0(2))	Centralized, replicated configuration database, distributed Web-based management consoles
Distinctive ring per phone	
html help access from phone	Configurable and default ringer WAV files per phone
Paperless phone-display driven	
QoS statistics at phone	Database automated change notification
Recent Dial list-calls to phone, from phone, auto-dial, edit dial	Debug information to common syslog file
Select specified phone to ring	
Single button data collaboration on SoftPhone–chat, application sharing	Device mapping tool–IP address to MAC address
Web services access from phone	JTAPI 1.3 computer telephony interface
	LDAP v3 directory interface (3.0(2))
	MGCP support to Cisco VG200 and AS2600 VoIP gateways
	Native supplementary services support to Cisco H.323 gateways
	QoS statistics deliver per call, per device

Continued

Table 5.2 Continued

CallManager 2.4 Admin Features	CallManager 3.0 Admin Features
	RDNIS-Redirected DNIS, outbound
	Single CDR per cluster
	Sortable component list by device and directory
	TAPI 2.1 computer telephony interface

Configuring the Bulk Administration Tool (BAT)

The Bulk Administration Tool (BAT) is an optional application for Cisco CallManager. After opening Cisco CallManager administration, select the Application drop down menu, and choose BAT. If you are administering a large number of phones at your site, you can use the BAT to perform batch add, modify, and delete operations for Cisco IP Phones. This saves a great deal of time over having to manually add and configure each phone using Cisco CallManager Administration.

With the help of Tool for Auto-Registered Phones Support (TAPS), BAT is capable of inserting a device record when the actual device does not exist. BAT also provides an option that allows you to create dummy MAC addresses. When the phones are ready to configure, administrators need to update the dummy MAC addresses with actual MAC addresses. With BAT, you are able to add up to 10,000 phones and users to the Cisco CallManager application.

BAT has three central menu options: Configure, Application, and Help. The Configure menu includes Phone Template, Phones, Users, and Phones/Users as submenu options. The Application menu returns you to the CallManager Administration Window. From the BAT window, the administrator can add, update devices, delete devices, and add users.

WARNING

Running the bulk transactions performed by BAT during the day may slow down the CallManager's performance. To avoid this problem, it is best to run BAT during off-peak hours. Any prolonged disruption in call processing is likely to lead to frustrated employees.

Adding Signaling System #7 (SS7) Using Cisco SC2200

Cisco's Signaling System 7 (SS7) works with both with dial access applications and H.323 VoIP. The SC2200 Signaling controller is what provides the ability for SS7 protocols to work with the Public Switched Telephone Network (PSTN).

An Introduction to Active Voice

Active Voice gives us a messaging solution that works along side CallManager to provide a full AVVID solution. Cisco has stated that "Active Voice offers a more complete Unified Messaging solution than uOne, and has decided to replace uOne with Active Voice's Unity." Unity is a Unified Messaging server that provides a wide range of messaging capabilities. Cisco acquired the Active Voice Corporation in November 2000. According to Cisco, "the acquisition of Active Voice's Unity operation represents an important step in the advancement of Cisco's Architecture for Voice, Video, and Integrated Data (AVVID) and underscores Cisco's commitment to delivering unified communications capabilities to the industry." For more detailed information on Active Voice and Unity, please refer to Chapter 6.

The Unity Product Line

Unity works with Exchange Server 5.5 using LDAP and MAPI. Unity uses Internet Explorer 4.01 and later versions to access the Unity Administrator Pages and Active Assistant pages for subscribers. IIS 4.0 hosts Unity's Active Server Pages. Microsoft Outlook 97, 98, and 2000 all support Unity's ViewMail application for subscribers. Other e-mail clients supported by Unity include Outlook Express, IMAP4 clients, POP3 clients, and Exchange's Web messaging client. Unity's product line includes:

- ActiveAssistant
- ViewMail
- ActiveFax

ActiveAssistant

ActiveAssistant is a Web site that you access by using your Web browser. It is a tool that allows users to set up or change their personal settings, such as call screening and message notification. Subscribers can record their own names and personal greetings by using either the Unity conversation or the ActiveAssistant. ActiveAssistant pages contain settings that control how you and your callers interact with Unity by phone. Users can customize Unity and drastically reduce their administrative workload.

The side bar menu for ActiveAssistant contains three setting groups: call settings, message settings, and personal settings. The call settings allow you to change your personal greeting and modify your call transfer and screening configurations. The message settings you are able to modify include your message notification, message playback, message addressing, private lists, and color options (to help identify what types of messages are in you in-box). Your name, telephones, directory listings, phone passwords, and language options are among the personal settings that you can modify within ActiveAssistant.

ViewMail

When a subscriber listens to a message, the voice message is sent as a message stream from the subscriber's Exchange home server, either to the Unity server or the subscriber's desktop from which it can be played using ViewMail. ViewMail allows users to control all e-mail, faxes, and voice mail from a messaging application on their PC, such as Microsoft Outlook. You can send, listen to, and manage voice messages from your Outlook Inbox.

When the recipient accesses messages from the desktop by using ViewMail, the messages are streamed from the Unity server. Streaming occurs on demand, regardless of network traffic, to give voice mail the proper sound quality. Without ViewMail, the message is sent as an e-mail with a .WAV attachment instead of being streamed. ViewMail uses a voice message form that works the same way as an Outlook e-mail message form. The ViewMail form also has a Media Master control bar which you use to record and play messages.

ActiveFax

ActiveFax is the optional fax component of Unity that provides fax service for the Unity server. Active Fax is similar to ViewMail in that users have the ability to control their fax and voice mail messages. Subscribers must have both a Windows NT or Windows 2000 account and an Exchange mailbox in order to receive faxes. ActiveFax provides more fax capabilities in that users can send faxes electronically and can use fax-on-demand. Fax-on-demand gives users the power to send faxes by using their regular telephone. When ActiveFax is installed on a separate server, the server handles only fax messages. These fax messages are routed to the message store on the subscriber's Exchange home server instead of being saved on the ActiveFax server.

When calling or logging on to Unity, subscribers see or hear their fax messages announced. ActiveFax lets subscribers deliver both fax and e-mail messages to any fax machine as well as forward a fax message to another subscriber. When a subscriber does access fax messages over the phone, he or she will hear a message summary and sometimes a voice annotation; however the contents of the fax message are not transferable over the phone (ActiveFax can't read your faxes to you). Notification of new fax messages is an available feature for subscribers through phones or pagers when not at a computer. Subscribers can also have their e-mail messages delivered to a fax machine. However, the only sendable e-mail attachments are .TXT, .TIF, and .DCX files. Other types of file attachments are removed, and the file names are listed at the end of the message. Moreover, your company must purchase a Text-to-Speech E-mail license for each subscriber who uses e-mail delivery to a fax machine.

Subscribers are able to set their fax message settings if ActiveAssistant is available. The Fax Server Monitor program and the Unity Administrator are used to set up ActiveFax. As an administrator, you can monitor outbound faxes through the *Status Monitor Fax Queue Status* page. The Status Monitor is a Web site that allow the administrator to view real-time information about Unity, such as port status, as well as use it to start and shut down Unity.

Internet Communications Software (ICS)

Internet Communications Software is Cisco's open model for allowing service providers and application providers to benefit from re-occurring revenue through innovative new products that they can offer their clients. Internet Communications Software is not to be confused with Integrated Communications Server, (also abbreviated as ICS)—it is a chassis-based device that has CallManager installed on it and can also function as a modular gateway. The Internet Communications Software consists of five components. These components include:

- ACD (Automatic Call Distribution)
- Cisco IP Contact Center Solutions
- ICM (Intelligent Contact Management)

- Customer Interaction Suite
- NAM

ACD (Automatic Call Distribution)

ACD is a service that automatically reroutes calls to customers within a distribution of locations that are served by the same CO. As part of the ICS, ACD is provided by Network Applications Manager (NAM). ACD delivers automatic call distribution through its remote agent support functionality. As an enterprise agent, it has tasks defined within the NAM. This enables ACD to participate with other ACD-based agents in system-wide virtual skill groups. This service is used to transfer, conference, and divert calls within an enterprise framework as well.

The combination of enterprise agents and ACD support provides the opportunity for service providers to enter the ACD business without limitations that come with the use of traditional Centrex ACD. All of the major ACD products integrate with the NAM which include both premise and office-based ACDs (Nortel DMS-100). Softphone and screen-pop applications are used for NAM enterprise agents and agents attached to CPE ACDs, providing for a uniform CTI solution. Queued calls are delivered to the customer site when an appropriately skilled enterprise agent or ACD-based agent becomes available. For Web-based calling, a *push to talk* button on a Web page allows a call to be established to an ACD agent.

Cisco IP Contact Center Solutions

The Cisco IP Contact Center (IPCC) is the combination of contact center solutions and Cisco IP telephony. Its products enable call center agents using Cisco IP phones to receive both plain old telephone service (POTS) and VoIP calls. IPCC was intended for integration with legacy call-center platforms and networks; therefore, it provides a migration path to IP-based customer contact while taking advantage of previous infrastructures.

Specific capabilities of IPCC include intelligent call routing, computer telephony integration (CTI), ACD functionality, and interactive voice response (IVR) integration. Some of IPCC's enhancements are as follows: data-rich screen pops, which is customer information delivered by ICM to the agents business application with call arrival; customizable agent desktop, which includes a fully functional SoftPhone; third-party call control, which allows agents to control actions such as answer, hold, conference, and transfer from within their desktop application; and agent statistics, which provide an agent with immediate feedback on personal statistics including the number of contacts handled, average call work time, average talk time, cumulative available time and total login time. Users who are being helped by an agent can use their Web browser to carry on a voice or text conversation with that agent.

Intelligent Contact Management (ICM)

Cisco's Intelligent Contact Management (ICM) software directs customer contact information to the appropriate resource. Customers can correspond via e-mail, the Web, or by telephone and be immediately routed to the most logical resource given a set of user defined roles. These roles are established via customer profiling combined with an up to date list of available resources. Cisco ICM software enables users to deploy a network-to-desktop CTI strategy, while managing the availability of real-time and historical information provided by multiple networks, ACDs, IVRs, Web servers, business applications, databases, and the system itself on the server. Contact, customer, and peripheral data are collected and stored in a Microsoft SQL Server database for use in the reporting.

Customers in need of information other than that provided on a corporate Web site can request assistance from a contact center agent via the Web. These requests are routed by the ICM system, with the accompanying customer-profile data collected over the Web, and are delivered to the most appropriate agent.

ICM software to control IVR scripting is enabled by a service control interface, which provides unified scripting. ICM 's open IVR interface enables communication between IVR applications and the Cisco platform. Therefore, the IVR may act as a routing client, managed resource, queue point, and an information source for consolidated real-time and historical reports.

Customer Interaction Suite

Cisco's Customer Interaction Suite provides companies with the ability to interact with consumers on the Web or network. Instead of the traditional procedure in which consumers point and click, send e-mail, and wait for a response, the Customer Interaction Suite provides the feeling of real-time interaction. Components of the Cisco Interaction Suite include the Cisco Media Manager, Cisco Media Blender, Cisco E-Mail Manager, and Cisco Collaboration Server.

The Cisco Media Manager is the component that allows companies to link customers the most appropriate and capable individual or resource for their given needs. It works in conjunction with The Cisco Collaboration Server intuitively combining human interaction with network resources.

The Cisco Media Blender combines network-initiated contact from customers with voice calls, text, and Web collaboration. This provides customers with great savings over traditional methods requiring the use of separate, often expensive, forms of media. Media Blender was developed to integrate into existing telephony infrastructures to keep the cost of deployment at a minimum.

Cisco E-Mail Manager intuitively directs incoming e-mail to the resource or individual best suited to respond. This of course cuts down on resources wasted on management of mail. Cisco Collaboration Server provides companies with the ability to respond quickly to customer requests not only with text, but with visual aides. Customers visiting the Interaction Suite receive a very personalized experience. Consumers are recognized for who they are, routed to the appropriate resource, and then receive a response that is catered to their individual needs. This is done quickly and with minimal human interruption.

Network Applications Manager (NAM)

Cisco's Network Application Manager (NAM) is an application that supplies service providers with the ability to offer a wide range of mission critical applications to customers. NAM is the only service platform specifically built to align a service provider's resources with the customer's own business applications. Some of the features include call blending, automatic call distribution and e-mail response collaboration.

The architecture of NAM is designed in a hierarchical structure. Users and customers can begin with relatively simple services and move up the chain to very complex services provided from service providers. Cisco stresses the need for a business partnership between customers and service providers as customers become more involved. This partnership is intended to lead to increased customer retention, loyalty, and satisfaction.

The NAM is flexible, scalable software that supports many services including: automatic call distribution (ACD), computer telephony integration (CTI), interactive voice response (IVR), Advanced services, Integrated customer relationship management (CRM), Web collaboration, e-mail response management, call blending, database routing, unified communications, Local number portability (LNP), Calling/pre-paid cards, and PSTN/VoIP. With the NAM platform, Service Provider hosted solutions are integrated with the customer's network. The NAM platform also enables a service provider to help its customers achieve objectives as their business grows and changes. Since NAM applications are developed by customers, the partnership with the Service Provider is strategic. The NAM architecture is flexible and can be deployed across many platforms. NAM can be deployed for use with Application Service Providers, Network Service Providers, and individual customers as well. NAM is secure and scalable providing room for growth as customers grow.

The Video Component of AVVID

The video components of AVVID discussed are IP Video Conferencing (IP/VC), and Content Delivery Networks (CDN). What sets the video component of AVVID apart from traditional methods is that it is packeted within IP, providing fast and reliable delivery of information.

IP Video Conferencing (IP/VC)

IP/VC Video Conferencing within Cisco's AVVID architecture provides for fast, reliable, and scalable video communication with a multitude of real-world applications. As businesses have grown to an international scale, it has become increasingly difficult for corporate managers to meet and discuss business strategies. As universities seek to increase student enrollment, they are often limited to geographical regions and staffing. IP/VC is a solution to these issues allowing for immediate "face to face" communication without the added expense of travel and accommodations. With IP/VC, corporate managers can communicate interactively with tier 2 managers on an international scale simultaneously. Universities and colleges can reach more students with less staff without dealing with the burden of geographical restrictions.

Video conferencing is certainly not a new technology; traditionally, it has been implemented over circuit switched networks and at a maximum of 128 Kbps video transfer. The systems were not reliable or redundant and have not "caught on" due to expense. IP/VC combines video, voice, and data in to one packet over the wire providing a cost-effective, quality-driven method of deployment.

Content Delivery Networks (CDN)

Cisco's Content Delivery Network (CDN) has been developed as an end-to-end solution providing increased availability, bandwidth, and response times for Web-based deployments. CDN has been developed to meet the needs of service providers and enterprises in moving audio, video, and data content to the edge of networks and closer to end users. CDN has been designed around five technologies:

- Content Distribution and Management
- Content switching
- Content Routing
- Intelligent network Services
- Content Edge Delivery

Content Distribution and Management equipment, such as the CDM4650, is capable of deploying up to 1000 content engines to content delivery nodes at the network edge. This is accomplished with centralized management and control. Content Switching is used for load balancing within a CDN and also provides the ability to process requests in the order of priority. Intelligent Network Services provides security and Quality of Service (QoS) within the CDN environment. The Content Edge Delivery is comprised of the content delivery nodes distributing content to end-users.

The CDN system works much like a department store. Consumers need not go to a corporate headquarters or warehouse to purchase a product. They need only to visit their local department store to purchase what they need, ultimately saving time and money. CDN accomplishes this same task by moving the desired content closer to the "consumer" saving time and money.

Utilizing WebAttendant

Being the first of many IP Telephony applications that integrate "Old World" and "New World" Telephony functions, WebAttendant is Cisco's solution to replace the PBX's traditional manual attendant console. Traditional manual attendant consoles can either be large phones with bulky attachments or proprietary expensive terminals. The Cisco WebAttendant is a client-server application that enables you to set up any Cisco IP Phone as an attendant console. It can be downloaded from the CallManager Web administration pages and can be installed either on the CallManager or any other system. The Cisco WebAttendant client provides a Graphical User Interface (GUI) to control a Cisco IP Phone when used as an attendant console, and includes speed dial buttons and quick directory access to look up phone numbers, monitor phone status, and direct calls. The Cisco WebAttendant client can be used by a receptionist or administrative assistant to handle the direction of calls for your entire company. In addition, it can be used by an individual to handle calls coming into a single Cisco IP Phone. It is an IP-based application, which is more scalable than the hardware-based line monitor devices used by PBXs. WebAttendant allows portability to various platforms including Windows 98, Windows NT, and Windows 2000. Working with the Cisco IP Phone, WebAttendant is able to monitor the state of every line in the system, while promptly and efficiently dispatching and accepting calls. Figure 5.2 shows you the WebAttendant interface.

Figure 5.2 The WebAttendant Interface

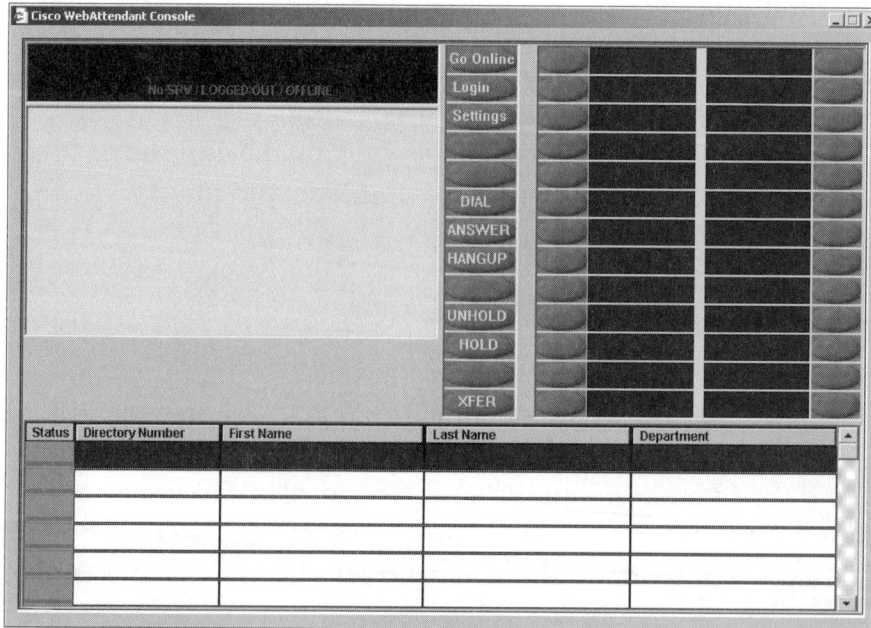

The Web Attendant interface includes the following components:

- Display
- Action Buttons
- Speed Dial Area
- Smart Line (SL) Area
- Status
- Directory

The WebAttendant Interface

The WebAttendant interface is a browser interface that is made up of six fields that help its user administer the incoming calls to an organization: the display, found in the upper left corner of the Cisco WebAttendant; the action buttons, found in the upper middle; the speed dial area, found in the upper right corner; the SL area, found on the left side beneath the display; the status field, found in the lower left corner; and the directory, found at the bottom. Refer to Figure 3.7 to reference the location of these fields.

The display on the Cisco WebAttendant, which looks much like the display on the Cisco IP Phone, shows you the state of the server and Telephony Call Dispatcher as well as any call actions in progress. The action buttons allow you to perform the attendant functions; you can go online, login to the WebAttendant console, modify the login settings, and perform the usual call operations such as dial, answer, hang-up, hold, unhold, and transfer. There are also unused buttons available to program for other actions that you may need. The speed dial area looks just like a regular speed dial menu, and is where you can set the speed dial numbers. You have room to program up to 26 different speed dial numbers in the two columns of speed dial buttons provided. The Smart Lines area has room for eight numbers to display smart lines that are available. The status of each smart line is indicated by a specific color: a flashing red button means a call on that line is on hold, a solid light blue button reflects an active line, and a flashing yellow button tells you a call is ringing on the SL button. The status area displays an entry for each phone being attended appears with the line state of each user's primary line. The Cisco CallManager database provides the directory information that you would see.

In order for the Cisco Telephony Call Dispatcher (receptionist) to route calls to Cisco WebAttendant, pilot points and hunt groups must be configured. A Cisco WebAttendant pilot point is a virtual directory number that receives and redirects calls to the members of its associated hunt group. A hunt group is a list of destinations that determine the call redirection order. The order in which the members of the hunt group are listed determines the call redirection order. The first available (not busy) member in a hunt group receives the call.

Utilizing Soft Phone

The Cisco IP SoftPhone is an application for a multimedia PC desktop. A user can use a microphone headset to send and receive calls on their computer. A laptop user can take their phone extension with them on the road. SoftPhone integrates easily with LDAP directories, allowing for the use of a global as well as personal address books. Conference calls can be made by simply dragging and dropping names onto the SoftPhone.

Summary

Many organizations are moving toward AVVID solutions to merge their phone and computer networks together. This centralizes the administration and can also save on long distance phone costs (especially when calling between office locations). Cisco's CallManager makes up and essential part of the AVVID solution by supplying call processing. Depending on size, one may choose to deploy CallManager on the MCS-7835 for medium to large-scale organizations, MCS-7822 for small to medium-scale organizations, or the IOS CallManager running on a Cisco 3640 Modular Router for small offices and remote sites. CallManager itself is a software application installed on a reliable Windows NT- or 2000-based server. Call Processing provides call control services for Cisco and third-party applications.

The CallManager was developed as a software-based call-processing component of Cisco's IP Telephony solution. Cisco's CallManager is central to the AVVID distributed architecture.

Active Voice gives us a messaging solution that works along side CallManager to provide a full AVVID solution. Unity is the Unified Messaging server developed by Active Voice, which provides a wide range of messaging capabilities. Cisco acquired Active Voice Corporation in November 2000. Unity works with Exchange Server 5.5 using LDAP and MAPI. Unity uses Internet Explorer 4.01 and later to access the Unity Administrator Pages and Active Assistant pages for subscribers. IIS 4.0 hosts Unity's Active Server Pages.

Internet Communications Software is Cisco's open model to service providers and application providers to benefit from re-occurring revenues through innovative new products they can offer their clients. The Internet Communications Software consists of five components that include:

- ACD (Automatic Call Distribution)
- Cisco IP Contact Center Solutions
- ICM (Intelligent Contact Management)
- Customer Interaction Suite
- NAM (Network Interactions Manager)

IP Video Conferencing (IP/VC) and Content Delivery Networks (CDN) are the video components of AVVID. What sets the video component of AVVID apart from traditional methods is that it is packetized within IP, providing for the fast and reliable delivery of information.

WebAttendant is Cisco's solution that replaces the PBX's traditional manual attendant console. The Cisco WebAttendant is a client-server application that enables you to set up any Cisco IP Phone as an attendant console. It can be downloaded from the CallManager Web administration pages and can be installed either on the CallManager or any other system.

The Cisco IP SoftPhone is an application for a multimedia PC desktop. Users have a microphone headset to send and receive calls on their computer. If using a laptop, users can even take their phone extension with them on the road.

FAQs

Q: Can I use CallManager 2.4 with many of the features described in this chapter?

A: No. In fact, CallManager 2.4 is no longer for sale, and if you are using CallManager 2.4, you should seriously consider upgrading to 3.06 or higher.

Q: What is the maximum number of IP Phones that a MCS-7835 cluster environment can support?

A: The MCS-7835 supports up to 2500 IP Phones and a cluster can support up to 10,000 IP Phones (2000 phones on each of five servers).

Q: What does the CallManager software rely on IIS to do?

A: It relies on IIS to publish a series of ASP pages by accessing SQL databases.

Q: What two components combine to make up the IPCC?

A: The Cisco IP Contact Center (IPCC) is the combination of contact center solutions and Cisco IP telephony.

Chapter 6

Utilizing Unified Messaging and Active Voice

Solutions in this chapter:

- **Understanding Unified Messaging**
- **What Is Active Voice?**
- **Configuring Active Voice**

Introduction

This chapter gives a comprehensive understanding of Unified Messaging and the components that make up this suite of services. We will talk about some real-world examples where Unified Messaging would be used, as well as show how to utilize the benefits of Voice Mail (VM) over IP in collaboration with fax and e-mail. Quality of Service (QoS) and how it factors in with Unified Messaging will also be covered in detail.

Cisco's latest Unified Messaging solution is derived from a company called Active Voice. Cisco purchased Active Voice in the fall of 2000 for its Unity software. Active Voice's Unity product will be replacing uOne as Cisco's Unified Messaging server because it offers a more complete solution. In fact, as of Call Manager 3.06, the "port" setup required to communicate to the Unity server is still denoted as a uOne port because Cisco technically is still selling the uOne product. More details about Unity, as well as its hardware platform requirements, will follow later in this chapter. We will also talk about the Unity scalability options.

We will discuss some of the software features and functionality offered through Active Voice, which enhance the AVVID architecture. Finally, we will examine how to configure Active Voice's Unity, and we will provide you with various examples of what you can accomplish in small and large corporate situations.

Understanding Unified Messaging

On its Web site, at this URL, www.activevoice.com/products/ phonesoft/lotus_wp.html, Active Voice defines Unified Messaging as "An advanced message management solution for all media types, providing access to any message, anytime, anywhere, from any device." Not long ago, voice, fax, and e-mail messages could only be delivered to different locations. The telephone was the sole means for providing access to voice messages. Faxes had to be manually retrieved from the nearest fax machine, forcing people to leave their cubicles to find their faxes (sometimes, being read by a co-worker no less!). What a dark time it was.

Now, the concept of Unified Messaging brings to light a whole new way of retrieving your messages. Unified Messaging is the combination of voice mail, e-mail, and fax messages in a single location. Figure 6.1 is an example of how Unified Messaging works. From this central location, administrators have an easier time controlling and maintaining communications on the network. For users, the ability to access all messages from one program is a fantastic time-saver. Not only do you have the ability to access all your messages from your computer, but you can review and reply to your voice mail, e-mail, and faxes anywhere on the Internet and over the phone as well.

Figure 6.1 The Benefits of Unified Messaging

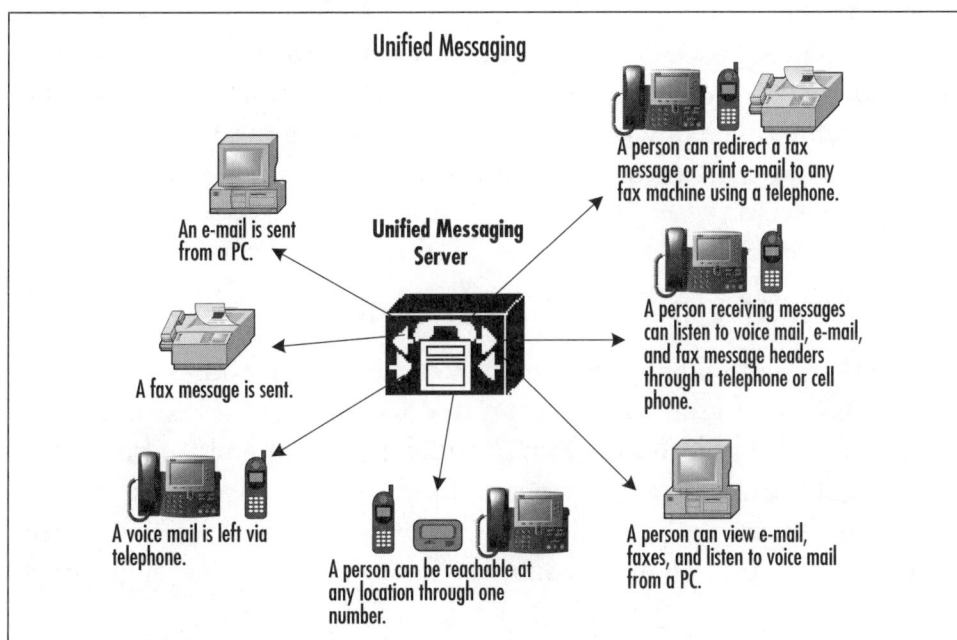

According to Cisco's Web site at www.ieng.com/warp/public/ 180/prod_plat/uni_com/unified_messaging.html, "Unified messaging offers all the benefits of a truly convergent technology; by bridging telephony and IP networks, Cisco allows users to send, receive and manage messages from any access device, regardless of the message type. That means users can listen to e-mail messages from the phone, voice messages through their PC, and forward fax messages to other e-mail users, in addition to a variety of other benefits. Unified messaging also offers cost-reduction benefits such as reduced long distance charges."

Unified Messaging creates a single infrastructure for managing e-mail, voice mail, and fax data, and it brings together voice telephony, wireless data, and Internet networking to allow users to access their messages however they prefer. Moreover, Unified Messaging is also the first step toward providing the same flexibility for broader collaborative technologies. The smart handheld wireless devices that are used to access Unified Messaging can now also be used to access other applications deployed on and accessible through the intranet. The IP telephony integration used to allow users to access all of their messages via the telephone can be incorporated to bring access to many other sorts of corporate information.

Also, as video conferencing and video-mail become more prevalent in many office environments, Unified Messaging lends itself very well to the integration of these and future communication media as they arise.

The Benefits of Unified Messaging

Can you imagine having the ability to access your e-mail over the phone, having it read to you or printed to the nearest fax machine, and then sending a reply? How about getting to the office on a busy morning, sitting down at your computer and seeing all your voice messages, faxes, and e-mail displayed before you—in one location? Unified Messaging allows for many ways to put your messages in and take your messages out of one central database.

My personal benefits from using Unified Messaging included a time when I was on my way to a client; I knew that I had received a fax with information that was important for my discussion with the primary contact at this particular client site. I was able to check my messages on my cell phone and forward the fax to my client's fax machine. This is just one example of time saved in today's hectic business world. In mid- to large-sized companies where it's hard to keep everyone up to date with what's going on, Unified Messaging leaves no excuses for your co-workers who didn't get that message you marked urgent yesterday.

In a large-scale corporate environment, employees may benefit from Unified Messaging through conference calls or video conferencing that may be saved and e-mailed to parties or individuals who were unable to attend. Another example of the benefit of Unified Messaging in the large-scale corporation that IT managers can relate to is the reduction in the number of products needing support. For example, Company X has voice mail on its PBX (or AVVID system), e-mail using Microsoft Exchange/Outlook, and faxes coming through another third-party application. In this situation, the telephony staff and the IT staff have to train each new employee on how to use at least three different systems instead of just one comprehensive system that is as simple to use as e-mail.

In many mid-sized organizations, administrators and branch managers have to travel from site to site. With Unified Messaging in place, a fax can be received at any location, no matter from where or to where it was originally sent. In addition, managers never have to worry about being away from the office and missing an important call or e-mail because all messages are accessible from any location, be it over the phone or at the nearest PC.

Utilizing Voice Mail (VM) over IP

Voice Mail over IP is the primary requirement most users have for Cisco's Unified Messaging suite. It allows users to check for and access messages from their mail client (Outlook) as well as any telephone on the IP telephony network or over the PSTN. Voice Mail over IP includes standard administration (which includes adding, modifying, and deleting users, changing greetings, and so on) and basic message management, all through an easy-to-use Web interface instead of the typical green-screen terminal stuffed in the MDF or telephone closet next to the PBX. Also included is Telephone User Interface (TUI) access to the service.

When setting up an IP phone for voice mail, users can apply the system greeting or record greetings that can be changed at any time. In addition, callers have an option of leaving multiple messages for a single person or leaving messages for multiple people during a single call. Callers may designate messages as urgent or private, and the system will inventory those messages accordingly. When they retrieve messages, users will be notified of message types. Users can listen to certain categories of messages in the order specified as well. This ensures that if they have only a few minutes in which to check messages, urgent messages get first priority. Also, callers have the option to transfer to another extension while leaving a message. Callers have no trouble locating a user's mailbox because name and numeric addressing can be used. This reduces the chance of being transferred to the wrong extension.

When using Call Services, users can even place a call within a messaging session. In order to do this, calls are placed by directly returning a call from a message using the ANI retrieved with that message or by dialing a number for the system to call. When the call is finished, the user returns to the mailbox "bookmark," which is the last message he or she heard before placing the call. This feature allows all messages to be handled and calls made from a single voice-mail session.

Voice messages can also be forwarded as e-mail attachments to any e-mail user with the use of Unified Messaging. This gives users with different voice-mail systems the ability to share voice-mail messages just as they would e-mail messages.

Users can be notified by the use of pagers, stutter dial tone, or message waiting indicator (MWI) on a telephone if Notification Services is running. This way, users never have to wonder if an important message has been received—no matter where they are when they receive it.

Utilizing Fax, Web, and E-mail over IP

Fax Mail over IP allows users (or "subscribers" in Unity) to receive and print faxes from their mailbox. Fax Mail over IP includes standard administration—such as adding, modifying, and deleting users—and basic message management. Also included is Telephone User Interface (TUI) and Web access to the service. Printing faxes from the user's inbox gives the user more privacy and ensures that faxes are not delivered to the wrong recipient.

Fax Mail over IP (FMoIP) allows you to view faxes as .TIF files from your e-mail. This allows you the ability to view your faxes whether there is a fax machine nearby or not. When checking your voice messages, Call Services lets you listen to fax headers from the telephone. FMoIP also allows a user to redirect a fax to any fax machine from the phone when using Call Services. Forwarding fax messages as e-mail attachments requires Unified Messaging. The advantage of this feature is that it ensures that faxes go to the intended recipient and are secure until viewed.

VMoIP users can be notified via pager, stutter dial tone, or message waiting indicator on a telephone set when new fax messages are received with the use of Notification Services. Cisco's Unified Messaging is based on Internet standards, and it allows the complete integration of voice and fax messages within a standard e-mail client interface. E-mail includes standard administration and basic message management. Also included is e-mail client and Web access to the service. For customers purchasing e-mail in conjunction with Voice Mail over IP, Telephone User Interface (TUI) access to the service is also included.

Support for post office protocol (POP) and Internet Message Access Protocol (IMAP) clients on PC- and Web-based clients gives users flexibility in choosing their components. Users have the ability to identify voice, e-mail, and fax messages in an e-mail inbox when Unified Messaging services are running. Voice Mail over IP lets you play voice messages as streaming audio or .WAV files through your PC. Users are more productive by using a single access device for voice and e-mail messages.

Call Services give you the ability to listen to e-mail messages from a telephone, allowing users to get important messages without requiring PC access. Users can be notified of new e-mail messages by way of pager, stutter dial tone, and message waiting indicator on a telephone when Notification Services is running.

Factoring in QoS Considerations

It is important to remember that running voice and data over a common infrastructure requires Quality of Service (QoS). QoS ensures that voice traffic will be transmitted before data traffic because voice packets are assigned a higher priority than data packets. QoS-aware devices recognize the priority of packets and transmit higher-priority packets first. IP phones, switches, and routers provide QoS at the Network and Data Link layers by using classification and queuing mechanisms. Classification marks voice and data frames differently so that they can be prioritized by the QoS-aware devices that make up the intelligent IP network. Catalyst switches have the appropriate queuing mechanisms to guarantee safe passage of voice traffic. An integrated Ethernet switch in a Cisco IP phone also has queuing mechanisms built in to ensure that the 80 Kbps voice stream will pass through before data.

What Is Active Voice?

In November 2000, Cisco Systems purchased Active Voice Corporation, along with its award-winning Unified Messaging solution, Unity. Unity will replace the first Unified Messaging solution offered by Cisco, uOne.

Unity's features complement Cisco's Voice over IP (VoIP) solutions by providing advanced capabilities that enable the unification of both text and voice. According to Cisco's press release regarding the acquisition of Active Voice (www.cisco.com/warp/public/146/pressroom/2000/nov00/corp_111000.htm), "The acquisition of Active Voice's Unity brings Cisco even closer to delivering a unified communications solution that will help businesses enhance productivity, lower cost of ownership, and provide better customer care."

Unity Enterprise

Unity Enterprise is a Windows NT-based messaging solution that delivers an automated attendant, Interactive Voice Response (IVR), voice mail, e-mail, and a fax server in a truly unified environment. Unity Enterprise is convergence-ready and works equally well with both traditional and IP-based telephone systems simultaneously. It is designed to give enterprise businesses the ability to allow users to access and manage their faxes, voice mail, and e-mail through a desktop PC, over the Internet, or even through a touch-tone telephone. Unity's true unified architecture minimizes installation, administration, and support costs, making life easier for system administrators The Unity Enterprise features visual management of voice and fax messages in Microsoft's Outlook, an HTML system administration interface, unified administration, desktop call control, and the ability to listen to e-mail via text-to-speech translation. Unity was designed to integrate with Microsoft Exchange Server, and Active Voice has embedded the Exchange Server within Unity. Users then have the ability to access one directory service for e-mail, voice mail, and fax. This translates into administration that is considerably easier. NT's native 32-bit architecture is used along with streaming media, scalability, networking, and Lightweight Directory Applications Protocol (LDAP) directory services so that Active Voice's Unity has a competitive marketing advantage.

You can access all your messages through Unity's ViewMail. ViewMail is an Outlook module that makes handling all your messages including voice, fax, and e-mail convenient and easy, no matter where you are. Whether you are in the office or on the road, Unity enables you to access all your messages through your phone, your e-mail, or your desktop PC. ViewMail gives you the ability to reply to, forward, and save your messages in public or personal Exchange/Outlook folders with just a click of the mouse. You know what type of messages you have received by the icons attached to each message. These icons give you instant visual descriptions, so you can see at a single glance the number, type, and status of all your communications.

One of the most interesting features of Unity is its text-to-speech capability. This allows you to hear the text portion of e-mail messages over the telephone. You can then respond with a voice message. Now that's convenience! In addition, if you use the optional

ActiveFax module, you can print e-mail and received fax messages on a nearby fax machine. For people who are forever forgetting to check their voice mail or need an e-mail reminder when they're out of the office, this really makes life easier.

Hardware and Platform Requirements and Recommendations

Active Voice built Unity from the ground up to take advantage of Microsoft Windows NT/2000 and BackOffice 4.5 and 2000. Unity is a software-based application that runs on its own server in your network. Currently, Cisco does not sell a server package with Unity installed, but this is expected to change shortly. Also in the works is a blade for the ICS7750 that will provide Unified Messaging. For now, there are a couple of different configuration variations to choose from when setting up a Unity server for Unified Messaging. These configurations are listed in the text that follows.

The 4-64 Port Voice Mail/ Unified Messaging System

A voice messaging port is where the phone lines come into the Unity server. Each of these ports handles one call at a time only. Therefore, you should plan for your system to have enough incoming lines to handle potential incoming calls and enough outgoing lines to handle potential outgoing calls. The voice ports are also needed to light message waiting indicators and to deliver message notification. It is how well you plan your port setup and allocation that will allow your system to work efficiently with the number of ports you set up. For that reason, if you plan to need 4-64 voice messaging ports for voice mail then the following platform is recommended:

- Windows NT hardware capability listing
- Dual SCSI hard drives (RAID optional)
- CD-ROM drive

- Monitor

- 256MB RAM

- 300MHz Pentium II processor

- Available ISA slot(s) required

- Internal or external modem, 33.6 Kbps or higher

- Approved voice board resources

Port allocation is also a factor when you assign class of service categories to your subscribers. The number of ports assigned to Media Master recording often determines how many subscribers can use the feature when recording their names and greetings, and how many can use ViewMail for Outlook with phone playback or use some of the recording features in ActiveAssistant.

Some organizations are smaller and do not have a strong need for a large number of ports. These companies may need only a few ports to accommodate the needs of the incoming and outgoing call traffic. In this case, smaller-scale organizations may do fine with only 12 ports or fewer. If this were your case, then the following would be the platform to choose.

The 4-12 Port Voice Mail/ Unified Messaging System

It is not cost-effective to run a server with more than 12 ports if you are a smaller organization. If your company does not have a high call volume, you should be able to support up to 150 people with a 12-port server. The recommended minimum for organizations with 50 users or fewer is four ports. Other factors can increase the need for more ports, including Auto Attendant, because you will need to consider the ports that will be used up by subscribers checking their messages and the volume of incoming or outgoing calls. The following is a list of some of the hardware specifications of the 4-12 Port Voice Mail/Unified Messaging System:

- Windows NT hardware capability listing

- IDE or SCSI hard drive

- CD-ROM drive

- Monitor

- 128MB RAM

- 233MHz Pentium II processor

- Available ISA slot(s) required

- Internal or external modem 33.6 Kbps or higher

- Approved voice board resources

Cisco will run Unity on the MCS-7822 or the MCS-7835. Although it is not recommended that you run Call Manager and Unity on the same server, this platform will probably be Cisco's initial recommendation. The MCS-7822 server is Cisco's low-end media convergence server that provides no redundancy. The MCS-7835 provides a hardware-based mirror of the system drive to provide greater system availability.

The MCS-7822

Smaller organizations working toward a Unified Messaging solution might want to incorporate the MCS-7822 as their Unity server. Chances are, it would be the same type of server running the Call Manager software for the network. It is Cisco's less expensive server option, specifically designed for small companies or remote sites in a large organization. For a main Unified Messaging server in larger organizations, you may want to install Unity on the MCS-7835. The following is a list of some of the hardware specifications of the MCS-7822:

- Pentium III 550MHz

- 512MB error-correcting RAM

- Single 9.1GB SCSI hard drive

- Single power supply

- Ability to run Call Manager 3.0(1)

- An additional internal or external modem, 33.6 Kbps or higher

The MCS-7835

Although the MCS-7835 usually comes with Call Manager installed, large corporations would benefit from using this model as the Unity server as well. This server is a rack-mountable chassis, and it is installed with Windows 2000 server. You would use this server at the same site as a Call Manager or running at a different location on the WAN. Either way, the MCS-7835 will give you a stable platform to rely on for running Unity. The MCS-7835, however, would probably be overkill for smaller organizations. Listed are some of the hardware specs for the MCS-7835:

- Pentium III 733MHz

- 1GB error-correcting SDRAM

- Maximum of 2500 IP phones per server

- Dual 18.2GB hot swap SCSI hard drives

- Hardware RAID controller

- Optional 12/24GB DAT tape drive

- Ability to run Call Manager 3.0 or uOne 4.1E, Corporate Edition

- An additional internal or external modem, 33.6 Kbps or higher

Unity also can be integrated with both a traditional, circuit-switched phone system and Cisco Call Manager simultaneously; this is referred to as a dual-switch integration. Any of the traditional phone systems Unity integrates with can be used in a dual-switch integration along with Cisco Call Manager. Call Manager works because it provides Unity with call information directly from the

TAPI (Microsoft's Telephony Application Program Interface) service provider in dual-switch integration. In addition, Unity does not support IP phone systems that send call information using serial packets.

It is important to remember that all extensions for subscribers and call handlers must be unique regardless of which phone system a subscriber uses. To transfer calls from one phone system to the other, Unity must dial the same access codes that a subscriber dials when calling someone on the other phone system.

WARNING

When setting up "dual-switch integration," specify settings for the traditional phone system before specifying settings for the IP phone system. You must proceed in this order, or the integration may not work.

Scalability and Redundancy

Unity is built using native 32-bit Windows NT services. It works together with an embedded Exchange Server to collect into one central message store and to provide a single address directory service. Unity uses TAPI to minimize the effects of audio messages on the network and to speed the system's performance. Using TAPI allows Unity to communicate with both traditional and IP phones systems.

Software Overview

The Unity software setup requires a layered approach. It runs with several applications, and all of these applications together form the base product, administration tools, and utilities.

Required Software

Software required to run Unity includes, but is not limited to, the following:

- Windows NT Server/Windows 2000 Server

- Exchange Server

- Internet Explorer

- Internet Information Server (IIS)

- Windows Messaging Client

- PC Anywhere

- Unified Messaging Software

- Cisco TSP

Again, please note that there is a layered approach to installing the Unity product, and should one piece of the installation be installed improperly, then the whole system may not function properly. Currently Cisco has not published an installation disk similar to Call Manager 3.X whereby the entire system (OS and subsequent applications) is preinstalled and the image is extracted to the Unity server. This installation disk is expected shortly.

The following information is not meant to replace the Unity documentation but to give you an overview of the requirements—a handbook of the basic pieces and conceptual understanding, plus some caveats not included in the current documentation releases.

Windows NT Server or Windows 2000 Server

Unity must run on either Microsoft Windows 2000 Server or Microsoft Windows NT Server version 4.0. In order to run Unity on Windows NT 4.0, Unity service pack 6A for Windows NT 4.0 or later is required. In order to run Unity on Windows 2000, Service Pack 1 for Windows 2000 is required.

Before installing Exchange on Windows 2000, be sure to configure IP services and install Active Directory. When installing Active Directory, configure the server to be part of a "New Forest," which will set up the server as a legacy domain controller. Set up the server to be a stand-alone system.

NOTE

Unity server must use Windows NT or Windows 2000 as an operating system. It has no problem, though, connecting to another network operating system that supports TCP/IP, such as Novell Netware or UNIX.

Exchange Server

Unity can run along side of Microsoft Exchange Server version 5.5, service pack 3 or later. Together, they both utilize the same address directory information and message storage. The role of Exchange is to provide an address directory for the subscriber information and talk to Unity by using LDAP. In fact, if the Exchange Services and the LDAP protocol are not enabled, then Unity will not even install.

NOTE

If LDAP is not detected to be running on the Exchange server during the Unity install, you may need to change the default port of 389 on the Exchange server as well as in the Unity configuration during install—my company uses port 1024.

LDAP Lightweight Directory Access Protocol is a format used to provide access to information directories; it supports TCP/IP. Unity functions by storing voice, fax, and e-mail messages in the Exchange information store. MAPI is used to access these messages.

MAPI Messaging Application Programming Interface is the Microsoft specification that allows different messaging and workgroup applications to work through a single client. In addition, Exchange provides gateway access to fax servers and the Internet.

Internet Explorer

In order to provide Web browser access, Unity requires Microsoft Internet Explorer version 4.01 or later. The Unity administration pages are accessed through the Internet Explorer browser; Netscape Navigator, however, is not supported. In addition, if you plan to run Status Monitor, you are required to run Internet Explorer 5.0 or higher.

NOTE

The Status Monitor is an application on the Unity server that runs separately from the Unity Administrator and displays information about the system. It contains six pages including a status information page, a ports information page, a reports information page, a license information page, a disk drive information page, and a fax queue information pager when ActiveVoice is installed.

Internet Information Server

Microsoft Internet Information Server (IIS) version 4.0 on Windows NT 4.0 is used to host the Active Server Pages that Unity administration pages will use, and Unity version 2.4 and later have been configured to use Microsoft Internet Information Server (IIS) version 5.0 on Windows 2000. IIS allows you to remotely administer Unity through the Web browser interface.

TIP

Active Voice recommends that the Unity server is not used to host any other Web pages or to be used with any other applications. It is viewed as an appliance—meant to do only one task—Unified Messaging.

Windows Messaging Client

After installing Unity server, you will need to install a Windows messaging client. Outlook 97, Outlook 98, or Outlook 2000 will do. The messaging client running on the Unity server is required for the testing of the Unity installation and for troubleshooting.

PCAnywhere

If a problem occurs on your Unity system that you or your reseller cannot fix, then Unity Technical Support requires PCAnywhere for troubleshooting. Therefore, it is important to install Symantec PCAnywhere32 v.9.0 or 9.2. It allows tasks to be performed remotely that otherwise would have to be performed locally on the Unity server. Unity residing on a 2000 server allows a terminal services connection to be made, but Cisco has not provided any details as to the future of remote support or servicing through its Technical Assistance Center (TAC).

Unified Messaging Software

You must install either Unified Messaging clients or e-mail clients on the subscribers' computers in order to access voice and fax messages when using Unified Messaging. If you are not running Unified Messaging, than you may use an e-mail client such as Outlook Express, IMAP4 clients, POP3 clients, and Exchange's Web messaging client. These e-mail clients will give you access to all of your voice and fax messages as well. In these clients, though, your voice messages will appear as e-mail messages with attached .WAV files, and fax messages will appear with .TIF files attached to them. Chances are, you may already have a good portion of these applications running on your network. The Unified messaging client applications include Microsoft Outlook 97, 98, and 2000. Outlook supports the ViewMail application for voice-mail access, and it also gives access to your fax messages.

NOTE

There will be great limitations in using clients other than Outlook—we do not suggest doing it. Consider a situation with a user using POP—when using POP, mail is no longer stored (by default) on the server. When a user retrieves his or her mail, it only resides on his or her PC, so if a user were to leave the computer on, where it constantly checks for new messages and then left the office—the user would not be able to check his or her voice mail via computer or phone.

Cisco TSP

After the Unity Server is installed, you must install the Cisco TSP. It is included on the installation CD-ROM, and a reboot is required to have the wave driver installation completed.

Features and Functionality

Unity's intelligent voice-mail capabilities allow you to customize settings and take advantage of features including automated attendant (which serves as an electronic receptionist, answering and routing incoming calls), tailored call handling, multiple message delivery options, multiple notification methods, and multiple personal greetings.

Figure 6.2 shows the Unity System Administrator. The navigation bar (located along the left side of the interface) shows links to categories of data pages. The main portion of the page is where Unity data is entered and displayed. You will see that the page name is highlighted at the top. The title bar displays the name of the record or of the group of settings that appear on the page. The title bar also has command icons such as saving, finding, adding, or deleting records, and generating reports. The two other command icons on the title bar open the online Help files.

Figure 6.2 The Web-Based Unity System Administrator Interface

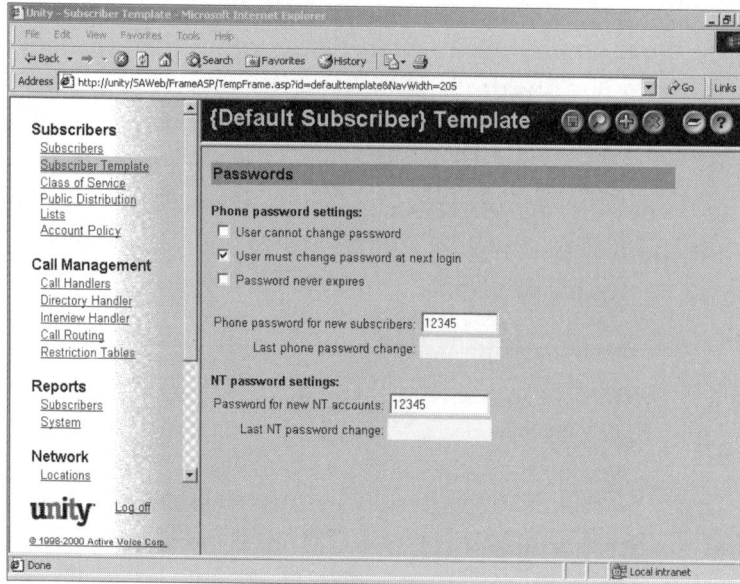

The Unity Administrator features five types of data that correspond to the categories on the Unity navigation bar. The first is subscriber data. The subscriber pages allow you to enter data related to individual users. This data also can be applied to subscriber templates that contain settings for subscribers belonging to a group. These settings include directory searches, caller prompts, call routing, direct and forwarded calls, pre-recorded caller interviews, call recording, and allowing or blocking certain dial strings.

The second data type is call management data. These pages are used to set how Unity answers, routes, transfers, and records all calls. The settings under call management data are directory searches, caller prompts, call routing, direct and forwarded calls, pre-recorded caller interviews, call recording, and allowing or blocking certain dial strings.

The third data type is report data. While providing options for generating reports of subscriber-based information, including message activity, distribution lists, phone logons, disk storage, and fax confirmation, these pages also include options for generating reports of system-based information.

Network data is the fourth data type. This page gives you the ability to add and view locations within your network. It is with these location objects that Unity enables remote messaging. The network data page is available only if digital networking is installed.

Finally, you have system data. This data type allows you to customize and view numerous system features including business schedules, annual holidays, fax settings, license counts, port settings, phone system settings, and diagnostic tools.

WARNING

Do not use Internet Explorer's *Back* button to return to a previously viewed page, or incorrect data will be displayed. Use the Unity navigation bar to return to a page that you viewed earlier.

Unity comes with a line of applications that include ActiveAssistant, ViewMail, and ActiveFax. Each application plays its part in the Unified Messaging suite.

Unity's ActiveAssistant is the computer interface used by subscribers to customize their Unity phone settings. By using ActiveAssistant, you can quickly and easily establish or change personal settings such as call screening, notification, and greetings. It allows for Web-based personal administration of voice mail. It also allows you to change your telephone password, transfer options, and directory listing status. This is where you would set fax delivery and message notification options as well.

Unity's ViewMail product works with Outlook and other e-mail clients to give you the ability to view all your messages at once. Rule-based messaging is used in ViewMail by placing an icon next to the message indicating what type it is. ViewMail gives you access to your messages from any computer or touch-tone phone.

ActiveFax is Active Voice's fax server application, and it is Unity's optional fax server component. ActiveFax can be installed on the Unity server or on another server. It allows Unity subscribers to manage their fax messages in much the same way as they manage other types of messages. Subscribers use the Unity conversation or the ActiveAssistant to set their fax message settings. Using ActiveFax allows you to send faxes from your computer, and it even gives you the ability to broadcast a fax to many people at once.

Text-to-speech is a feature that allows you to listen to your e-mail over a touch-tone phone. Unity reads the text portion of e-mail messages and provides information including message length, the sender's name (if the sender is a subscriber), the subject, time, and date the message was sent, as well as any attachments.

Most third-party fax servers that can install an Exchange fax gateway work with Unity. When an installation includes integrating a third-party fax server with Unity, the fax server software is installed on the fax server, not on the Unity server. Installation and administration are controlled by the fax server software and not by Unity.

Live record allows subscribers to record a conversation while talking to a caller. The recorded conversation is stored as a message in the subscriber's inbox and can be reviewed later, redirected to another subscriber, or redirected to a group of subscribers.

Unity's ActiveNet Digital Net- allows subscribers to send voice messages to people at other locations and to include them on distribution lists. In addition, if Unity is integrated with a networked phone system, you can set up Unity so that subscribers at other locations receive calls and voice messages from subscribers and outside callers. With ActiveNet, you can set up Unity so that voice messages can be sent between Unity servers in the same Exchange site, in different Exchange sites, or Unity servers and computers that do not use Exchange. The networking option is typically used by organizations that have more than one site or that have subscribers who work at another location. If you also have the FaxMail and text-to-speech e-mail options enabled on the system key, subscribers can use the phone to forward fax and e-mail messages to subscribers at another location.

NOTE

If you plan to use ActiveFax, your organization must purchase a text-to-speech e-mail license for each subscriber who will use e-mail delivery to a fax machine.

Configuring Active Voice

Unity can be configured in several ways—from a stand-alone voice messaging server to a Unified Messaging server connected to several Exchange servers on a network. A requirement for all configurations of Unity, including the stand-alone voice messaging server, is Exchange which is used for address directory information and for message storage.

Unity uses LDAP when accessing address information from an Exchange directory. Settings for subscribers, call handlers, interview handlers, location objects, and other entities are stored in the Exchange directory along with the address information. For accessing voice and fax messages in an Exchange message store, MAPI is used. Using Exchange gives Unity access to the same address directory and message store used by e-mail clients.

NOTE

When Unity is installed, LDAP is enabled, and it must remain enabled. You can use the Exchange Administration to check the Protocols section to verify that LDAP is enabled.

Unity suggests that there are four ways in which a Unity server can be configured to run on your network:

- Stand-alone voice messaging server

- Stand-alone voice messaging server with LAN administration
- Unified Messaging with one Exchange server
- Unified Messaging with more that one Exchange server

Stand-Alone Voice Messaging Server

The stand-alone voice messaging server configuration sets up the Unity server to handle voice messages only. Therefore, the server does not need to be connected to the network. This method also works along-side a legacy PBX. In fact, Active Voice Unity includes documentation on connecting to many legacy PBX systems from Lucent, Nortel, and other systems.

Stand-Alone Voice Messaging Server with LAN Administration

In the stand-alone voice-messaging server with LAN administration configuration, the Unity server will still handle only voice messages. It is connected to the network, however, and can provide remote administration capabilities. If your future plans are to install additional Unity servers, the Unity servers can be installed at the same Exchange site or different sites. Routing and replication between two stand-alone Unity servers can also be set up, as can connectors to other e-mail systems.

Unified Messaging: One Exchange Server

In this type of configuration, the Unity server is also the only Exchange server at the location. Note that this Exchange server is not to be used as a primary mail server for general SMTP user messages—it is meant only as a message database repository and relay for the Unity product. It has the ability to handle voice, fax, and e-mail messages, making it a Unified Messaging server. The single server stores the messages for all subscribers who can access them from anywhere.

When you add Unity to an existing Exchange network, you can expect an increase in the number of messages and the size of the messages. The impact Unity has on your network will depend on many factors, including your network topology. If you have a fast connection that Exchange can run across without problems, then the additional message traffic should not have much effect on your network's performance.

If you are introducing Unity into a multi-site Exchange network in which messaging and directory replication connectors have been set up, the MTA will route voice messages automatically, according to the settings for e-mail. Additionally, Exchange directories containing subscriber addressing information also replicate to each location.

Unified Messaging with More Than One Exchange Server

When using Unified Messaging with more than one Exchange server, the Unity server obviously connects to other Exchange servers in the same location. Because of this, the Unity server will process voice and fax messages, but most often, they are stored on other Exchange servers with all the e-mail messages. Exchange servers at the same location automatically route messages and replicate directories. In order for message routing and directory replication to occur among Exchange servers in separate locations, you must set up messaging and directory replication connectors.

Each of these configurations is upgradeable or expandable when your business messaging needs expand. Unity gives you the ability to add a stand-alone voice messaging server to the network and set it up to be a Unified Messaging server. Or if need be, you can add another Exchange server along side your Unified Messaging server. This allows you to provide more disk space for messages by moving subscriber's mailboxes. In addition, multiple Unity servers can be installed on an Exchange network in either the same location or in different locations. Figure 6.3 provides you with an idea of how an Active Voice Unified Messaging environment can be set up.

Figure 6.3 An Example of How to Set Up a Unity Installation

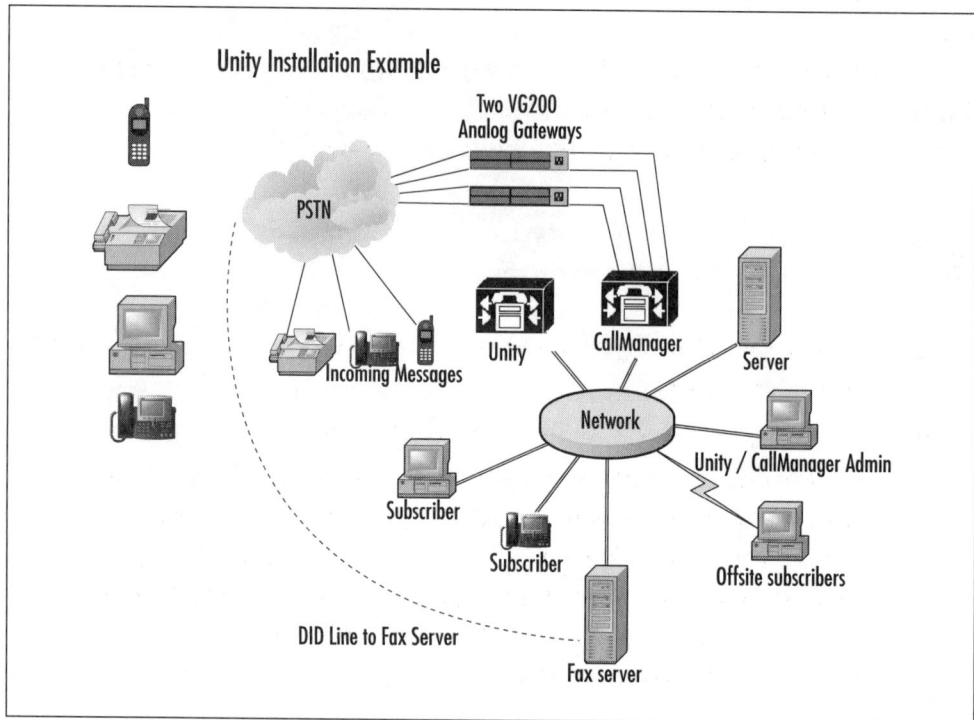

Unity Installation Example

Summary

Because of some shortcomings in their own uOne product, Cisco has decided to acquire companies with mature offerings in the voice mail and Unified Messaging arena. With the Active Voice acquisition and Unity product assimilation into AVVID, Cisco has solidified its intention to dominate the IP telephony and Unified Messaging arena.

Configuration of the Unity product is currently not trivial, and we must take a layered approach to the installation until Cisco provides a simple, all-in-one solution, as it has done so often with its routers and switches through IOS. Shortly after installation, the benefits of Unified Messaging become abundantly apparent.

Maintenance of the users of the Unified Messaging system is easier than in many other voice-mail systems through the Web interface; it provides a wealth of other functionality that only IP telephony can provide because only then are all communications are digital.

From this first look at Unified Messaging, we begin to grasp the immense impact on corporate communications that this relatively new technology will have in the next few years.

FAQs

Q: Can I use Unified Messaging with any legacy PBX or IP telephony solution?

A: Yes, Unity, for instance, works with Cisco's Call Manager as well as many other legacy PBX vendors' products. Unity is natively compatible to an IP telephony system because it is a computer using TCP/IP. If you wish to use Unity with other legacy PBX products, often, you will need additional communications cards to be installed on the Unity server to interface with the legacy PBX.

Q: Should I configure my Unity Server to participate in the Corporate Tree (Active Directory)?

A: No, not unless you *really* know what you are doing! Active Directory Services changes the basic domain settings and can negatively affect the functionality of the Call Manager. This may change shortly as Cisco more tightly integrates their product with Windows 2000.

Q: Are Unified Messaging and its implementation worth it?

A: Yes, everyone who uses Unified Messaging agrees—they gain functionality yet sacrifice nothing. Unified Messaging takes a little longer to install, but many IT staff save countless hours of time in training and support.

Q: Can you receive fax messages in your e-mail if you don't have a Unified Messaging e-mail client?

A: Yes, fax messages will appear with .TIF files attached.

Q: For what reason does Unity use TAPI?

A: Unity uses TAPI to minimize the effects of audio messages on the network. Using TAPI also allows Unity to communicate with both traditional and IP phones systems.

Q: Why is the "port" setup required to communicate to the Unity server called the uOne port on Call Manager 3.06?

A: Cisco's original Unified Messaging product was called uOne, and Cisco technically is still selling the uOne product. The uOne port setup is required to provide for the TAPI interface with the Unity Unified Messaging server.

Chapter 7

Design Considerations in a WAN/Campus Environment

Solutions in this chapter:

- Traffic Engineering Principles for Packet Voice Networks

- Quality of Service

- Designing Enterprise Dial Plans

Introduction

Designing a solid infrastructure plan is the foundation of any network. Other considerations come into play when specifically designing an AVVID network solution. Traffic Engineering, QoS, traffic prioritization, maximizing bandwidth efficiency, and a scalable dial plan are just some of the issues involved in designing an AVVID voice architecture. A sufficient network capacity is required to handle voice traffic on a converged network. In this chapter, we will discuss traffic engineering principles and some of the considerations involved in designing a scalable AVVID infrastructure. Lastly, we will cover some of the requirements in designing an enterprise dial plan.

Traffic Engineering Principles for Packet Voice Networks

Whether it's Voice-over IP (VoIP), Voice-over Frame Relay, Voice-over ATM, or Voice-over HDLC, traffic engineering is a major issue that needs to be examined quite closely before an IP telephony or Voice-over network can be implemented. *Traffic engineering* refers to the process of determining the required trunk capacity that will meet the projected call volumes within a telephony network. In a circuit-switched network, the number of trunks required equates to the number of DS0 facilities that are required in the WAN. For a Voice-over data network, the required number of trunks must then be multiplied by the amount of bandwidth that will be required per call. This result will then be used to determine the total amount of bandwidth required for WAN facilities to support both voice and data on the same network. There are essentially two approaches to determine the maximum number of simultaneous calls that must be supported in the WAN. The easiest approach is to plan the IP voice network capacity based on the existing network. An alternate and perhaps more precise approach is to apply traditional traffic engineering principles.

Analyzing Existing WAN Facilities

The first approach can be used when a legacy PBX system is being upgraded to an IP telephony/CallManager solution. In this case, the simplest strategy is to examine the existing voice network facilities and use this as a guideline for provisioning the required Voice-over data bandwidth. Consider a simple example: if an organization currently has a full T1 facility between PBXs at only two locations, they can currently support up to 24 simultaneous calls between the two sites. If the trunking in the existing network is sufficient, this provides a reasonable basis for the calculation to determine the amount of bandwidth required for voice. For now, we will assume that each voice call will consume 12 Kbps, based on the selected voice coder and other parameters. Supporting 24 simultaneous calls at this rate will require a minimum of 288 Kbps in the WAN. This amount must then be added to the minimum bandwidth required for the existing data applications that require WAN bandwidth. Finally, an additional 25 percent should be added to accommodate overhead traffic such as routing protocols, SNMP management traffic, layer 2 link maintenance (keepalives), and so on.

Applying Traffic Engineering

The second approach to determining the required WAN bandwidth is to use classic traffic engineering principles to determine the trunking capacity in the WAN. Although a complete discussion of traffic engineering is beyond the scope of this text, we will take a look at the basic process.

This approach can be used for existing systems that are migrating to a VoIP system, or for new installations. The first step in traffic engineering is to either gather or estimate the required data to understand the traffic patterns in the entire voice network. For simple topologies with only two sites, this process is relatively straightforward. For more complex topologies, a matrix must be constructed to evaluate traffic volumes between all sites. Gathering data from an existing installation involves collecting the call detail records (CDR) from existing PBXs and analyzing billing records for external calls that utilize the PSTN between sites. When analyzing CDRs and other call accounting data, it is important to base calculations on attempted calls if possible, rather than completed calls. The risk in analyzing only completed calls is that the statistics will not reflect any blocked call attempts, which may hide the fact that the existing network is under-provisioned. The goal of this phase of traffic engineering is to reduce call volumes to a standard unit of measure known as *Erlang*. An Erlang is simply the total traffic volume of a single channel for a period of one hour, or 3600 seconds. You may commonly see Erlangs expressed in units as CCS (centrum call seconds), or 36ccs for 1 Erlang. Call volumes are reduced to this standard unit of measure in order to evaluate call volumes according to different statistical distribution models.

Once call volumes have been determined, the busy hour must be identified; busy hour is simply the term that is used to designate the busiest calling time of the day. Capacity planning is based on busy hour traffic (BHT) volumes since this is when attempted calls have the greatest chance of failing due to insufficient capacity. One other required parameter is the blocking factor; this term refers to the maximum number of failed call attempts that will be tolerated. The acceptable blocking factor is typically expressed as a percentage. For example, if a maximum of three out of 100 attempted calls fail due to insufficient capacity, this would be expressed as a blocking factor of .03. Most organizations will tolerate a blocking factor within the range of .01 to .03.

When the BHT and blocking factors are known, the required number of trunks can then be looked up in an Erlang distribution table. There are different distribution tables used depending on the calling patterns of a given organization. The most commonly used distribution table for most organizations is the Erlang B model. There are many telephony references available that include Erlang tables. There is also a Web site at www.erlang.com that has an online calculator that will provide the required number of trunks based on the BHT and blocking factors that are supplied as input.

After determining the required number of trunks through traffic engineering, the required bandwidth must be then be calculated as described previously.

Quality of Service

One of the greatest challenges when deploying voice services over a converged data network is maintaining voice quality for all callers that is on par with circuit-switched facilities. Packet, cell, or frame-based networks all have the potential for introducing quality impairments such as loss of payload, excessive delay, or jitter. Fortunately, the equipment that is used to build these networks has the ability to provide preferential treatment to voice payload over other types of traffic, thus leading to a Quality of Service (QoS) for the voice traffic.

Supporting voice and data traffic simultaneously on a converged network infrastructure requires careful planning and design in order to meet the required service levels for all types of traffic. Data traffic is inherently bursty and sacrifices timeliness for accurate, reliable delivery. Voice and video traffic, however, tends to have the exact opposite characteristics. These real-time types of traffic are sensitive to delay, and traffic streams are more predictable rather than being bursty. Tools are available today to provide the required service levels for all traffic types when deployed properly in the network infrastructure. The greatest enemies to providing acceptable-quality voice services on a converged network are packet loss, delay, jitter, and echo.

Providing QoS in a packet voice network must be accomplished on an end-to-end basis. That is, there are many points in the network along the transmission path that can cause impairments; thus, there are tools that can be used to minimize these impairments throughout the network. In this section, we will discuss QoS tools that are available for the local and wide area portion of the voice network.

QoS Issues in the WAN

The wide-area portion of the voice network generally receives the greatest focus when considering which QoS tools are required. The reason is quite simple: here, the pipes are generally the smallest and where they cost the most money. Many QoS issues can be solved to a certain extent by just adding more bandwidth; however, in the WAN, this is generally an impractical approach. Therefore, we must apply greater intelligence in the network to solve the QoS issues.

Minimizing Loss, Delay, and Jitter

Congestion management tools must be utilized on WAN devices that will be carrying multiservice traffic in order to prioritize real-time traffic and minimize loss, delay, and jitter. These are all potential impairments to achieving acceptable voice quality in a VoIP network. Congestion management is achieved first through classifying traffic based on certain characteristics, then managing queues based on the classification.

Traffic Classification

One of the fundamental requirements for providing QoS in a network infrastructure is the ability to classify traffic based on certain characteristics of the packets being transmitted. Packet classification allows network traffic to be separated into multiple classes of service with each class receiving a different level of service. Once traffic has been classified, it is then up to the network devices to provide prioritization using advanced queuing techniques. There are multiple tools available to classify traffic, as described in the following sections. These tools are often referred to as QoS signaling tools since they are used to signal which class of service is required for a given datagram.

IP Precedence

One of the simplest and most common ways to define multiple classes of service is by using IP precedence. This classification tool uses three bits that are already present in all IP packets to indicate the relative level of service required by the data contained in the packet. The primary advantage of using IP precedence is that there is no extra overhead incurred since it only involves setting the value of the precedence bits in the header that will exist for all IP traffic. No additional signaling protocols are required to implement IP precedence. For this reason, IP precedence is considered an in-band QoS mechanism. Figure 7.1 illustrates the location of IP precedence values in the IP header.

Figure 7.1 Traffic Classification with IP Precedence

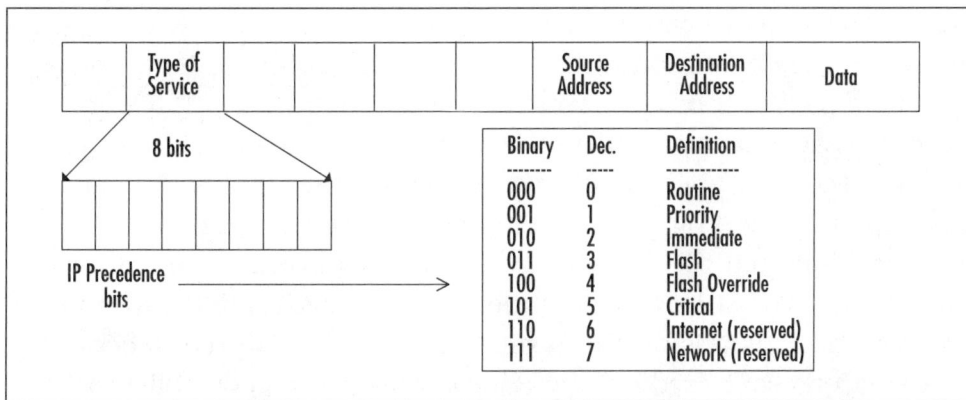

IP precedence uses three of the bits in the type of service (ToS) field of the IP header, which means that there can be up to eight possible values ($2^3 = 8$) using the precedence bits. This allows for up to six classes of service to be defined, since two of the values generally are reserved for routing protocols, ICMP messages, and other network overhead. Packets with a higher precedence value will then have higher priority in the network. Once the IP precedence values have been set, QoS features enabled on network devices such as routers can use this information to determine the type of service that is required for an individual packet. For example, Cisco routers can use IP precedence to control the behavior of QoS features like weighted fair queuing (WFQ) and weighted random early detection (WRED).

The actual value and meaning of the precedence bits are established by the local network administrator. The traditional meaning of IP precedence values is defined in RFC 791; however, there is no requirement that all IP networks must use the same values. These values were set in the context of a DoD messaging system where large surges of traffic and significant damage to the network were expected. Although today's networks can handle large volumes of traffic, the application of the IP precedence bits can still be useful in the event of congestion.

In general, IP precedence levels should be set as close to the source as possible; this allows other network devices to observe the classification as the packets travel from the source to destination across the core of a network. The value of the IP precedence bits can be set on the endstation at the source of the traffic, or it can be set as traffic passes through a router. Cisco's 7900 series IP telephones mark all packets at precedence level 5 before transmission. It may be useful to set IP precedence values on a router if endstations are not capable of setting the value directly before transmission. Another time that routers may be used to set precedence is to override the values set by an endstation. Access control lists are used to set precedence levels on Cisco routers. This means precedence levels can be set based on any criteria that can be controlled with access lists, such as source/destination address, application, or an individual user. Precedence levels can also be set in Cisco routers using dial-peer statements to route individual calls. This means that precedence levels can be set based on a destination phone number. By default, Cisco routers do not modify IP precedence levels.

The actual priority values selected for voice traffic by a network administrator will depend on the characteristics of the network traffic. For example, if voice is the only priority traffic type in the network, voice may be assigned a precedence level of five and all other traffic will be treated as routine. In another example, if the network will carry video and SNA in addition to traffic, a different prioritization scheme will be required. Voice may be assigned a level of five, video may be assigned a value of four, SNA will be assigned a value of three, and all other traffic will be treated as routine.

Although IP precedence can be simple to implement, it may actually be too simple in some cases. Since there is no means available to control which stations are allowed to set elevated IP precedence levels, any user with the proper knowledge can change IP precedence values as they see fit for their purposes. For example, a power-user that knows how to configure his workstation to do so can set all of his IP traffic with an elevated precedence level. This may not be a common scenario, but it is possible. It would be up to network engineers to prevent this situation by reclassifying the traffic at the router.

Differentiated Services (DiffServ)

DiffServ is a newer method for classifying traffic, defined by the Internet Engineering Task Force (IETF) in RFC 2474. Similar in concept to IP Precedence, DiffServ has been put forth by the IETF to supersede IP precedence since it provides greater flexibility for classifying traffic. DiffServ defines a differentiated services (DS) field for IPv4 and IPv6 packet headers, which contain the DiffServ Code Point (DSCP). One of the major differences between DSCPs and IP precedence values is the number of possible combinations. The DS field uses six bits for the DSCP, yielding 64 possible values, whereas IP precedence is limited to three bits, or only eight possible values.

Traffic Prioritization

These classification techniques described previously will not solve congestion problems on their own. Traffic classification must be combined with a prioritization technique that can manage queues in the event that congestion occurs in the WAN. Four different queuing techniques can be implemented on WAN interfaces to prioritize traffic: first-in, first-out (FIFO); weighted fair queuing (WFQ); custom queuing (CQ); and priority queuing (PQ). In addition, a new queuing technique known as low latency queuing (LLQ) has been introduced, which combines characteristics of WFQ and PQ on the same WAN interface. WFQ and Low Latency Queuing are the two preferred queuing methods that can be used on Cisco routers to provide prioritization of voice traffic.

Weighted Fair Queuing

The objective of WFQ is to provide a more fair allocation of available bandwidth to low-volume or interactive traffic types to improve performance on congested WAN links without having to add additional bandwidth. The WFQ algorithm can dynamically classify traffic into flows based on packet header characteristics such as source/destination addresses, protocols, and port/socket numbers. Layer 2 characteristics may also be used to classify the traffic such as source/destination MAC address or Frame Relay DLCI. The weighting refers to the fact that the traffic classification can be controlled to a certain extent using classification techniques like IP precedence or RSVP. Since WFQ is able to *see* IP precedence values, it can schedule these packets for faster transmission to improve delay and response times. As IP precedence levels increase, the WFQ algorithm allocates more bandwidth to this traffic when congestion occurs. WFQ can prevent a high-volume application such as FTP from consuming all available bandwidth on a link and starving out other low-volume traffic such as voice.

Multiple variations of the WFQ algorithm can be implemented. The simplest form is sometimes referred to as flow-based WFQ to reflect the method of traffic classification that is used. Flow-based WFQ is enabled by default on WAN interfaces at speeds equal to or less than 2 Mbps and provides 256 queues per interface by default. A key advantage to WFQ over other queuing techniques is that it does not require configuration of access lists in order to classify the traffic. One disadvantage of WFQ is that it may become too fair if there are a large number of flows in the network at a given time. Also, there is no way to use WFQ to guarantee bandwidth for a specific type of traffic.

Another variation of the WFQ algorithm is class-based WFQ (CBWFQ). With CBWFQ, network administrators have more control over the classification of the traffic. Multiple traffic classes can be defined based on protocol, access control lists (ACLs), and input interfaces. Up to 64 classes of traffic can be defined in this fashion using CBWFQ. Additionally, once traffic has been assigned to a class, bandwidth can be assigned to a class and guaranteed during periods of congestion. The ability of CBWFQ to guarantee bandwidth for a specific traffic type makes it the preferred form of WFQ to implement for voice. CBWFQ currently is not supported with traffic shaping, however.

Low Latency Queuing (LLQ)

The queuing features listed previously, including PQ, CQ, WFQ, and FIFO, are all limited to one of these features being enabled on a given interface at any one time. LLQ overcomes this limitation by providing both WFQ and PQ on a single interface at the same time. This combination of queuing techniques offers the best possible solution for all traffic types: guaranteed bandwidth for voice traffic and WFQ for the remaining traffic. For example, voice traffic could be directed to the PQ within LLQ by assigning voice an IP precedence level of 5. On the same interface, SNA traffic for a mission-critical application could also be directed to the PQ within LLQ. Lastly, all remaining traffic on the interface would be handled with WFQ. LLQ is a relatively new feature for Cisco IOS, which was first introduced in IOS release 12.0(7). However, the initial release of LLQ supported VoIP only on serial WAN interfaces and ATM PVCs. To use LLQ on Frame Relay interfaces requires a minimum of IOS release 12.1(2)T.

Fragmentation and Interleave

A potential source of delay on low-speed WAN links is serialization delay, which is the amount of time required to place bits from an output buffer onto the transmission media. The amount of delay experienced will be fixed, depending upon the link speed and the size of the transmitted datagrams—the lower the speed, the greater the delay. In a data-only network, serialization delay is tolerated for most traffic types. For a converged network supporting real-time voice traffic along with data packets, serialization delay will negatively impact voice quality. For example, consider a scenario where voice and data traffic is being transmitted over a 64 Kbps WAN link. If a voice sample is awaiting transmission behind a data packet with an MTU of 1500 bytes, the voice sample will be delayed for a minimum of 188 ms:

$$\frac{1500 \text{ bytes x 8 bits/byte]}}{[64,000]} = 0.188$$

Considering that the maximum end-to-end delay for a voice call should be within the range of 150–200 ms, this would nearly exceed the maximum tolerable delay on a single WAN link. The way to combat this situation is to break up large data packets into smaller packets and interleave them with interactive traffic types like voice before transmission.

In general, it is desirable to keep serialization delay below 10 ms per link. A simple rule of thumb is that fragmentation will be required for link speeds of 768 Kbps or less. At speeds above 768 Kbps, a 1500 byte packet causes less than 10 ms of delay. However, when using LAN media such as Token Ring, MTU sizes can exceed 1500 bytes and fragmentation may be required at link speeds higher than 768 Kbps. Cisco offers multiple options for fragmentation and interleave, as described in the following sections.

Link Fragmentation and Interleave (LFI)

For low-speed point-to-point serial links, Cisco uses the Multi-Link PPP (MLP) standard defined in RFC 1717 to reduce serialization delay on these interfaces. This feature also requires that weighted fair queuing (WFQ) be supported and enabled on the WAN interfaces. Without a special queuing technique like WFQ to move small voice samples to the front of the line, the voice samples would have to wait until all of the data fragments are transmitted. Thus, fragmentation alone will not solve the problem of serialization delay; it must be combined with a queuing technique that gives priority to the voice traffic. A limitation of the LFI feature is that it can be implemented only on PPP WAN links; this rules out use on links utilizing Frame Relay, HDLC, and any other WAN protocol besides PPP.

RFC 2686, "The Multi-Class Extension to Multi-Link PPP," September 1999, defines a similar method for fragmenting serial links that utilize the PPP protocol.

Frame Relay Forum Implementation Agreement FRF.12

When procedures were defined initially by the Frame Relay Forum for encapsulating multiprotocol data over Frame Relay services, voice was not one of the included payload types. As a result, there were no provisions for dealing with the fragmentation issue. With the FRF.12 implementation agreement (IA), there is now a standard mechanism available for fragmenting large chunks of data on frame relay interfaces that will support voice traffic.

The FRF.12 IA defines multiple ways to implement fragmentation in a Frame Relay network. One method is to handle the fragmentation across the UNI interface, which would be between the router interface and the Frame Relay switch. Implementation of this method would require support on both the router and the switch. Effectively, this means that the router would fragment the datagrams and the local switch would be responsible for reassembly before transmission across the network. This method of fragmentation at the UNI interface is not supported on Cisco routers. The other fragmentation method defined in FRF.12, which Cisco does support, is simply referred to as end-to-end, which would be between the two routers on either end of a permanent virtual circuit (PVC). The primary advantage of this method is that it requires support only on the routers and not the Frame Relay switches, and it is completely transparent to the Frame Relay network. This is the method that is supported by Cisco.

De-jitter Buffers

As digitized voice payload travels across a packet network, there will be a certain amount of fixed delay incurred from transmission delays, coding/decoding algorithms, and other sources. There will also be variable sources of delay that will change over the duration of a voice conversation, thus causing variation in the inter-arrival times between voice samples. If these voice samples were played out with the variable inter-arrival times, there would be breakups in the voice conversation, leading to reduced quality. De-jitter buffers can be used in the playback device in order to smooth out the voice playback by retiming and adjusting for the variable delay incurred during transmission. De-jitter buffers can be found in endstations such as voice gateways and IP telephones.

De-jitter buffers must adapt to the dynamic conditions in the packet voice network. If buffers are too small, packet loss may result if the buffers are overrun. If the buffers are too large, excessive delay in the voice conversation may result.

Traffic Shaping

ATM and Frame Relay network technologies are commonly referred to as non-broadcast multi-access (NBMA) networks. Because of the inherent nature of NBMA networks, there is a potential for a speed mismatch across the WAN between sites. A speed mismatch refers to a situation unique to NBMA networks where one location may have a high-speed access connection to the network, while other sites have lower speed connections. For example, consider a large organization with a headquarters location and multiple remote branch offices. If the headquarters site has an access link into the network at a rate of 768 Kbps and the branches offices have lower speed access links such as 256 Kbps or 384 Kbps, a speed mismatch exists between headquarters and the remote sites, as shown in Figure 7.2. This can create problems when NBMA networks are used to transport VoIP between sites as the potential for congestion and delay exists when a speed mismatch exits. If congestion occurs as a result of this speed mismatch, the network will then have to discard traffic; this will have obvious consequences on voice quality if voice traffic is discarded as a result of congestion. Traffic shaping provides a solution to this potential problem and will be required if using Frame Relay or ATM to transport VoIP. Traffic shaping is used in VoIP networks to prevent packet loss and can also be used to control jitter that may result on an NBMA network.

Figure 7.2 A Non-broadcast Multi-Access Network

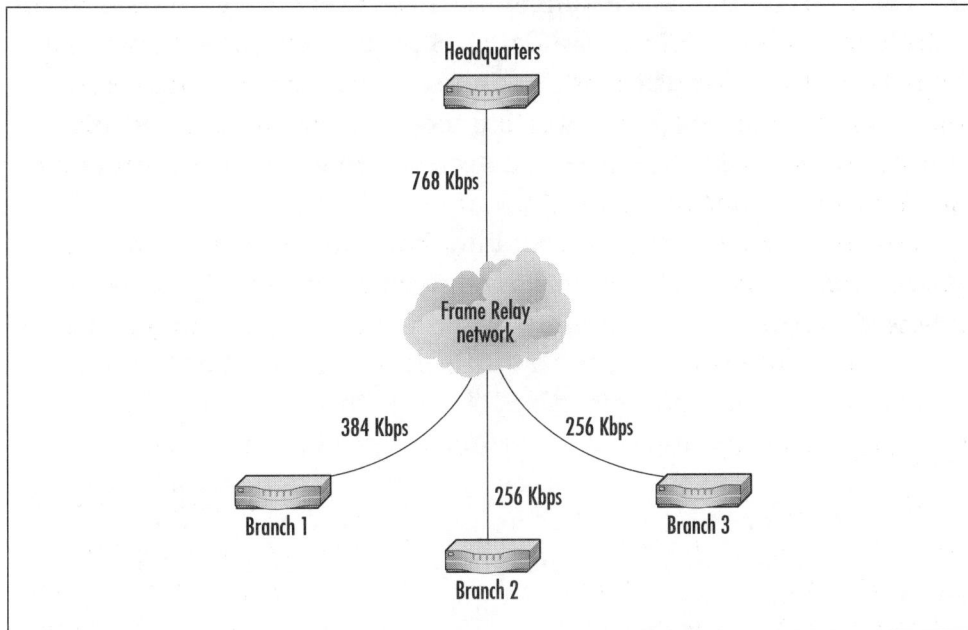

Traffic shaping is used to limit that rate at which traffic is transmitted toward the lower speed side of a connection. For example, if the access link at a headquarters location is 768 Kbps and a branch office access link is only 256 Kbps, shaping must be done at headquarters for traffic destined to the branch office. The router at the headquarters location will transmit at a full line rate of 768 Kbps if possible; this traffic will obviously run into a bottleneck at some point if it is destined for a target interface that is only 256 Kbps. This bottleneck will lead to buffering, packet drops or both. To prevent this, traffic from the headquarters site must be shaped to a rate of 256 Kbps or less. It may also be necessary to shape in the direction of the headquarters site to guard against the potential of several remote sites simultaneously bursting in the direction of headquarters. For example, if there are multiple branch offices that link to headquarters and the aggregate of the access links is greater than the capacity of the headquarters access link, it may be necessary to shape from the branch offices in the direction of headquarters.

Traffic shaping can be implemented on Cisco routers using Generic Traffic Shaping (GTS) or Frame Relay Traffic Shaping (FRTS). Both methods are similar with the exception of how they handle queuing of delayed traffic. GTS uses weighted fair queuing (WFQ) for delayed traffic; FRTS can use WFQ, custom, priority, or FIFO queuing for delayed traffic (support for WFQ along with FRTS requires IOS version 12.0(4)T or later). Another important difference is that FRTS supports shaping on a per-PVC basis, whereas GTS is implemented per interface or subinterface. However, GTS can be made to act on a per-PVC basis by configuring each PVC on a separate subinterface. One last significant consideration between the two methods of traffic shaping is that FRF.12 (fragmentation) is supported only in conjunction with FRTS. For this reason, FRTS is currently the preferred method to use for traffic shaping.

When traffic shaping is implemented with Frame Relay, traffic is shaped based on the CIR value for a given PVC. The flow rate can be set manually, or can be configured to adapt dynamically based on FECNs/BECNs received by the router.

Maximizing Bandwidth Efficiency

A common objective for any network manager is to optimize the use of available bandwidth on WAN circuits. This becomes especially important when considering a multi-service network that will support VoIP. If a single WAN infrastructure will be used to support voice and data traffic, a design objective should be to utilize the WAN to support as many voice calls as possible and avoid toll charges for using PSTN facilities. Another constraint that many organizations face is that WAN bandwidth is very expensive, so adding extra bandwidth to support voice traffic on an existing network will mean additional costs. In addition to supporting low bit-rate voice coders in IP telephones and voice gateways, other tools are available within Cisco IOS to help network managers achieve better utilization from the available WAN bandwidth.

RTP Header Compression

The Real-time Transport Protocol (RTP) is an industry standard protocol defined by the IETF that is used to carry packetized audio traffic between endpoints in an AVVID network. RTP is defined in RFC 1889 and primarily is intended to carry real-time types of traffic such as audio and video in unicast or multicast networks. RTP header compression is a complimentary standard (RFC 2508) that defines a method for reducing the size of RTP packet headers to achieve greater bandwidth efficiency when transporting audio and video traffic over low-speed WAN links. A secondary benefit is that there will be a reduction in serialization delay on links where RTP header compression is enabled. RTP header compression is also referred to as compressed RTP (cRTP).

When transporting audio samples between endpoints using RTP, the digital audio samples are encapsulated with a 12-byte RTP header, an 8-byte UDP header, and a 20-byte IP header for a total of 40 bytes of packet overhead. Considering that the size of a typical digital audio sample is in the range of 20 to 160 bytes, transport of RTP traffic with full headers is relatively inefficient. For example, a G.729 audio sample that is 20 bytes in size will be stuffed into an RTP/UDP/IP header that is twice the size of the payload. RTP header compression can reduce the size of a full header down to approximately two to four bytes. In terms of bandwidth per voice channel, a single G.729 voice call using full RTP headers may consume approximately 24 Kbps; this would be effectively cut in half to approximately 12 Kbps when using compressed RTP headers.

The compression technique applied to RTP headers is similar to the technique defined for TCP header compression (also known as Van Jacobson header compression, for the author standard) in RFC 1144. The basic principle behind these compression techniques is that a significant portion of the full header information remains constant for the duration of a connection. After the first packet with an uncompressed header is sent, the redundant information can be stripped from the headers of packets that follow. Additional compression can be achieved on the remaining fields by reducing their size even if their values are changing.

Originally intended for dial-up modem links in the range of 14.4 to 28.8 Kbps, RTP header compression may also be beneficial for WAN links up to 512 Kbps. RTP compression should be considered for low-speed links to improve link efficiency when there is a significant amount of RTP traffic. Enabling RTP compression is done on a hop-by-hop basis, not end-to-end. Cisco routers can support RTP compression on serial WAN links using Frame Relay, HDLC, or PPP encapsulation and ISDN interfaces.

Voice Activity Detection

One of the advantages often claimed for migrating to Voice-over IP is that bandwidth can be used more efficiently than in a circuit-switched voice network. Voice activity detection (VAD) is a bandwidth savings tool that can be enabled in packet-based telephony networks to recover unused bandwidth for use by other applications or additional voice traffic. VAD can effectively reduce WAN bandwidth requirements by approximately one half when utilized in an AVVID network.

In a legacy voice network, a single voice call over a digital facility typically consumes 64 Kbps. This is the amount of bandwidth available in a single DS0. The amount of bandwidth required for a circuit-switched call remains constant, regardless of the amount of silence during the call. In other words, no efficiencies can be realized when there are periods of reduced voice activity on the call.

Migrating to a packet-based infrastructure instead of a circuit-switched infrastructure allows bandwidth to be recovered when either party in the conversation is silent. Statistically, the average human voice conversation is idle in either direction for approximately 30 to 60 percent of the duration of the call. If there is no human voice traffic to encode and send over the link, it is not necessary to fill up the WAN with empty voice samples.

VAD is actually one of three techniques that occur simultaneously by the DSP, which collectively are referred to as silence compression. VAD is simply the ability of a voice coder to recognize when a talker is silent or actually talking into the handset. This is coupled with discontinuous transmission (DTX), which is the ability of the coder to stop sending frames when the VAD process has determined that that talker is silent. Some coders do not actually stop transmitting, but will reduce the rate at which they transmit during periods of silence. Lastly, if all sound is removed from one side of the conversation, the listener may perceive that the talker has been disconnected. To counteract this negative consequence of silence compression, comfort noise generation (CNG) is performed to regenerate background noise for the listener. Comfort noise can be generated in one of two ways. The first method involves playing back a calculated sample of background noise that was captured during active periods of the conversation. Other coders will send a minimal amount of information that can be used to regenerate the original background noise. Cisco's IP phones can use either approach, depending upon the actual endpoints in the conversation.

Cisco's 7900 series telephones can generate comfort noise when VAD is enabled (the default setting). The white noise, as it is referred to, is generated locally by the listener's handset; it is not transmitted across the link. The information used to create the background noise is sent in silence information description (SID) frames when a call is placed between two Cisco 7900 series phones. If the call is between a 7900 series phone and some other device that does not send SID frames, the 7900 series phone will calculate the proper noise levels based on information from previous voice samples received.

In general, VAD is a useful tool for conserving WAN bandwidth, and it is recommended that VAD remain enabled whenever possible. There may be some side effects when using VAD, however, that may require disabling VAD. One side effect of VAD is *clipping*, which refers to the first few milliseconds of voice being lost due to the VAD process on the DSP. In addition to being an annoyance for humans, clipping may also cause problems when using mid-call DTMF tones if the first few milliseconds are truncated.

Reducing Echo

Echo is a necessary evil that exists to some extent on all voice calls that cross analog components or wiring at some point. In many cases, the echo that is present on the line is not detectable by human ears. When the delta between the echoed sound and the original sound is small enough, it will not be perceived.

The primary type of echo in most conversations occurs when the transmitted signal is reflected back to the person talking, which is referred to as *talker echo*. The amount of echo will vary depending upon how far the transmitter is from the point of reflection. If the point of reflection is close to the talker, the echo may be barely noticeable. If the point of reflection is far away from the talker, the echo will be a nuisance to the talker and may be severe enough to disrupt the conversation. Another less common type of echo is referred to as listener echo and occurs when reflected images affect the listener on the far end. Echo is caused by impedance mismatches between analog components. A common culprit is a device known as a hybrid where a two-wire circuit is converted to a four-wire circuit.

In a legacy voice network, echo may not be a problem since the end-to-end delays are negligible. However, echo will always be a problem in VoIP networks when traversing analog facilities since the process of packetization and compression combined with transit delays will always cause sufficient delay to make the echo very noticeable. This may even be true for local calls that go through a local VoIP gateway to the PSTN. It is important to realize that echo will be a problem only for VoIP calls that traverse analog facilities at some point. For a pure VoIP call end-to-end (such as a call from one IP phone to another), it is impossible to experience echo since IP packets cannot be reflected back to the source. The most common sources of echo in a VoIP network are gateways to the PSTN or a PBX.

Dealing with echo in a legacy voice network involves inserting echo suppressors or echo cancellers into the circuit. These devices will insert loss into the circuit or disrupt the return path so that reflected images cannot be returned to the talker. For VoIP networks, echo can be dealt with, to a certain extent, at the DSP level. Understanding that echo is simply the same audio played back at a delayed period in time at a reduced level, the echo can be detected and cancelled out by the DSP before playback. The DSPs used in Cisco's voice gateways can perform this function. Extreme cases of echo will require further troubleshooting and inserting additional attenuation into the circuit to reduce the echo.

QoS Issues in the LAN

With the advent of switched Fast Ethernet and Gigabit Ethernet LANs, some may argue that QoS is not a concern in the LAN. However, considering critical points in the LAN such as uplinks and campus backbones, there is a potential for over-subscription as organizations deploy more and more bandwidth-hungry applications. This will eventually lead to a requirement for QoS tools in the LAN.

Classification

Classification of traffic in the LAN becomes important when voice traffic needs to be protected from data traffic in a converged LAN environment. Similar to WAN QoS, once the traffic has been classified, different service levels can be applied based on traffic requirements. An industry standard mechanism for classifying traffic in the LAN is the IEEE 802.1Q standard. The 802.1Q standard was developed as a standard mechanism for tagging Ethernet frames to identify VLAN membership at layer 2. The ability to classify layer 2 frames to request priority service using three of the bits within the 802.1Q tag is defined by the IEEE in the 802.1p standard. Similar to IP precedence values in the IP ToS field, there are eight possible values for 802.1p tags.

Classification of traffic at layer 2 using 802.1Q/p tags generally is referred to as class of service (CoS); classification at layer 3 using IP precedence bits generally is referred to as type of service (ToS). One of the advantages of classifying traffic at layer 3 is that the classification will be persistent end-to-end regardless of media, since IP is a media-independent protocol.

Conversely, when classification is performed at layer 2, it will not be persistent. The first router that is encountered along the transmission path will remove and discard layer 2 headers from the IP packet. Since the 802.1Q/p classification is contained in the layer 2 header, the classification will be lost as soon as an Ethernet frame crosses a router. There are a couple of workarounds to this situation. The first is simply to use layer 3 ToS classification at the source of the traffic; Cisco's IP phones are capable of doing this. The other workaround is to reclassify traffic at a layer 3 switch or router by rewriting the layer 3 ToS value based on the incoming CoS value in the layer 2 frame.

Prioritization

QoS in the LAN is delivered by examining traffic as it enters a switch, classifying the frame based on some specified criteria, and then queuing the important data for prioritized transmission. The way the queuing is actually handled can vary based on the particular switch that is being used. Layer 2 LAN switches such as Cisco's Catalyst 2900XL and 3500XL support two separate queues per physical interface. The switches can classify traffic based on the 802.1p/Q tagging method described previously, or the classification can be done on a per-port basis as defined by the network manager for frames that are untagged. Once the traffic has been classified, high priority traffic (CoS = 4-7) can be sent to the expedite (high priority) queue and the low priority traffic (CoS = 0-3) to the normal queue. This scheduling mechanism is essentially a priority queuing algorithm, so there is a potential for starvation of the normal queue. Starvation would result in the event of a constant stream of traffic for the expedite queue. Prioritization based on MAC addresses or characteristics from layer 3 and above is not possible with these switches.

Layer 3 LAN switches that may be used in the core of a campus network, such as the 4908G-L3 and the Catalyst 6500 provide additional QoS features for prioritizing voice traffic. Since they are layer 3 switches, they can support classification using IP precedence. They also provide multiple queues per interface and support scheduling techniques such as weighted round robin (WRR) and weighted random early detection (WRED), a congestion avoidance mechanism.

LAN Infrastructure Basics and IP Telephony

One of the fundamental requirements for an IP telephony infrastructure is that it be built on a combination of layer 2 and layer 3 switches and routers, with switched connectivity to the end-stations. Shared LAN technologies have the potential for collisions, ultimately leading to packet loss, which cannot be tolerated in an IP telephony network. Cisco will not support AVVID installations on shared LAN devices such as hubs or repeaters. In addition to this fundamental requirement, there are other considerations that must be addressed in the LAN in order to provide a reliable infrastructure.

Inline Power

Powering a telephone handset is something that many of us take for granted. This is a by-product of how legacy telephony solutions operate today. For example, in our residences, power for the phones is provided centrally from the CO. In a business telephony environment, power to the handsets can be provided from the PBX. IP telephones will also need power and there are some unique logistical issues that must be addressed. First, an IP telephone requires both a data network connection as well as a connection to a power source. For first generation IP telephones, this required a connection to the Ethernet switch port for the data network connection and a separate connection to an AC power outlet by way of an outboard power adapter. In this case, when the power is provided from an AC outlet, if phone service is required in the event of a power outage, every AC outlet that powers an IP telephone must have a backup power source. This would be very cost-prohibitive for most organizations.

One other consideration has to do with the actual placement of IP telephones. If a phone will require an AC power outlet, then phones can only be placed within reach of a data network connection and an AC outlet. This may not always be possible for areas such as break rooms, lobby areas, hallways, etc. Because of these restrictions, the industry is developing a standard for providing power inline over the Ethernet cabling to eliminate the requirement for an external power source. This will also increase flexibility for placement of the IP telephones. Additionally, inline power increases reliability since the power can be backed up much easier from a single central location.

Although the proposed industry standard for inline power (IEEE 802.3af) has not yet been finalized, Cisco has implemented a solution for inline power in their current generation of 7900 series IP telephones (see Figure 7.3). There are two key issues to be addressed when providing power over the Ethernet cabling. First is actually how the power is supplied on the connection. The proposed standard calls for supplying power on the unused pins (4, 5, 7, 8) within the cable. Cisco provides support for this method, but also can provide power over the same pairs that are used for the actual Ethernet signaling (pins 1, 2, 3, 6). The advantage of utilizing the same pairs as the Ethernet signaling is that all cable plants will have these pairs available. Conversely, not all cable plants have the unused pairs available since they are not required for Ethernet to function properly. For example, some cable plants use a single UTP cable with eight wires to provide connectivity for two stations. The other issue that is addressed by the 802.3af standard is known as phone discovery. This part of the standard defines a process used by a switch that provides inline power to ensure that an IP phone is connected before applying power. The purpose of the phone discovery process is to prevent damage that may result if power is applied to a standard Ethernet device that does not support inline power.

Cisco switches that support inline power include the Catalyst 3524-PWR fixed-configuration switch and the Catalyst 4000 and 6000 modular switches. An additional consideration for the modular

Figure 7.3 Inline Power Strategies for IP Phones

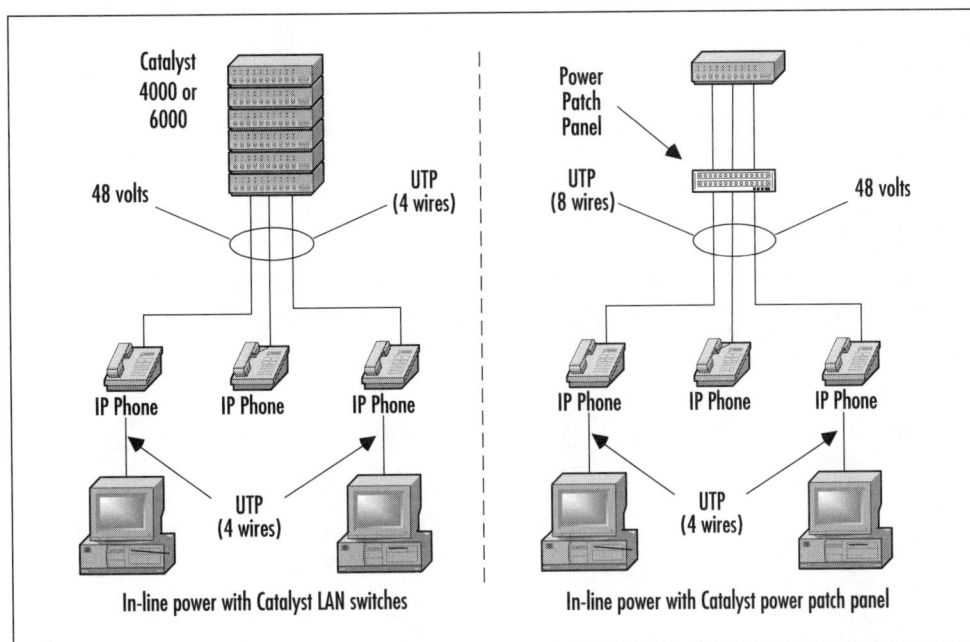

In-line power with Catalyst LAN switches   In-line power with Catalyst power patch panel

switch platforms is that inline power to the IP phones means that the power will actually be supplied centrally from the LAN switch. This will obviously increase the current draw for the entire switch. Care must be taken to select the proper power supply to support all installed line cards in the switch as well as all of the IP phones that are connected to the switch. In addition, sufficient power must be provided for the switch, which may require installation of 220V circuits instead of the standard 110V circuits used in the US.

For Catalyst switches and other vendors' switches that do not have direct support for inline power, a power patch panel is available. This patch panel essentially injects power into the cable by connecting to the network between the existing switch and the stations that require power. The availability of the patch panel means that organizations with existing switches do not have to replace them in order to provide support for inline power.

Design Tip: Which Power Supply?

When using the Catalyst 6000 modular LAN switch with inline power capability, there are three different power supplies to choose from: 1050W, 1300W, and 2500W. Determining which of these power supplies is appropriate requires developing a power budget. Three factors must be considered in the power budget: how many phones will be connected, what are the power requirements for other cards in the switch, and what is the total capacity of the switch? Each phone will require a maximum of 6.3W; this value is multiplied by the total number of required phones to determine the total current draw for phones. Next, the current draw for each supervisor module and other line cards must be added. Once the total power budget is known for the switch, the required power supply can be selected.

Power Supply	Maximum Amperage
1050W	20A
1300W	27A
2500W	55A

Redundant power supplies can be provisioned for the Catalyst 6000 LAN switches. When two power supplies are installed in the Catalyst 6000, they can be used in redundant or non-redundant mode. Non-redundant mode essentially doubles the available power for the switch.

Reliability and Availability

Many organizations considering VoIP within their network are reluctant to put their voice traffic over the data network because of concerns about availability of the data network. There is a perception by many that data networks are inherently less reliable than voice networks. Although there are, in fact, many data networks that are not reliable enough to support voice traffic, it is certainly possible to build data networks with sufficient reliability to support voice. The way to achieve a highly available network is to design and build the network using the proper tools to provide the required level of reliability. This section details some the tools that are available today for building reliability into the network from the ground up.

Hot Standby Router Protocol (HSRP)

A basic premise in network design is to provide redundancy of critical components in the event of failure of such a device. Within a VoIP network, LAN switches would certainly qualify as critical components as they will provide the connectivity between IP phones and the rest of the world. Using redundant layer 3 LAN switches such as the Catalyst 2948G-L3, 4908G-L3, or the Catalyst 6500 series enables the use of HSRP between these switches. HSRP provides redundancy between two routers' layer 3 LAN switches by sharing a virtual IP address and MAC address between the two devices to appear as a single virtual device to endstations. In the event that one of the devices should fail, the other device in the HSRP group can take over for the failed device.

Redundant Physical Links

Redundancy at the physical level should be used at all levels of a hierarchical network design. At the workgroup/wiring closet level, redundant uplinks to core or backbone switches should be utilized. Catalyst workgroup LAN switches such as the 2900XL and 3500XL have multiple uplink ports available that can be used for providing redundant paths to the core of the network.

Spanning Tree Protocol (STP) Enhancements

The spanning tree protocol is implemented on layer 2 switches to enable redundant connections between devices, but avoid looping and broadcast storms that would otherwise occur. Although STP helps in this regard, there are some negative consequences. For example, in the event of a topology change, it may take a significant amount of time for STP to reconverge and restore connectivity to the LAN. The actual convergence time may take nearly a full minute due to the default settings of STP timers. To improve convergence times with STP, Cisco has implemented enhancements to STP on Catalyst LAN switches that can substantially reduce convergence times to less than five seconds. Specifically, these features are known as PortFast, UplinkFast, and BackboneFast. The basic premise behind these features is that they "break the rules" when it comes to reconverging in the event of a link failure. The STP algorithm specifies a certain order of transition between states that ports must follow when devices detect a failure. By altering the order of transition and the time required, connectivity can be restored much quicker than the STP default behavior.

PortFast PortFast can be implemented on individual switch ports to speed up the initial connectivity or startup delays that may occur when an end-station initially connects to a switch port. There may be several causes of this delay, including STP, EtherChannel negotiation, trunking negotiation, and full/half-duplex negotiation. Negotiating all of these parameters upon initial connection can take nearly one minute. Of the four causes listed, STP causes the greatest delay in port initialization. When using the default settings for STP, a switch port would normally have to transition from a blocking state to a listening state, then from listening to a learning state, then finally to the forwarding state before the port becomes active. To transition from one state to the next, a delay timer must expire, which leads to long initialization time to ultimately reach forwarding state. With PortFast enabled, a switch port can transition directly from blocking state to forwarding state to minimize the initialization time required for the port. Enabling PortFast on a switch port transitions the port immediately and permanently to the forwarding state. PortFast should be used only on nontrunking ports where a single end-station connects to the switch, not for uplinks to other switches. Loops may result if PortFast is enabled on uplink ports between switches or other network devices.

UplinkFast This feature is most useful on wiring closet or workgroup switches where endstations connect into the network. The UplinkFast feature would be implemented on redundant uplinks between workgroup/access layer switches and the core/backbone switches by creating an uplink group of multiple ports, only one of which is forwarding. Within two seconds of a link failure, UplinkFast will restore connectivity to the network backbone. UplinkFast can also provide load balancing between redundant uplinks. UplinkFast is not intended for backbone or distribution layer switches.

BackboneFast Connectivity to a backbone switch can be restored rapidly with the BackboneFast feature. BackboneFast can detect a link failure on a link that is not directly connected to the switch by listening for certain types of STP messages. When a failure is detected, the switch can immediately transition a port from blocking to forwarding mode in order to provide an alternate path around the failed link. This capability allows a switch connected to the backbone to react much faster to indirect failures. In order for BackboneFast to work correctly, it must be enabled on all switches within the network.

Per VLAN Spanning Tree (PVST)

Redundancy and load balancing can be implemented on connections between access layer and core network switches using the PVST feature. PVST can also help to reduce STP convergence times since the PVST topologies should be smaller than if a single spanning tree topology was used in the network.

EtherChannel

Fast EtherChannel (FEC) and Gigabit EtherChannel (GEC) enable multiple physical connections between devices to be aggregated or bundled into a single logical channel. The primary benefits of using FEC and GEC are increased bandwidth and redundancy between switches, and the ability to load balance traffic on uplinks between switches. FEC and GEC can be implemented on connections between LAN switches, routers, servers, and workstations using standards unshielded twisted pair (UTP) or fiber optic cabling. Some LAN switch platforms allow up to four physical connections per EtherChannel and others allow up to eight physical connections per EtherChannel.

Security

Some basic security mechanisms are available in LAN switches to prevent unauthorized users from gaining access to the network or attempting to capture data or voice traffic. These basic tools combined with normal physical security measures, such as placing equipment in locked rooms or closets, can increase the security of the LAN infrastructure.

Port security is a feature that can be used to prevent potential intruders from gaining access to the network for purposes of capturing traffic. This feature works by mapping a specific layer 2 MAC address to a specific switch port. If the switch detects a different MAC address on a given port, or detects that a MAC address has moved to a different port, the switch automatically can disable the ports in question.

Protecting the actual network devices themselves can be achieved with the Terminal Access Controller Access Control System (TACACS) protocol. TACACS provides an authentication mechanism that can prevent unauthorized users from gaining Telnet access or direct console access to a switch or router to make configuration changes that would disrupt the network. Deploying TACACS will require the protocol to be enabled on the LAN switches as well as a separate TACACS authentication server. Another benefit of using TACACS is that userid/password administration can be centralized on the TACACS server instead of maintaining userids on each individual device.

Private VLAN edge is another security feature that can be enabled on workgroup Catalyst LAN switches such as the 2900XL and 3500XL. This feature essentially prevents forwarding of unicast, broadcast, or multicast traffic directly between switch ports. Instead, the traffic must be forwarded through a router or layer 3 switch, which would allow ACLs to be used to filter the traffic before being forwarded. Using private VLAN edge ensures that voice traffic will travel directly to its destination without the potential to be redirected to another port. This feature can be enabled or disabled on individual switch ports.

Designing Enterprise Dial Plans

Just as an IP data network needs an IP address plan, a voice network needs a dial plan. Constructing a dial plan involves assigning unique addresses (phone numbers) to each handset or terminal, and determining how calls will be routed between all possible destinations. A dial plan must support routing of external calls to the PSTN or a separate CallManager cluster. Calls to internal destinations must also be supported, which is typically accomplished with abbreviated dialing. Although the IP network will be the preferred path for WAN calls, the dial plan should also support dynamic rerouting of calls in the event of a failure of the IP network.

A dial plan not only provides the addresses required for each device, but also implements the logic that is used to route calls to both internal and external destinations. Call routing logic is implemented in a CallManager dial plan with a combination of routing decision points and the capability to modify dialed numbers. A dial plan can also incorporate restrictions on calling. Before constructing a dial plan, it is important to understand the terminology that is used by the Cisco CallManager.

Dialed Numbers and Number Modification

One of the functions of call processing in a voice network is to interpret the digits that are dialed by the telephone user and set up a call to the requested destination. Although we generally don't think of this as we dial the phone, the dialed digits are actually a form of signaling to the network about the destination we are requesting. Once the network receives the dialed digits from the user, the may modify the number before completing the call processing. The following is an explanation of the terminology that is associated with this phase of call processing.

> **Dial String** Dial string is the set of digits that a user dials to initiate a call. For example, this may include a local extension, a full E.164 number, or some prefix digits followed by a full E.164 phone number. The length of the dial string used for internal calls must be determined when creating a dial plan. In general, the number of digits used should minimize the number of digits that users must dial for internal calls while allowing enough flexibility to support growth of the organization. Dial strings can be manipulated by the system, transparent to users, with digit manipulation and digit translations.

> **Digit Manipulation** Digit manipulation entails adding or stripping a prefix or suffix to a dial string. Digit manipulation can be applied to outbound external calls only, and may be applied at within route patterns or route groups. This may be necessary when alternate routes to a given destination exist. For example, when calling to a branch office location with a five-digit internal extension, the preferred route for the call would be on-net over the IP WAN. If the IP WAN is congested or unavailable, the call can be routed over the PSTN. If a user dialed only five digits and the call must go over the PSTN, digit manipulation can be performed to add the required prefix back on to route the call over the PSTN. Digit manipulation is performed transparently to the user.

> **Digit Translation** Digit translation is applied to outbound or inbound external and internal calls, as well as both the calling and called party numbers. The three types of digit translation that can be applied, in order of processing, are discarding digits, transformations, and adding prefixes. A common application of digit translation for incoming calls is to transform calls to unassigned direct inward dialing (DID) numbers to roll to an attendant automatically.

Call Routing Decision Points

Receiving a string of dialed digits from a user is only the beginning of the call processing function. There are many potential destinations that can be reached by callers using a voice network. The call processing device (the CallManager in an AVVID network) must be programmed to deliver calls to the proper destination and in the most efficient manner. A series of decisions must be made during call processing in order to accomplish this part of the call setup. For example, should a call be handed off to a local PSTN trunk, or will the call be completed over the IP WAN using a voice gateway? The CallManager has several levels of decision logic that can be used to control these decisions. The following section describes the call routing decision points that must be configured in the CallManager.

Route pattern Defined in the CallManager to identify or match a dial string that was dialed by a user for external calls only. Route patterns can consist of a single explicit number or can contain wildcards to define a range of numbers to minimize the required entries and simplify the dial plan. When a dial string matches a route pattern, the call is handed off to a route list to determine how the call will be routed. Before handing the call off to the route list, digit manipulation can be performed to add or strip dialed digits as required to process the call. Route patterns are not used to process local calls between two IP phones on the same CallManager or cluster of CallManagers. Typically, a single route pattern is used for external calls to the PSTN.

Route list An ordered list of potential routes that a call may take to reach the required destination. A route list determines how a call will be routed according to the listed order of preference. In the simplest case, a route list may point to a preferred route group to reach the IP WAN, or may secondarily point to a route group to reach the PSTN for fail-over purposes. Multiple route patterns can point to a single route list. Previous to CallManager version 3.x, route lists were referred to as route points.

Route group One or more devices that can be used to handle a given call. Devices can be listed within the route group in order of preference. Digit manipulation can also be performed within a route group, and can override the manipulation performed by a route pattern. If a route group contains multiple devices, all devices will have the same characteristics, such as digit manipulation. In legacy telephony lingo, a route group can essentially be viewed as a trunk group.

Devices Includes IP telephony gateway endpoints such as H.323 gateways, MGCP gateways, and Skinny Gateway Protocol gateways.

Figure 7.4 shows a sample dial plan that may be implemented on the San Jose CallManager.

Figure 7.4 A Sample Dial Plan for San Jose CallManager

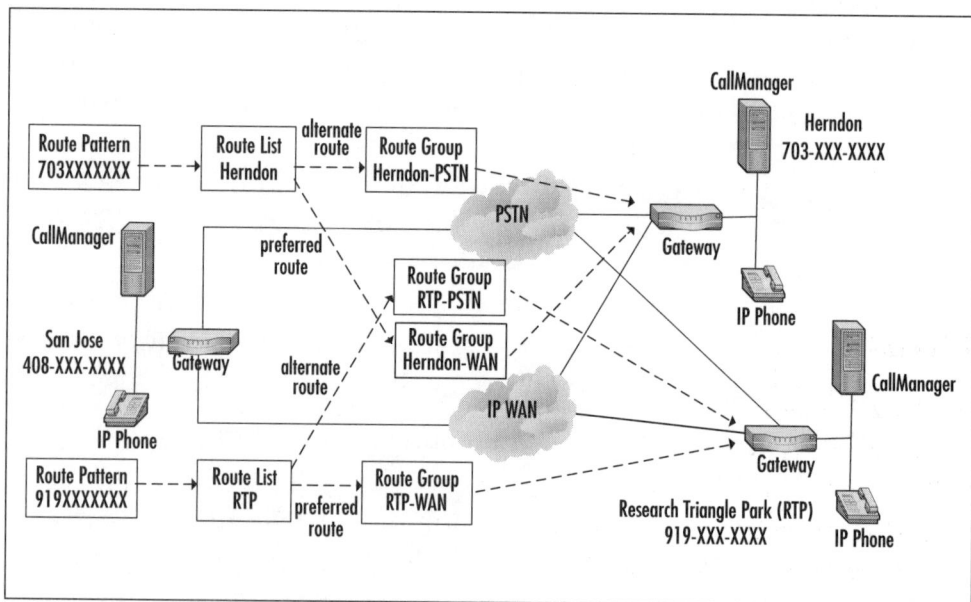

Dial Plan Groups and Calling Restrictions

Calling restrictions and class of service can also be incorporated into the CallManager dial plan for IP phone users. These features of the dial plan will require configuration of partitions and calling search spaces.

Partitions A collection of devices and associated route patterns with similar call processing characteristics. A partition contains directory numbers, route patterns, and IP telephones.

Calling Search Space A list of partitions that is searched in a specified order before allowing a call to be completed. Any device that can initiate a call may be subject to the restrictions of calling search spaces, including IP phones, SoftPhones, and VoIP gateways. Users can only dial DNs within a partition in the calling search space that they are assigned; this is how calling restrictions can be implemented. Restricting calls in this fashion is also commonly referred to as class of service in a telephony system. For those familiar with the data routing capabilities of Cisco routers, calling search spaces are somewhat analogous to using access control lists to restrict reachability to certain parts of the network.

Summary

An AVVID voice network will only be as good as the infrastructure upon which it is built. Designing a solid foundation begins with providing sufficient network capacity to handle voice traffic on a converged network. Once sufficient capacity has been provisioned, the proper QoS tools must be deployed in the WAN and LAN in order to guarantee voice quality end-to-end through the network. Lastly, a scalable dial plan must be implemented that supports required user services.

FAQs

Q: Which is the preferred method of implementing traffic shaping in a Frame Relay network, generic traffic shaping (GTS) or Frame Relay traffic shaping (FRTS)?

A: FRTS and GTS are similar in the way that they are implemented. However, since FRTS works in conjunction with FRF.12 for fragmentation and GTS does not, FRTS is the better solution.

Q: Are new LAN switches required in order to support inline power to IP telephones?

A: No, Cisco provides an inline power patch panel that can be used to supply inline power when existing LAN switches do not have inline power capabilities.

Q: Can the new 7900 series phones be used if inline power is not available?

A: Yes, the 7900 series phones support both inline power and external power from AC wall outlets.

Q: Must I acquire additional IP addresses from my ISP in order to support new IP telephones within the network?

A: No. Private IP addresses (RFC 1918) can be used internally within the organization for IP telephones.

Chapter 8

The Cisco AVVID Fast Track

Solutions in this chapter:

- A Hardware Overview
- A Software Overview
- AVVID Design Considerations

Introduction

As with any new technology, there are going to be shortfalls. Some of the products will not have all of the features or functions that are currently offered by some of the legacy systems. Some of the products may not scale to all expectations or needs, and information may sometimes be hard to come by. With Cisco's AVVID model, we are seeing some of these expected problems, However, by carefully considering your options and putting together a solid design, an AVVID infrastructure will give you a 100 percent reliable solution with many benefits that are not offered by your current legacy systems. As we reviewed, Cisco has introduced a line of software applications that will help make your call center and employee productivity increase. Cisco has also developed a sound hardware product offering with product enhancements that are being delivered every day. Cisco Systems, Inc. is definitely on their way to changing the way the world does business.

A Hardware Overview

As a review of the AVVID architecture, let's take a look at some of the current hardware offerings and their main features and functionality.

IP Phones

One of the main benefits of an AVVID infrastructure is the flexibility of the solution set. Even down to the handset, Cisco has multiple offerings that the end user can choose from ranging from a low-end "lobby" handset to an executive level handset with multiple lines and a larger display.

7910 IP Telephony Handset

The entry line to Cisco's IP telephones are the 7910 and 7910+SW which provide a low-price unit for areas where phone usage and functionality are less of a need. Typical implementations of the 7910 series are placements in shop areas, lobbies, break rooms, and so forth. No two-way speakerphone support is offered.

The key features of this phone are a new wider 24-character screen, plus four buttons statically defining hold, transfer, call park, and end call. The 7910 and 7910+SW phones are identical, with the exception that the 7910+SW offers a two-port 10/100 switch rather than a 10 Mbps hub.

7940 IP Telephony Handset

The 7940 IP telephone is Cisco's mid-level device that provides all of the capabilities of the 7910 series phone with an integrated two-port 10/100 switch and adds programming capabilities. The integrated switch natively supports 802.1q and gives network administrators the ability to assign both the phone and the user's PC to separate VLANs.

Currently, the 7940 supports the following functionality controlled though the LCD menu:

- Message notification and message storing

- Direct-dial callback to numbers with Caller ID

- Directory information, such as services by Lightweight Directory Access Protocol 3 (LDAP3)

- Configuration settings, such as display contrast, ringer tone, handset, headset, ringer, and speaker volume

- Network configuration including DHCP and TFTP settings and network status

- Call status

- Information services, such as those provided by the system administrator using Extensible Markup Language (XML), such as stock market quotes, weather reports, company information, and so forth

- Online help with any of the above described functions

7960 IP Telephony Handset

The 7960 IP telephone is essentially the same as the 7940 with the exception that it includes six lines or speed dial buttons rather than two.

7935 IP Telephony Conference Station

The 7935 IP conference station is Cisco's answer to corporate needs for an all-encompassing solution to service meetings and conference events. Composed of a desktop architecture, Cisco's 7935 provides features similar to those of the 7910 telephone. The primary differences are, of course, in design for a speakerphone and lack of a handset. Cisco's 7935 provides a digital Polycom-designed speakerphone that utilizes three microphones to service a room in 360 degrees.

Routers & Modules

Cisco voice-enabled routers are more than simply IP-enabled devices that provide encapsulation and compression. In fact, these routers provide host capabilities to link both analog and digital telecommunication technologies together.

Cisco offers highly flexible solutions for which a modular router can support any number of interface types, software functionality, and protocols. Cisco 1750, 2600, and 3600 series routers share common boards that any of these routers can use.

MCS 3810

The MCS 3810 is Cisco's all-encompassing flexible solution for media convergence. This router was Cisco's first unit to provide AVVID support, and it is tightly integrated with Cisco IGX.

While common at facilities where AVVID has been deployed in early configurations, this router is no longer very popular as it is too expensive and has little advantage over routers such as the 2600 series at its cost point and throughput (about 15,000 packets per second) or the 3600 for an equivalent cost.

The MCS 3810 combines switched voice, LAN traffic, and legacy data over Frame Relay or leased lines at speeds up to those of T1/E1. As with most of Cisco's routers, the 3810 is based on IOS and offers available support for Voice over IP, Voice over ATM, IPSec, and H.323 compatibility.

2600 Series Modular Router

The 2600 series of routers consists of eight different models fulfilling three different performance levels. All 2600 series routers include two WIC slots, a network module slot, and an advanced integrated module (AIM) slot and are available with AC, DC, and redundant power supplies.

3600 Series Modular Router

The 3600 series routers functionally are identical to the 2600 series with the exception of greater capacity and faster processing. The 2600 series router, while powerful, is not considered a core operations router. Like the 2600, all 3600 series routers are available with AC, DC, and redundant power supplies.

Switches & Modules

In addition to router technology, Cisco has also introduced several "voice friendly" Catalyst switches. Some of the unites we have reviewed are a fixed configuration, while a great deal of the switching products are modular in design and can accommodate some of the newer voice modules as well as enhanced Quality of Service (QoS).

Catalyst 3500 Series Switch

The Catalyst 3500 series is designed as "scaleable" entry-level switches that provide interoperability to additional Cisco devices via fiber or copper connection. The 3500 series switches provide the ability to interlink to one another through gigabit uplinks. Each

3500 series switch utilizes 4MB of memory, used to buffer between all ports beyond the 8MB used for IOS and its 4MB flash. With the release of the new 3524 XL PWR switch, line power is now supported over existing data cabling (Category 5).

Catalyst 4000 Series Modular Switch

The Catalyst 4000 series is made up of four switches: the 4003, the 4006, the 4840G, and the 4908G. Cisco has positioned these switches as an advance modular step above the 3500 series and an answer to the significantly higher costs of the 6000 series. The 4000 series maintains ground as an extremely capable switch when compared to similar competitors. The mainstays of the 4000 line are the 4003 and 4006 switches, providing three and six modular slots, respectively. In a typical configuration, the 4003 utilizes a supervisor I module, while the 4006 utilizes a supervisor II.

Catalyst 6000 Series Modular Switch

The Cisco 6000 series of switches is based on four entirely modular, highly available configurations—the 6006, the 6009, the 6506, and the 6509. As you have probably already determined, the last number in the model number specifies the number of module switches while the 60 and 65 prefixes designate performance. All 6000 series have modular power supplies offering varying wattage and redundancy. Furthermore, this series boasts functional capabilities such as standby supervisor modules and integrated routing. Routing in the 6000 series has grown from a module that requires its own slot—multilayer switch module (MSM) that forwards at a rate of five million packets per second (pps)—to a multilayer switch feature card (MSFC) that resides directly with the supervisor module that nearly triples the forwarding rate to 15 million pps. Effectively, the routing of the 6000 series functions similar to a Cisco 4500 router.

The 6000 series offers complete AVVID support by providing inline power at 48 ports per blade directly to second-generation IP phones. In many environments, where a cleaner solution is required, it is not desirable to use the Catalyst inline power patch panel or an external power adapter for the phone. The extra link in the wiring from the switch to the panel, then to the computer can easily become overwhelming. To address the needs of such customers, Cisco offers the Catalyst inline power patch panel as an integrated 48-port blade for the Catalyst 6000. The Catalyst 6000 version of the power panel offers an additional key advantage of automatically segregating IP phone sets to a separate VLAN. By virtue of being integrated into a Catalyst 6000 series switch, additional 10/100 48-port inline powered blades can be in a single unit. For example, the nine-slot Catalyst 6509 can support eight–48 port blades, totaling 384 ports in a single unit.

MCS

The Cisco Media Convergence servers are PC-based systems that operate on Windows 2000 operating systems to supply call management control and unified messaging services to AVVID clients. Cisco currently offers two MCS platforms to choose from, the MCS 7822 and the MCS7835. Table 8.1 outlines the details on the two products.

Table 8.1 A Comparison of the MCS 7822 and the MCS 7835

	MCS 7822	MCS 7835
Processor	Pentium III 550Mhz	Pentium III 733Mhz
Cache	512Kb secondary	256Kb secondary
RAM	512MB 100Mhz ECC SDRAM	512MB 100Mhz ECC SDRAM
Network Adapter	10/100 TX Fast Ethernet	10/100 TX Fast Ethernet
Storage	One 9.1G Ultra 2 SCSI	Dual 18.2G Ultra 2 SCSI Hot-Plug
Floppy Drive	1.44MB Standard PC Floppy Drive	1.44MB Standard PC Floppy Drive
CD-ROM	High Speed IDE	High Speed IDE
Power Supply	Fixed	Hot-plug redundant
Operating System	Windows 2000	Windows 2000

IPVC

Cisco's IP/VC 3500 series defines the AVVID solution for video conferencing. Essentially a hardware-based solution, Cisco's video conferencing offers H.323 and H.320 compatibility for interaction with applications such as Microsoft's NetMeeting or solutions by PictureTel, Polycom, Tandberg, Sony, and others.

IPVC 3510 MCU

The Cisco 3510 is at the heart of the video conferencing architecture by providing a multipoint control for all video conferencing communications. By defining a single control point, video conferencing controls can be enabled that govern establishing, joining, and terminating a meeting.

IPVC 3520 and 3525 Gateway

The video conferencing functionality is extended with the 3520 and 3525 gateway products, which provide protocol translation for H.323 and H.320, allowing video conferencing to extend beyond the network. Using these standard protocols, not only can network meetings be established, but also, extended conferences with systems via ISDN or other connectivity can be set up. As a gateway, calls can be placed between H.320 and H.323 end points and need not require video, such as linking a telephone conversation. The IP/VC 3520 gateway is designed as a modular unit that provides for five configuration options composed of two or four ISDN BRI ports, two or four V.35 ports, or a combination of two ISDN BRI and twp V.35 ports. As you may have surmised, lower-bandwidth links—64, 128, 256, and 384 Kbps—are established via ISDN using aggregated or bond lines, while the V.35 provides the higher-speed 768 Kbps connections. Sessions established at higher speeds through the v.35 port utilize RS-366 signaling so that a circuit-switched connection through an inverse multiplexor (IMUX) is used. On the network, through the 3520's 10/100 Mbps Fast Ethernet interface, the IP/VC 3520 enables full end-to-end T.120 support for data conferencing.

The IP/VC 3525 is very similar to the 3520, except that it is designed for a large volume of calls through its ISDN PRI interfaces. Unlike the 3520, which can support only four simultaneous sessions, the 3525 can support up to eight at 128 Kbps each; however, it also supports higher quality through multilinked or bound lines yielding up to three sessions at 384 Kbps on a PRI-T1 or four on a PRI-E1.

IPVC 3520 VTA

Finally, the IP/VC 3530 video adapter allows a company to preserve investments in older technologies that support only H.320. Through a conversion process, legacy equipment signals are converted to H.323 so that they operate correctly over an IP-enabled network. Video throughput varies according to user-specified settings at rates as low as 112 Kbps and at a maximum of 768 Kbps.

IP/TV

Cisco's IP/TV server product line provides video broadcasting services very similar in nature to television, which provides a solution to issues such as information dissemination, poor communications, and other problems of this nature with regard to scheduling issues.

All of the IP/TV servers are delivered with a pre-configured software load according to their function on a Windows NT/2000 Platform. IP/TV provides scalability, integration, support of industry standards, and ease of use.

In addition to providing video services, the IP/TV servers can also provide audio services similar to those of radio technologies. Cisco currently provides support for pulse code modulation (PCM), Global System for Mobile Communication (GSM), 8- and 16-bit linear (many sampling and frequency rates), DVI, True-speech, MPEG, MPEG-1 Layer 3 (MP3), and Microsoft Audio.

Cisco's television series systems consist of five different specialties as summarized in Table 8.2.

Table 8.2 Cisco's Television Series

Server	Primary Function
3411 Control Server	Management of broadcast services including scheduling, control of video types, access to archive servers, and more
3415 Video Starter System	All-in-one, small-scale video services including control functionality, storage, and broadcast functionality
3422 Broadcast Server	Provides streaming real-time or prerecorded video services via MPEG-4 over low-bandwidth links
3423 Broadcast Server	Similar to the 3422 Broadcast Server offering MPEG-1, MPEG-2, MPEG-4, Indeo, and H.261 compression with more of a focus on performance over bandwidth
3431 Archive Server	Repository for pre-recorded video services

Voice Trunks and Gateways

Products such as Cisco voice gateways enable the communication between voice and data networks. These voice gateways serve to provide connectivity between your private network and conventional telephone trunks, legacy voice-mail systems, and other analog devices that are not capable of direct communications.

Voice gateways are available in two flavors—analog and digital. Depending on the equipment to which you are connecting, your choice will be determined by the accommodation of the available interface.

Digital gateways typically provide for two types of transports. These transports are provisions for T1 and E1 circuits. In the United States, Canada, Japan, and a few other countries, T1 lines are common and use μ-law encoding. In most of Europe and part the rest of the world where E1 lines are used, a-law encoding is employed. All Cisco digital voice gateways support these standards as common functionality including the mapping of IP addresses to phone numbers and vice versa.

Cisco provides a number of products for gateway services. Some of these devices are analog only; others are purely digital, and some support both.

Catalyst 6000 Series Gateway Modules

The Catalyst 6000 series of switches can operate as voice gateways for AVVID networks and legacy PBX's or the PSTN. In this capacity, this series permits a large-capacity voice gateway, allowing up to 24 FXS analog ports or eight T1/E1 PRI ISDN interfaces per blade.

Catalyst 4000 Series Gateway Modules

As noted earlier, the 4000 series switch is a scaled-down version of the 6000 that lacks certain functionality. Of that service that had been removed, Cisco adds the 4000 access gateway module. This module provides field office support for network voice services, voice gateway functionality, and IP routing.

Through the use of the access gateway module, a 4000 series router gains the capability of direct use of many functions primarily reserved for routers. This access gateway module provide two VIC or WIC slots, a dedicated VIC slot, a high-density analog slot, and direct support for integrating with the switch itself. Configuration of the access gateway module is very similar to that of a Cisco router and offers a common console port for easy access.

DT-24+ & DT-30+ MCS Gateway Modules

The DT-24+ and DE-30+ represent Cisco's solution to interfacing a legacy PSTN- or ISDN (PRI)-based digital trunk to a Cisco AVVID telephone network whereby either solution is controlled via Cisco's Call Manager. The DT-24+ is design for United States standards where T1 is used; the D-E30+ is design to operate with the European E1 circuit. Both T1 and E1 lines are channelized within all gateway solutions as 24 and 31 channels, respectively. Because clocking for each channel of the digital line is handled out of band, one channel per T1 or E1 line is removed. As such, a T1 link that is composed of 24 channels will effectively allow for utilization of 23 for communication while an E1 permits 30.

VG200 Voice Gateway

Cisco's VG200 is an advanced Voice Gateway interface that allows communications between an IP-based phone system and analog telephony devices. In this capacity, the VG200 allows users on the IP-based system to both make and receive calls with seamless integration to an existing legacy phone system.

Like other Cisco AVVID devices, the VG200 is controlled through Cisco's Call Manager application. Like its router counterparts that utilize Cisco IOS, it also provides for a command-line interface. The command-line interface can be accessed in all the ways common to IOS devices such as Telnet, serial cable, and so forth.

As a modular unit, the VG200 shares a common architecture with the 1750, 2600, and 3600 series routers whereby other network modules and voice interface cards are interchangeable, allowing all the flexibility that is inherent to its router counterparts. For example, the VG200 can be used to provide analog and digital dial access services, in addition to PBX or PSTN connectivity, as well as other devices, such as legacy voice-mail systems.

ICS 7750

Like other Cisco products, the ICS 7750 uses a modular design that allows for the integration of both WIC and VIC options. WIC options are reasonably standard, providing high-speed and asynchronous serial interfaces, ISDN BRI support, and 56 Kbps and fractional T1 with integrated CSU/DSU provisions. Similarly, the VIC options are on par with the 2600, providing capabilities for digital multiflex trunks (one or two ports) and analog two ports for E&M, FXO, and FXS.

The ICS 7750 is a six-slot modular-based router that provides functionality as required by adding cards, memory, and processors.

Each of the slots can be expanded to use either Cisco's Multiservice Router Processor (MRP) or System Processing Engine (SPE) option. The MRP comes standard with 64MB of RAM and is expandable to 96MB, enabling it to support either two WICs or VICs and two PVDM (packet voice/fax DSP).

The SPE is perhaps the greatest feature of the ICS 7750. In a remote field office, it is often not feasible to utilize a Call Manager installation at the corporate office. Essentially, the SPE provides for this. Fundamentally, the SPE is a single-board computer that is capable of running Cisco Call Manager as well as voice-mail, call routing, and attendant and interactive voice-driven functions.

A Software Overview

As a review of the AVVID architecture, let's take a look at some of the current hardware offerings and their main features and functionality

CallManager

Installed on an MCS Hardware platform, Cisco CallManager 3.X provides PBX functionality to a Cisco IP Telephony network. With the newly enhanced 3.0 version, we are seeing more standard telephone features as well as improved scalability. CallManager 3.0 servers can be clustered and administered as one entity, which greatly improve administration. The current release of Call Manager 3.06 supports MGCP, Web Attendant, and a host of gateways previously unsupported (the 2600, the 3600, and so on). CallManager can supports up to 2500 IP Phones, and a cluster of CallManager servers can support up to 10,000 IP Phones (2000 phones on each of five servers).

Active Voice

Active Voice is Cisco's answer to voice mail. One of the key items and major benefits of Active Voice and Cisco's IP Telephony solution is the unified messaging direction. With Unified Messaging, Active Voice (Voice Mail) can be integrated with standard e-mail applications (Microsoft Outlook) to provide a system that will allow e-mails to be checked via voice mail and voice mail to be checked via e-mail. Fax is also supported within Unified Messaging.

Soft Phone

The Cisco IP SoftPhone is an application that can be loaded on any networked attached PC. As long as the user has a legal IP address, a microphone and headset available, they can use this application to send and receive calls on their computer via the IP Telephony model that Cisco has implemented with their hardware handsets. A traveling user now has the ability to take their direct telephone number with them on the road. SoftPhone integrates easily with LDAP directories, allowing for the use of a global as well as personal address books. As with most applications, drop and drag functionality adds a feature to this application. Conference calls can be made by simply dragging and dropping names onto the SoftPhone.

WebAttendant

WebAttendant is Cisco's solution to replace a legacy voice system's traditional manual attendant console. Traditional manual attendant consoles can either be large phones with bulky attachments or proprietary expensive terminals. The Cisco WebAttendant is a client-server application that enables you to set up any Cisco IP Phone as an attendant console. It can be downloaded from the CallManager Web administration pages and can be installed on any system. The Cisco WebAttendant client provides a Graphical User Interface (GUI) to control a Cisco IP Phone when used as an attendant console. WebAttendant also includes speed dial buttons and quick directory access to look up phone numbers, monitor phone status, and direct calls. It is an IP-based application, which is more scalable than the hardware-based line monitor devices used by PBXs. WebAttendant allows portability to various platforms including Windows 98, Windows NT, and Windows 2000. Working with the Cisco IP Phone, WebAttendant is able to monitor the state of every line in the system, while promptly and efficiently dispatching and accepting calls.

AVVID Design Considerations

Migration from legacy PBXs and voice messaging systems to IP telephony systems is a challenge for many organizations. It would be unrealistic to expect any organization looking to deploy IP-based voice systems to immediately replace all of their installed legacy voice systems when the decision is made to implement an AVVID solution. Therefore, we can expect that we will be faced with the challenge of integrating legacy systems with the respective AVVID components. In addition to making the proper physical connections, system applications and user features must also be preserved. This can be achieved with different levels of compatibility depending of the method of integration that is available. Selecting the best migration strategy involves understanding the capabilities of the existing equipment and the AVVID components, as well as understanding what features and applications are most important to users.

PBX Migration Strategies

Migrating to a converged AVVID network will mean different things to different organizations based on the amount of legacy equipment currently installed and the network size. There are some generalizations that can be made, however, that will help identify a few strategies that can be used when an organization is faced with migrating to an AVVID network.

New Installations

The migration to a CallManager system will be simplest for those organizations that do not yet have any voice network equipment installed. This may include new start-up businesses, small businesses previously using Centrex services, or any other organization that has not yet invested in a phone system. Since there will be no existing equipment on-hand, the only real integration that will be required is to the PSTN for calls to outside users.

Immediate Migration

Some organizations may choose to do an immediate migration of all users from the legacy system to a new AVVID system. The advantage of this approach is that it will minimize integration issues with legacy equipment since the cutover to the new system will be immediate. For example, if an organization is implementing a CallManager system to replace a legacy PBX, there will be no need for the legacy components to co-exist. This will eliminate any interoperability issues when preserving calling features and messaging waiting indications.

Summary

No matter what type of business you are currently in, or what type of data, voice, and video network you are currently running, technology is taking us is towards the converged infrastructure model. Cisco has been on the leading edge of this technology. They are continuing to introduce optimal products in this space as well as revise and enhance their existing product line. It will only be a matter of time before a great majority of the industry is running on a Cisco Systems AVVID network.

FAQs

Q: What is unified messaging?

A: Unified messaging is the integration of e-mail, voice mail, and fax capabilities. It allows all of these services to be accessed through and e-mail client or through a phone.

Q: If my voice mail is treated like e-mail, can I forward it to someone?

A: Yes. You can even forward it to individuals who are not running AVVID. The voice message is treated as a .WAV file attachment. Virtually any computer should be able to play it.

Q: What industry standard protocols are available for integrating legacy voice systems with IP telephony systems?

A: Three are several industry standards have been defined for integrating between legacy systems and IP telephony systems, including SMDI, AMIS, and VPIM. However, vendor support for these protocols must be verified for all of your system components as they have not yet been universally adopted.

Q: Why should I choose to go with Cisco Products as opposed to other systems and products out there out there?

A: Cisco has made a concerted effort, through internal product development and key corporate acquisitions, to establish themselves as leaders in integrating voice, video, and data technology. In addition to great product support, Cisco has made a commitment to AVVID, believing that this truly is the future of networks and business communications. As market leaders in providing much of the backbone that comprises the Internet and corporate networks today, it is pretty safe to say that Cisco's AVVID product development will be a driving force in computing for years to come.

Optimizing Network Performance with Queuing and Compression

Solutions in this appendix:

- WAN Connection Requirements

- WAN Topology and Specifications

- Network Planning and Design

- Considerations Before Installation

- Selecting Cisco Access Servers and Routers

- Implementation Considerations

Introduction

Today's networks are coping with ever-increasing traffic and applications that require more bandwidth and faster response times. As we start connecting these networks together and allow remote users to dial in and access them, it is unlikely that will will have unlimited bandwidth available, due to cost constraints. It is the network designer's job to ensure that the applications running across these links can maintain a satisfactory level of performance and responsiveness, as well as make efficient use of the available bandwidth.

To improve responsiveness in congested networks, Cisco has provided congestion management and avoidance techniques. Congestion management, or queuing features, include first-in, first-out queuing (FIFO), priority queuing (PQ), custom queuing (CQ), and weighted fair queuing (WFQ). IOS version 12.x also introduces a new class-based weighted fair queuing feature (CBWFQ), Versatile Interface Processor (VIP), and distributed weighted fair queuing (DWFQ) for the Cisco 7000 series products.

In addition, Cisco empowers network architects with congestion avoidance techniques. These mechanisms monitor the traffic load in an attempt to anticipate and avoid bottlenecks before they occur. This is accomplished using random early detection (RED) algorithms.

Using compression is an effective way to make more efficient use of bandwidth by reducing the amount of data that needs to be transmitted between endpoints. Cisco provides a number of different compression techniques and options, which will be covered in this appendix.

Network Performance

Managing congestion over wide area network (WAN) links is important due to the mismatch in speed between input ports (10 Mbps Ethernet) and output ports (56 Kbps serial link). One way that network devices can handle overflow of arriving traffic is to use a queuing algorithm to sort and prioritize outbound traffic, and then prioritize the traffic on the output link as indicated. It is important to note that queuing/prioritization works most effectively on WAN links that experience bursty traffic. If a WAN link is congested 100 percent of the time, queuing/prioritization may not remedy the issue—look to additional bandwidth instead.

The Cisco IOS software includes the following queuing tools:

- FIFO
- WFQ
- PQ
- CQ
- CBWFQ

Each queuing algorithm was designed to solve a specific network traffic problem and each will have a different effect on network performance. As described in the following sections, queuing is an effective way to control the order of traffic.

Queuing Overview

Many applications currently in use are of an interactive, transaction-based or time-sensitive nature. These applications are commonly referred to as *real-time* applications. An example of a real-time application is *Voice over X (VoX)*. VoX can refer to voice over IP, voice over Frame Relay, voice over Asynchronous Transfer Mode (ATM), or an AVVID solution. Voice traffic does not tolerate excessive delays because it is transported between endpoints. Therefore, Quality of Service (QoS) mechanisms need to be provisioned to reduce end-to-end delay or jitter.

Cisco routers route IP packets from input ports to output ports based on the most specific route entry found in the routing table. During periods when interface traffic volumes are low, packets traverse a given interface in a first-in, first-out manner. As packets arrive faster than they can be forwarded out of an interface, they are placed in a queue. Therefore, queuing happens when network congestion occurs (that is, the queue depth is greater than or equal to 1), otherwise all packets are forwarded out an interface as they arrive.

Various queuing methods have been developed and implemented for the Cisco series of routers. We will explain how the queuing algorithms work, and how each method increases performance, allowing improved access to the outgoing interface. Queuing algorithms allow different traffic streams to be prioritized on network interfaces. These queuing algorithms can allow real-time traffic to be transmitted before other, less time-sensitive traffic. By using queuing techniques, the network manager can optimize network traffic flow resulting in better traffic management and support of all end-user applications.

Queuing Methods and Configuration

There are five network queuing techniques that we will cover: FIFO, WFQ, PQ, CQ, and CBWFQ. Each of these queuing techniques has advantages and disadvantages pertaining to the design and configuration of each individual network. We will examine the way each queuing method works, then develop a flowchart for selecting which queuing scheme should be enabled.

First-In, First-Out Queuing (FIFO)

The first queuing method is FIFO. Packets arrive in sequential order at the network interface. They are then inserted into the output buffer in the order in which they were received, and processed in the exact order that they arrive at the buffer. The packet buffer or processor on the interface does not give precedence to the type of packets or traffic arriving or when it needs to exit the interface. All packets exit the interface sequentially, in the same order in which they arrived. This is the default queuing method for all interfaces, except for serial interfaces operating at a rate of 2.048 Mbps and slower. Figure A.1 illustrates FIFO queuing.

Figure A.1 FIFO queuing.

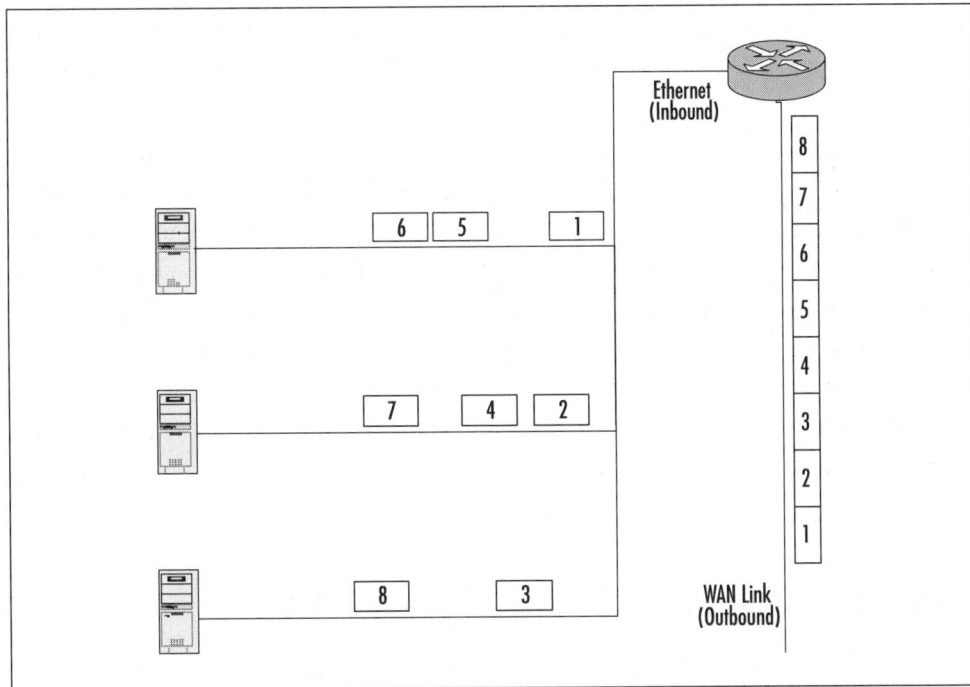

When designing router hardware and software, a methodology had to be derived to allow all packet flows to have fair access to an outgoing interface. A packet flow can be described as a conversation between two end stations. Problems occur when large continuous packet transfers, sometimes called packet troops or packet trains (for example, a large file transfer), consume the majority of network resources and prevent other traffic from using the link. (Under sustained heavy utilization, time-sensitive traffic like voice, video, and Telnet may not reach its destination in a timely manner. Failure to reach a destination on time may cause unacceptable user results. In theory, this file transfer could decrease its utilization of the network link and allow time-sensitive traffic fair access to interface bandwidth. The four queuing algorithms described in the next sections were implemented to give network managers the ability to balance interface bandwidth allocation between multiple applications and assign priority to mission-critical applications.

Weighted Fair Queuing (WFQ)

WFQ is a queuing method that automatically provides even allocation of bandwidth to high-bandwidth traffic flows, and prioritizes low-bandwidth connections to each network resource. This algorithm dynamically tracks traffic flows and allocates bandwidth accordingly. WFQ is the default queuing mechanism for all serial interfaces operating below 2.048 Mbps that do not use Linked Access Procedure, Balanced (LAPB), X.25, and Synchronous Data Link Control (SDLC) encapsulations.

WFQ interweaves low-volume traffic flows with high-volume traffic flows, resulting in the breakup of packet trains that restrict lower bandwidth traffic's access to network resources, as shown in Figure A.2. WFQ automatically places interactive low-volume traffic at the front of the queue (to reduce response time) and allows high-volume traffic to compete for the remaining capacity. When WFQ is running in conjunction with Frame Relay, the algorithm will adjust the queuing schedule to compensate for link congestion, as identified by the receipt of forward explicit congestion notification (FECN) and backward explicit congestion notification (BECN) frames. This function is enabled by default and requires no manual configuration.

For example, assume we have a mid-sized hub-and-spoke network design topology for a national retail chain. The links between the hub and spokes are T1 circuits. Users primarily use FTP for batch processing and Telnet for access to their order entry system located at the hub site. Remote users have been complaining about intermittent response time problems resulting in a loss of revenue. Assuming the role of network operator, we suspect batch processing is degrading performance of the more interactive applications. By enabling WFQ, Telnet is automatically given priority over FTP, resulting in improved response time.

WFQ has three important user-configurable parameters. The interface command used to enable and configure WFQ is **fair queue**. It has several optional parameters such as congestive discard threshold, number of dynamic queues, and number of reservable queues.

Figure A.2 WFQ.

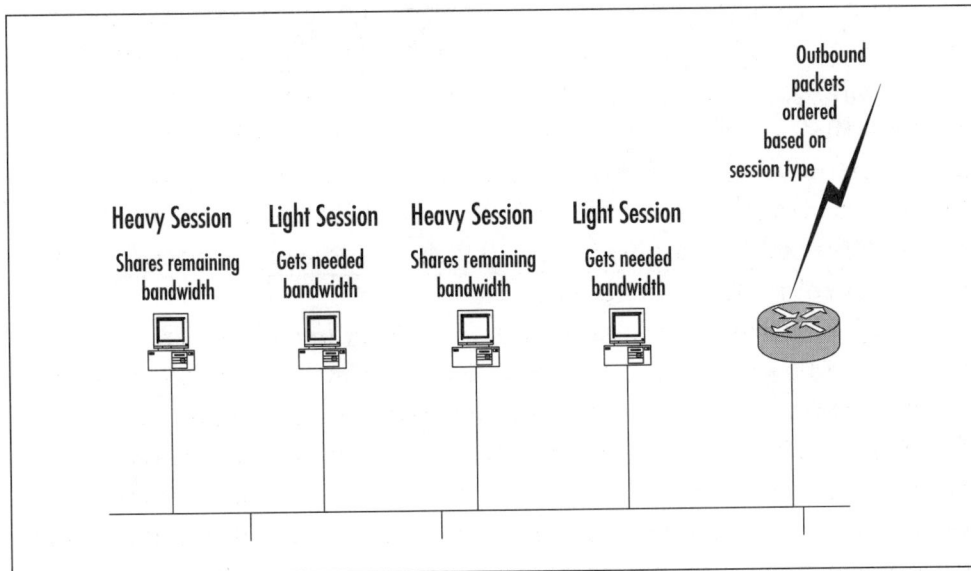

The congestive discard threshold is set to 64 by default. This means that once 64 messages (packets) are queued as part of a flow, new packets belonging to that flow will be discarded. A network manager/administrator can select to change this parameter to an integer based on a power of 2 from a range of 16 to 4096. Changing this parameter should be considered only after completion of a traffic analysis. If this parameter is changed, the router should be carefully monitored for memory issues. In most networks, this variable should remain unchanged.

Dynamic queues are used to support best-effort conversations. The default number of dynamic queues allocated is directly proportional to the configured interface bandwidth, as listed in Table A.1:

Table A.1 Allocation of Dynamic Queues

Bandwidth Range	Number of Dynamic Queues
Less than or equal to 64 Kbps	16
More than 64 Kbps and less than or equal to 128 Kbps	32

Continued

Table A.1 Continued

Bandwidth Range	Number of Dynamic Queues
More than 128 Kbps and less than or equal to 256 Kbps	64
More than 256 Kbps and less than or equal to 512 Kbps	128
More than 512 Kbps	256

The last parameter (reservable queues) is used to define the number of flows reserved for features such as Resource Reservation Protocol (RSVP). The default value is determined by dividing the configured interface bandwidth value by 32 Kbps. The value can be statically defined as an integer from 0 to 1000. In practice, this value should not be changed unless an accurate traffic analysis has been performed. The following is an example of a serial interface being configured for WFQ using all default configuration values:

```
interface Serial0

 ip address 10.10.10.1 255.255.255.252

 fair-queue
```

The next example illustrates a serial interface configured for a congestive discard of 100 and 128 dynamic queues:

```
interface Serial0

 ip unnumbered Ethernet0

 bandwidth 384

   fair-queue 100
```

In summary, WFQ can identify and prioritize mixed traffic streams to more fairly allocate access to an interface rather than just servicing packets in FIFO fashion. WFQ is designed to minimize configuration efforts and automatically adapt to changing network traffic conditions.

Resource Reservation Protocol (RSVP)

RSVP is an Internet Protocol (IP) service that guarantees, or "reserves," bandwidth across a network. RSVP is an ideal QoS method for real-time traffic (audio and video). Real-time traffic is consistent and very sensitive to latency; therefore, it requires a guaranteed network consistency. Without this consistency, there is risk of jitter, delay variations, and information loss due to insufficient bandwidth.

RSVP supports two types of real-time traffic: *multicast traffic*, primarily a flow in one direction from a single host sending packets to many hosts, and *unicast traffic*, for guaranteed bandwidth between two hosts.

There are three RSVP-supported reservation styles: wildcard-filter style, fixed-filter style, and shared-explicit style. A reservation style is a set of control options that specify a number of supported parameters. There are two groups of reservation styles: *distinct* and *shared*. A distinct reservation notes each individual flow, as in a video stream. A shared reservation notes a group of flows, as in an audio environment.

The three types of reservation styles are:

- **Wildcard-filter (WF) style** is a shared reservation style. A single reservation is created, into which flows from all upstream senders are mixed. The reservation is extended to new senders.

- **Fixed-filter (FF) style** is a distinct reservation style. A distinct reservation request is created for data packets from a particular sender.

- **Shared-explicit (SE) style** is a shared reservation style. A single reservation is created, into which flows from all upstream senders are mixed. The scope is explicitly specified by the receiver.

As discussed in the previous section, WFQ is RSVP-aware. The bandwidth reserved by WFQ can be statically defined or dynamically allocated.

Planning Considerations

How much bandwidth is needed for your application? If you are running VoIP and using a G.729a codec, then, depending on your configuration, you may need from 6.3 Kbps to 17.2 Kbps. As you can see, if you plan for 10 Kbps you could be shocked when it is time to test.

How much bandwidth is available? The default for a Cisco router is 75 percent of available bandwidth is reservable.

How much bandwidth is needed for other data traffic? You do not want to squelch your other traffic.

WFQ and IP Precedence

When queuing IP traffic, WFQ uses the IP precedence field from the QoS portion of the IP packet header in its algorithm to allocate bandwidth. The IP precedence bits are located in the type of service (TOS) field of an IP packet and have a value between 0 (default/low) and 7 (high). In practice, the precedence values of 6 and 7 are reserved. Please review Table A.2.

Table A.2 IP Precedence Values

Precedence Number	Value Name
0	Routine
1	Priority
2	Immediate
3	Flash
4	Flash-override
5	Critical
6	Internet
7	Network

As IP precedence values increase, the algorithm allocates more bandwidth to the flow. This results in higher-precedence traffic being served in the queue before lower-precedence traffic. Once the IP header has this value set, the value will traverse the network intact unless explicitly changed. This allows packets with higher precedence/priority to be serviced throughout a network (end-to-end) based on their IP precedence.

A benefit of using IP precedence is that WFQ is IP precedence-aware. The higher the value of IP precedence, the more bandwidth allocated to the IP traffic flow by WFQ. Non–real-time traffic flows normally have an IP precedence value of 0. Assigning real-time applications an IP precedence value greater than 0 ensures they will be serviced as high priority by the queuing algorithm.

The method that WFQ uses to calculate flow priority is complex. The following examples should help to simplify understanding.

In WFQ, each IP flow is given a percentage of the total interface bandwidth based on precedence level and the number of flows assigned to each precedence level. The following formula simplifies the issue:

Percentage of interface bandwidth assigned to a flow =

$$\frac{\text{Precedence level}+1}{\text{The sum of [(each flow's precedence level}+1) * \text{(the number of flows at that precedence level)]}}$$

To further clarify, consider the following two examples. In the first example, our object is to determine what percentage of bandwidth is assigned each flow with a precedence value of 0 and 4. We have eight flows using precedence levels 0 through 7 with one flow allocated per precedence level.

$$\frac{\text{precedence level}+1}{(0+1)*1+(1+1)*1+(2+1)*1+(3+1)*1+(4+1)*1+(5+1)*1+(6+1)*1+(7+1)*1}$$

To determine the bandwidth for precedence 0, we will insert 0 for precedence level and calculate the lower half of the formula:

$$\frac{0+1}{1+2+3+4+5+6+7+8} = 36$$

To determine the bandwidth for precedence 4, we will insert 4 for precedence level and calculate the lower half of the formula:

$$\frac{4+1}{1+2+3+4+5+6+7+8} = 36$$

In the formulas above, precedence 0 traffic will be allocated 1/36 of the interface bandwidth and precedence 4 will receive 5/36 of the interface bandwidth.

In our next example, we have adjusted the formula to represent 12 traffic flows and three individual precedence levels. Our objective is to determine the amount of interface bandwidth assigned to a single flow at each precedence level.

Example criteria:

Five flows with a precedence of 0

Ten flows with a precedence of 2

Two flows with a precedence of 4

$$\frac{precedence\ level+1}{(0+1)*5+(2+1)*10+(4+1)*2}$$

To determine the bandwidth for precedence 0, we will insert 0 for precedence level and calculate the lower half of the formula:

$$\frac{0+1}{(1*5)+(3*10)+(5*2)} = 45$$

To determine the bandwidth for precedence 2, we will insert 2 for precedence level and calculate the lower half of the formula:

$$\frac{2+1}{(1*5)+(3*10)+(5*2)} = 45$$

To determine the bandwidth for precedence 4, we will insert 4 for precedence level and calculate the lower half of the formula:

$$\frac{4+1}{(1*5)+(3*10)+(5*2)} = 45$$

The output of the formula states that precedence 0 flows receive 1/45 of the interface bandwidth, precedence 2 flows receive 3/45 of the interface bandwidth, and precedence 4 flows receive 5/45 of the interface bandwidth.

For example, assume we have two locations interconnected via a T1 circuit, as illustrated in Figure A.3. By default, WFQ is enabled on each WAN interface. Traffic is distributed between Voice over IP (VoIP) and Internet traffic, with 10 flows of VoIP traffic and 70 flows of Internet traffic, respectively.

Figure A.3 IP Precedence Used to Allocate More Bandwith to Voice Traffic

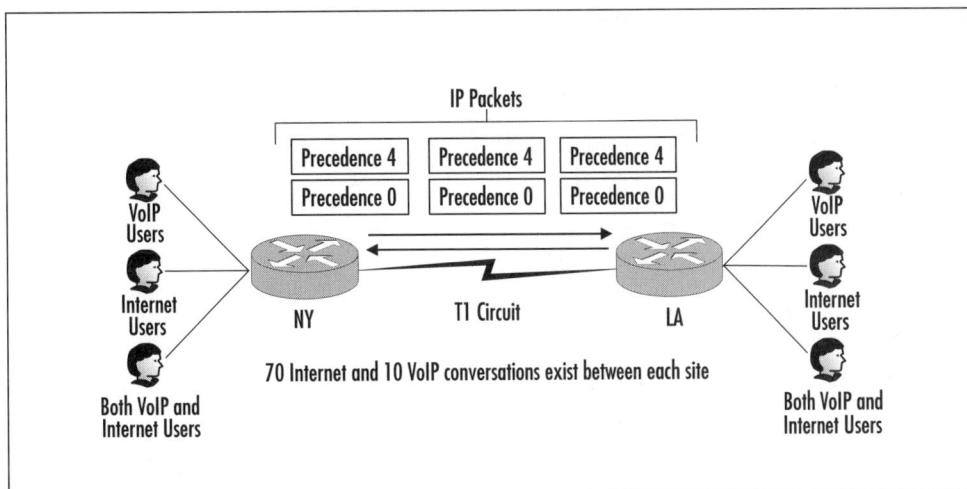

All voice traffic has been assigned an IP precedence value of 4 and all Internet traffic a precedence value of 0. During periods of congestion, using the formula above, WFQ will allocate 1/120 of the interface bandwidth to each precedence 0 flow and 5/120 or 1/24 of the interface bandwidth to each Internet flow. This equates to about 64 Kbps per VoIP session and 12.8 Kbps per Internet session.

VIP DWFQ

VIP DWFQ can be described as the high-speed version of WFQ. This version requires the use of a Cisco 7000 series router using VIP2-40s or later interface processors. Although the VIP2-40 is the minimum required interface processor to run DFWQ, it is recommended to deploy VIP2-50s when the aggregate port speed on the VIP exceeds 45 Mbps. In addition, distributed Cisco express forwarding (dCEF) is required to run DWFQ.

dCEF provides increased packet routing performance because the entire route forwarding information base (FIB) is resident on each VIP card. Therefore, routing table lookups happen locally on the VIP card without querying the centralized route switch processor.

In flow-based DWFQ, all traffic flows are equally weighted and guaranteed equal access to the queue. This queuing method guarantees fair access to all traffic streams, thus preventing any single flow from monopolizing resources.

To enable DWFQ, activate fair queuing by enabling "IP CEF" in global configuration mode and "fair-queue" under the VIP2 interface configuration.

Review the following example:

```
version 12.1
!
ip cef
!
interface FastEthernet0/0
 ip address 172.20.10.2 255.255.255.0
 full-duplex
!
interface Hssi4/0
 ip address 172.20.20.2 255.255.255.0
 fair-queue
!
router ospf 100
 network 172.20.0.0 0.0.255.255 area 0
!
router#
```

DWFQ also has the following limitations:

- Can be configured only on main interfaces; per IOS 12.1.0, there is no sub-interface support.

- Can be configured only on an ATM interface with AAL5SNAP encapsulation. Per IOS 12.1.0, there is no support for AAL5MUX or AAL5NLPID encapsulations.

- Is not supported on any virtual, tunnel, or Fast EtherChannel interfaces.

- Cannot be configured in conjunction with RSP-based WFQ, PQ, or CQ.

Priority Queuing (PQ)

PQ provides a granular means for the network administrator to determine which traffic must be queued and serviced first. With priority queuing techniques, the network administrator must understand all the traffic flows within the network. This type of control is important when specific mission-critical traffic must receive servicing. The network administrator has the control to create different interface packet queues that are serviced in a hierarchical order. Each network flow can be categorized by the following:

- Protocol or sub-protocol type
- Incoming interface
- Packet size
- Fragments
- Access lists

The queues are known as high, medium, normal, and low. The router services the queues from highest to lowest priority. The service order on the four queues works such that if the high queue has traffic in it, the normal queue cannot forward any packets until all packets in the high-priority queue are transmitted. This is a major issue when designing a queuing strategy for a network. The network administrator may inadvertently starve a certain network stream, making users unable to use applications and services on the network. However, this may be ideal for networks in which critical applications are not able to run because network users are running "less important" applications. Figure A.4 illustrates the PQ packet flow.

Figure A.4 PQ packet flow.

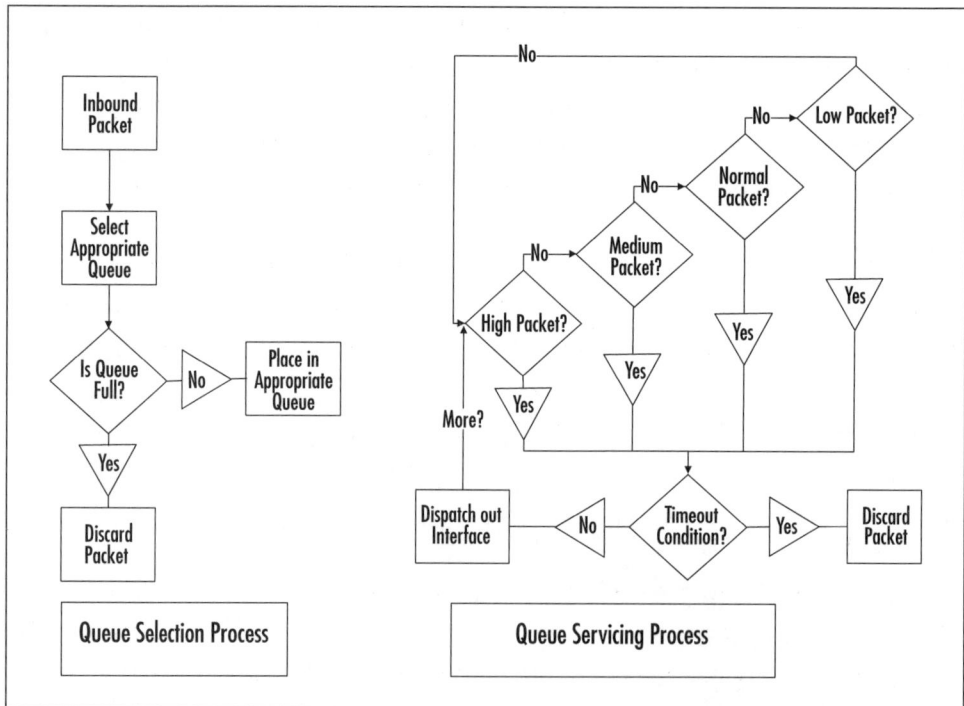

When using PQ, packets are compared with a statically defined priority list. If there is any capacity in the priority queue associated with the incoming traffic, the packet is placed in the designated queue and waits to be serviced out the interface. If there is no room left in the queue, the packet is dropped.

WARNING

Packets that are dropped do not go into another queue.

Since the definitions for queues are defined, a packet either fits into that queue, or it does not. Even though packets are sent into queues, there is no guarantee they will be processed in time to reach their destination. This process enables network administrators to control the priority of mission-critical network traffic, but also requires a good understanding of its effect on the flow of other network traffic. Networks implementing priority queuing require constant reassessment, since traffic pattern requirements may change as well. Traffic that was once considered high priority may become a low priority at some point.

It is important to note that priority queuing can affect CPU utilization. Cisco routers will process switch packets on interfaces that have priority queuing enabled. The packet-switching performance will be degraded compared with other interfaces using caching schemes. Also note that priority queuing is not supported on tunnel interfaces.

Priority Queuing Examples

In a mainframe environment, there may be a lot of users "surfing" the Web and downloading files, causing performance problems with time-sensitive Software Network Architecture (SNA) traffic and other tn3270 (Telnet) traffic. The following situation allows the SNA traffic (using Data-Link Switching (DLSw)) and the Telnet traffic to have high priority where the reset of traffic is considered low. There may be some exceptions that can be controlled using an access list to make a normal priority.

```
!
priority-list 1 protocol ip normal list 100
priority-list 1 protocol ip high tcp telnet
```

```
priority-list 1 protocol dlsw high
priority-list 1 default low
!
```

To use an extended access list to make specific IP traffic have normal priority on the interface, the **priority-list 1 protocol ip normal list 100** command is used.

To configure Telnet traffic as high priority, the **priority-list 1 protocol ip high tcp telnet** command is used.

To configure DLSw traffic as high priority, the **priority-list 1 protocol dlsw high** command is used.

To configure traffic that does not match any of the previous statements, the **priority-list 1 default low** command will set a default priority. If no default queue is defined the normal queue is used.

```
!
interface Serial0
 priority-group 1
!
```

The interface **priority-group 1** command is configured under the whole interface to specify that priority list 1 is used for that interface.

```
c2507#show interface serial 0
Serial0 is up, line protocol is up
  Hardware is HD64570
  MTU 1500 bytes, BW 1544 Kbit, DLY 20000 usec, rely 255/255, load
1/255
  Encapsulation FRAME-RELAY, loopback not set, keepalive set (10
sec)
  LMI enq sent  0, LMI stat recvd 0, LMI upd recvd 0, DTE LMI up
  LMI enq recvd 0, LMI stat sent  0, LMI upd sent  0
  LMI DLCI 1023  LMI type is CISCO  frame relay DTE
```

```
   Broadcast queue 0/64, broadcasts sent/dropped 0/0, interface
broadcasts 0
   Last input 00:00:03, output 00:00:03, output hang never
   Last clearing of "show interface" counters 00:00:03
   Input queue: 0/75/0 (size/max/drops); Total output drops: 0
   Queueing strategy: priority-list 1
   Output queue (queue priority: size/max/drops):
      high: 0/20/0, medium: 0/40/0, normal: 0/60/0, low: 0/80/0
   5 minute input rate 0 bits/sec, 0 packets/sec
   5 minute output rate 0 bits/sec, 0 packets/sec
      0 packets input, 0 bytes, 0 no buffer
      Received 0 broadcasts, 0 runts, 0 giants, 0 throttles
      0 input errors, 0 CRC, 0 frame, 0 overrun, 0 ignored, 0 abort
      0 packets output, 0 bytes, 0 underruns
      0 output errors, 0 collisions, 0 interface resets
      0 output buffer failures, 0 output buffers swapped out
      0 carrier transitions
      DCD=up  DSR=up  DTR=up  RTS=up  CTS=up


c2507#
```

Using the **show interface serial 0** command, the type of
queuing is displayed on the queuing strategy line of the interface
output. The syntax for queues is size/max/drops, where size is the
current used depth of the queue, max is the maximum depth of the
queue before packets are dropped, and drops is the number of
packets dropped after the max has been reached. The size and
drops reset to 0 when the counters are cleared.

```
!
priority-list 1 queue-limit 30 60 60 90
!
```

The command **priority-list 1 queue-limit <*high*> <*med*> <*norm*> <*low*>** configures the different queues to different depths.

Custom Queuing (CQ)

CQ is a method used to statically define your own queuing parameters. Before enabling CQ, a traffic analysis needs to be performed. To define CQ parameters you need to know the packet sizes being used for each application. This data is necessary to configure CQ effectively.

CQ is the next progression of PQ. It guarantees some level of service to all created queues. With PQ, you can end up servicing only your high priority queue and never service the low priority queue. CQ takes the other queues into consideration, allowing a percentage of the other queues' traffic to be processed. The percentage can be defined by the protocol, source/destination address, or incoming interface. This ability to assign a percentage of the output interface ensures that each queue will be serviced regularly and guaranteed some level of bandwidth. Figure A.5 illustrates CQ serving process.

Figure A.5 The CQ servicing process.

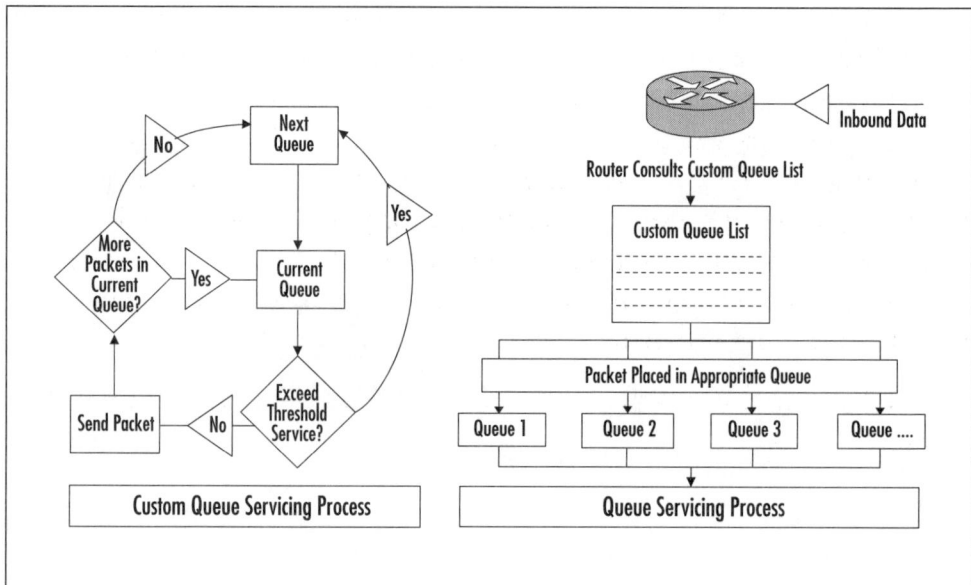

There are 17 queues defined in CQ. Queue 0 is reserved for system messages such as keep alives and signaling, and queues 1 through 16 are available for custom configuration. The system queue is always serviced first. The algorithm will allow you to specify the number of bytes to be serviced by the queue and/or the number of packets to be forwarded by the queue before moving to the next sequential queue. The result is a queuing mechanism that services each queue sequentially for the predetermined byte and/or packet count before cycling to the next queue. Bandwidth to each queue is indirectly configured in terms of byte count and queue length. When using CQ, no application receives more bandwidth than configured in the custom queue under congestive conditions.

It is important to set the byte count parameters correctly to achieve predictable results. Assume that you want to engineer a custom queue that divides the effective interface bandwidth evenly across four different applications. Now, also assume that you have not performed any traffic analysis and have configured four CQs with a byte count of 250 under the assumption that all the applications are similar. Now suppose that each application transmits 100-, 300-, 500-, and 700-byte frames consecutively. The net result is not a 25/25/25/25 ratio. When the router services the first queue, it forwards three 100-byte packets; when it services the second queue, it forwards one 300-byte packet; when it services the third queue, it forwards one 500-byte packet; and when it services the fourth queue, it forwards one 700-byte packet. The result is an uneven distribution of traffic flowing through the queue. You must pre-determine the packet size used by each flow or you will not be able to configure your bandwidth allocations correctly.

To determine the bandwidth that a custom queue will receive, use the following formula:

(queue byte count / total byte count of all queues) * bandwidth capacity of the interface.

Custom Queuing Examples

In an environment where there is a low-speed serial connection handling all of the network traffic and more control over the different traffic types is necessary, CQ may be most suitable. In an environment where users are having problems getting Dynamic Host Configuration Protocol (DHCP) information when booting up, create a configuration that allows for DHCP traffic to have a higher priority. The following configuration shows Telnet and bootpc with the highest priority and an access list with the lowest priority.

```
!
queue-list 1 protocol ip 1 list 100
queue-list 1 protocol ip 2 tcp telnet
queue-list 1 protocol ip 3 udp bootpc
queue-list 1 default 4
!
```

To use an extended access list to make specific IP traffic flow into queue 1, the **queue-list 1 protocol 1 list 100** command is used.

To configure Telnet traffic to flow into queue 2, the **queue-list 1 protocol 2 tcp telnet** command is used.

To configure UDP bootpc to flow into queue 3, the **queue-list 1 protocol 3 udp bootpc** command is used.

For all other traffic not defined in any of the CQs, a default queue should be configured as in the **queue-list 1 default 4** command. If there is no default queue configured, the router will assume that queue 1 is the default.

```
!
queue-list 1 queue 1 byte-count 1000
queue-list 1 queue 2 byte-count 4000
queue-list 1 queue 3 byte-count 4000
queue-list 1 queue 4 byte-count 2000
!
```

Queue 1 has been configured for 1000 bytes to be drained per cycle, queue 2 has been configured for 4000 bytes, queue 3 has been configured for 4000 bytes, and default queue 4 has been configured for 2000 bytes. Configuring the byte count of the different queues controls which queue has high priority. The higher the byte count, the more bandwidth is dedicated to that queue.

```
!

interface Serial 0

  custom-queue-list 1

!
```

To apply CQ to a specific interface, the **custom-queue-list 1** command is used.

```
c2507# show interface serial 0

Serial0 is up, line protocol is up

  Hardware is HD64570

  MTU 1500 bytes, BW 1544 Kbit, DLY 20000 usec, rely 255/255, load
1/255

  Encapsulation FRAME-RELAY, loopback not set, keepalive set (10
sec)

  LMI enq sent  0, LMI stat recvd 0, LMI upd recvd 0, DTE LMI down

  LMI enq recvd 0, LMI stat sent  0, LMI upd sent  0

  LMI DLCI 1023  LMI type is CISCO  frame relay DTE

  FR SVC disabled, LAPF state down

  Broadcast queue 0/64, broadcasts sent/dropped 0/0, interface
broadcasts 0

  Last input 00:00:07, output 00:00:07, output hang never

  Last clearing of "show interface" counters 00:00:03

  Input queue: 0/75/0 (size/max/drops); Total output drops: 0

  Queueing strategy: custom-list 1

  Output queues: (queue #: size/max/drops)
```

```
   0: 0/20/0 1: 0/20/0 2: 0/20/0 3: 0/20/0 4: 0/20/0
   5: 0/20/0 6: 0/20/0 7: 0/20/0 8: 0/20/0 9: 0/20/0
   10: 0/20/0 11: 0/20/0 12: 0/20/0 13: 0/20/0 14: 0/20/0
   15: 0/20/0 16: 0/20/0
 5 minute input rate 0 bits/sec, 0 packets/sec
 5 minute output rate 0 bits/sec, 0 packets/sec
   0 packets input, 0 bytes, 0 no buffer
   Received 0 broadcasts, 0 runts, 0 giants, 0 throttles
   0 input errors, 0 CRC, 0 frame, 0 overrun, 0 ignored, 0 abort
   0 packets output, 0 bytes, 0 underruns
   0 output errors, 0 collisions, 1 interface resets
   0 output buffer failures, 0 output buffers swapped out
   2 carrier transitions
   DCD=up  DSR=up  DTR=up  RTS=up  CTS=uph


c2507#


!
queue-list 1 queue 1 limit 40
!
```

The **queue-list *<list>* queue *<queue#>* limit *<depth>*** command configures the queue depth for each custom queue.

Class-Based Weighted Fair Queuing (CBWFQ)

CBWFQ is an extended version of the standard WFQ functionality, with support for user-defined traffic classes added. With CBWFQ, the network administrator has the ability to separate traffic and place it into queues based on criteria such as protocol, access control lists (ACLs), or originating interface. Each packet is analyzed in an effort to match a defined traffic class. The packet is then forwarded to the appropriate queue for servicing.

Classes are defined by parameters called *class characteristics*. Examples of class characteristics are bandwidth, weight, and maximum packet limit. The bandwidth assigned is the minimum bandwidth required for that specific class of service during periods of congestion. The weight value is derived from the bandwidth value assigned to each class. In addition, the weight value is used to help calculate the average queue length and packet limit. The packet limit defines the queue depth in packets. The queue is designed to drop all packets that exceed the configured queue depth or packet limit unless a policy is applied to the class. An example of such a policy is weighted random early detection (WRED), which we will discuss a bit later.

CBWFQ does not allow more than 75 percent of the interface bandwidth to be assigned to classes. The additional 25 percent is reserved for overhead such as routing updates. The network administrator can override this threshold, but must first take into account all the bandwidth required for routing protocol updates.

A good example is an ATM-based interface. This network administrator would need to take into account the overhead required to package data into ATM cells at Layer 2, in addition to any control packet flows traversing the link.

The advantage to using CBWFQ is that it is not bound to packet flows. In CBWFQ, up to 64 classes can be defined to a more granular level than traditional WFQ. CBWFQ is not affected by the total number of flows traversing an interface, and classes do not compete for bandwidth with other classes. The caveat is that multiple flows can compete for bandwidth within a defined class; therefore, significant thought is required when defining your queuing strategy.

CBWFQ is not supported in conjunction with traffic shaping or ATM unspecified bit rate (UBR) permanent virtual circuits. Please review Figure A.6, which illustrates CBWFQ operation. CBWFQ allocates bandwidth to a queue by guaranteeing the minimum amount of bandwidth defined for each class. There are 64 definable queues; WFQ is used to allocate bandwidth within each class or queue, unlike CQ, which services each queue defined in a FIFO manner.

Figure A.6 CBWFQ.

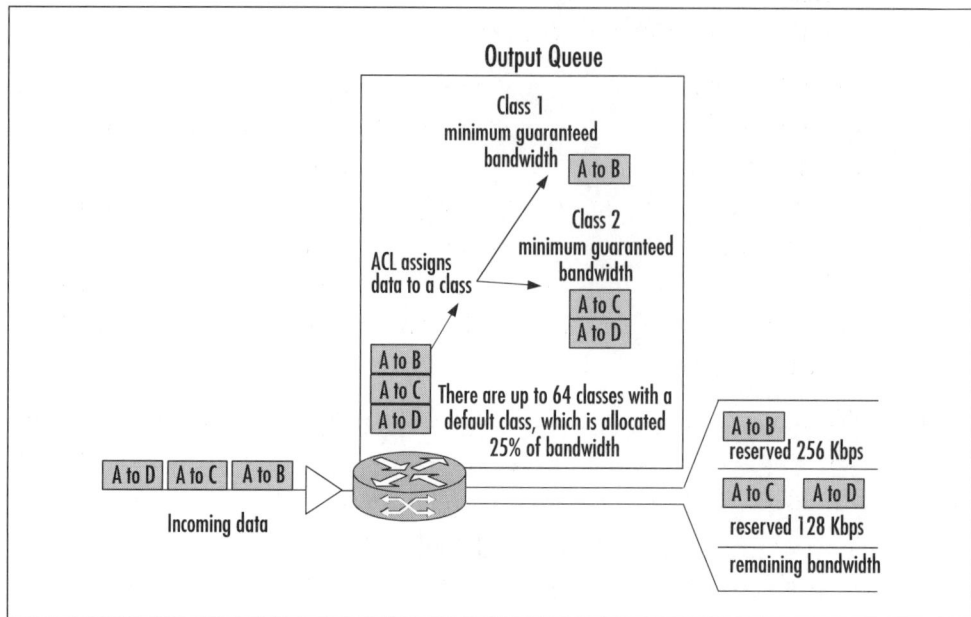

Selecting a Cisco IOS Queuing Method

Steps 1 through 6 should be followed when determining which queuing option to implement:

1. Is the WAN link congested with network traffic? If there is no congestion on the link, there is no need to sort the traffic into queues. If the link is consistently congested, traffic queuing may not resolve the problem. If the link is only congested for short periods of time, queuing may resolve the flows.

2. What type of traffic is traversing the network and is it congested? The network administrator must learn traffic flows and study the link during peak usage. This will help determine what traffic is utilizing the link and what can be done with that traffic. The network administrator needs to determine whether control over individual streams has to be enforced and/or if generic protocols need to be queued to

improve response time. Remember, traffic utilization is dynamic and will need to be analyzed often to determine whether changes are required.

3. After the traffic analysis is completed, can traffic be serviced by WFQ? This step is done to determine whether packet trains are utilizing the link during peak times. If so, automatic queuing provided by WFQ may be able to meet current needs. Remember, traffic patterns are dynamic and subject to change. It is recommended that a regular traffic analysis be performed to determine whether queuing optimization is required.

4. What is your organization's queuing policy? Queuing policies are based on application requirements in conjunction with a detailed traffic study. All interfaces require basic queuing configuration. These configuration values may need to be adjusted based on application requirement or location.

5. Does control over individual streams need to be taken into account? If certain applications are failing but enough bandwidth exists, CQ, WFQ, or CBWFQ can be utilized. This will allow the network administrator to select the critical traffic to be serviced while the other network flows will utilize the remaining bandwidth.

6. Can network delay be tolerated? If so, the network administrator can develop PQ schemes. The network administrator will need to determine which flows need servicing first and then determine how the other flows can be divided into the remaining queues. If the network cannot handle delays in packet arrival, then CQ can be used. CQ can guarantee that all applications gain some access to the link. Please review the queuing selection flow chart in Figure A.7.

Figure A.7 Queuing selection.

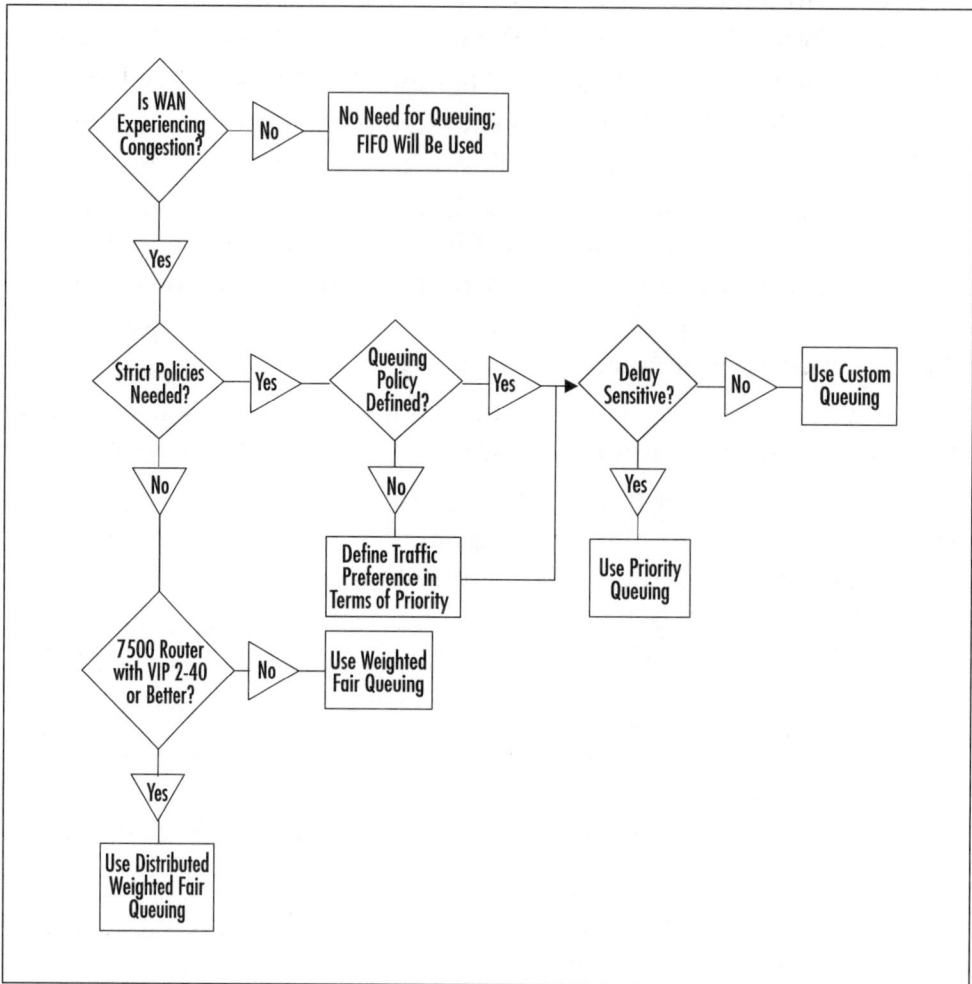

NOTE

When addressing congestion on links that have very low physical bandwidth, consider the amount of bandwidth being used by the routing protocol selected. For locations that are stub sites (have only one link connected to the backbone), consider using a default route or gateway of last resort. This will avoid the overhead associated with dynamic routing protocols.

Other things to consider are dynamic routing protocol selection, such as Routing Information Protocol (RIP) versus Open Shortest Path First (OSPF). Distance Vector protocols such as RIP will propagate the entire routing table every 30 seconds, requiring more bandwidth than link state protocols such as OSPF, which propagate changes in a given topology as they occur.

Table A.3 provides a comparison of queuing techniques.

Table A.3 Queuing Technique Selection

Weighted Fair Queuing	Priority Queuing	Custom Queuing
No queue lists	4 queues	16 queues
Low volume given priority	High queue serviced first	Round-robin service
Conversation dispatching	Packet dispatching	Threshold dispatching
Interactive traffic gets priority	Critical traffic gets through	Allocation of available bandwidth
File transfer gets balanced access	Designed for low-bandwidth links	Designed for higher-speed, low-bandwidth links
Enabled by default	Must configure	Must configure

Verifying Queuing Operation

To properly verify queuing operation, use the **show queuing** command to identify discards in both the input and output queues.

```
Router1#show queuing


Current fair queue configuration:
Interface Serial 0
```

```
   Input queue: 0/75/0 (size/max/drops); Total output drops: 0
 Output queue: 18/64/30 (size/threshold/drops)
    Conversations 2/8 (active/max active)
    Reserved Conversations 0/0 (allocated/max allocated)
 (depth/weight/discards) 3/4096/30
 Conversation 117, linktype: ip, length: 556, flags: 0x280
 source: 172.16.128.110, destination: 172.16.58.90, id: 0x1069,
ttl: 59,
  TOS: 0 prot: 6, source port 514, destination port 1022
  (depth/weight/discards) 14/4096/0
 Conversation 150, linktype: ip, length: 1504, flags: 0x280
 source: 172.16.128.110, destination: 172.16.58.90, id: 0x104D,
ttl: 59,
  TOS: 0 prot: 6, source port 20, destination port 1554
```

Weighted Random Early Detection (WRED) Overview

WRED is Cisco's version of RED. When this service is used, routers will attempt to anticipate and subsequently avoid network congestion. This differs from queuing techniques that attempt to control congestion after it has occurred on an interface.

RED is designed to make packet-switched networks aware of congestion before it becomes a problem. RED tries to control the average queue size while indicating to the end host if it should stop sending packets using Transmission Control Protocol's (TCP's) congestion control mechanisms.

RED will randomly drop packets during periods of high congestion. This action causes the source machine to decrease its transmission rate. Since TCP restarts quickly once a packet is lost, it can adapt its transmission rate to one the network can support.

RED is recommended only for TCP/IP networks. It is not recommended for protocols such as AppleTalk or Internetwork Packet Exchange/Sequenced Packet Exchange (IPX/SPX), which respond to dropped packets by retransmitting the packets at the original rate.

Tail Drop

Tail dropping occurs when the egress queues become so congested that no more packets can enter the queue. These packets have nowhere to go so they are dropped from the tail end of the queue. Once packets start to tail-drop, the current network session will go to timeout mode. These timeouts can cause each sender to simultaneously retransmit. Since all TCP sessions restart at the same time, more packets get congested in the queue at approximately the same interval, essentially causing a cyclic effect. In other words, traffic can go through a wave of congestion that increases and decreases at regular intervals, and is commonly referred to as a *global synchronization problem.*

Weighted Random Early Detection (WRED)

WRED tries to overcome the problem seen with tail dropping by randomly discarding packets before the buffers get congested. WRED determines when to start dropping packets based on the average queue length. Once the packet count within the queue exceeds the defined upper queue threshold, WRED begins dropping packets in the upper queue range. The dropping of packets is totally indiscriminate to the network flow. Since packets are dropped at random within the queue, this causes only a few sessions to restart. This gives the network a chance to drain the queues. Since the remaining sessions are still flowing, the buffers can empty and allow other TCP sessions a chance to recover.

NOTE

WRED, CQ, PQ, and WFQ are mutually exclusive on an interface. The router software produces an error message if you configure WRED and any one of these queuing strategies simultaneously.

Flow-Based WRED

Flow-based WRED takes into account the types of packets and protocols it attempts to drop while keeping track of flow states. If it needs to drop any flows, it will look for new flows within the queue rather than sacrificing a currently connected flow.

To allow for irregular bursty traffic, a scaling factor is applied to the common incoming flows. This value allows each active flow to reserve a number of packets in the output queue. The value is used for all currently active flows. When the scaling factor is exceeded, the probability of packets being dropped from the flow is increased.

Flow-based WRED provides a more fair method in determining which packets are tail-drops during periods of congestion. WRED automatically tracks flows to ensure that no single flow can monopolize resources. This is accomplished by actively monitoring traffic streams, learning which flows are not slowing down packet transmission, and fairly treating flows that do slow down packet transmission.

Data Compression Overview

Traffic optimization is a strategy that a network designer or operator seeks when trying to reduce the cost and prolong the link life of a WAN—in particular, improving link utilization and throughput. Many techniques are used to optimize traffic flow, which include PQs (as we described earlier), filters, and access lists. However, more effective techniques are found in data compression. Data compression can significantly reduce frame size and therefore reduce data travel time between endpoints. Some compression methods reduce the packet header size, while others reduce the payload. Moreover, these methods ensure that reconstruction of the frames happens correctly at the receiving end. The types of traffic and the network link type and speed need to be considered when selecting the data compression method to be applied. For example, data compression techniques used on voice and video differ from those applied to file transfers.

In the following sections, we will review these compression methods and explain the differences between them.

The Data Compression Mechanism

Data compression works by providing a coding scheme at both ends of a transmission link. The coding scheme at the sending end manipulates the data packets by replacing them with a reduced number of bits, which are reconstructed back to the original data stream at the receiving end without packet loss.

The scheme for data compression is referred to as a *lossless compression algorithm*, and is required by routers to transport data across the network. In comparison, voice and video compression schemes are referred to as *lossy* or *nonreversible compression*. The nature of voice or video data streams is that retransmission due to packet loss is not required. The latter type of compression allows for some degradation in return for greater compression and, therefore, more benefits. The Cisco IOS supports teleconferencing standards such as Joint Photographic Experts Group (JPEG) and Moving Picture Experts Group (MPEG).

Lossless compression schemes use two basic encoding techniques:

- Statistical compression
- Dictionary compression

Statistical compression is a fixed, non-adaptive encoding scheme that suits single applications where data is consistent and predictable. Today's router environments are neither consistent nor predictable; therefore, this scheme is rarely used.

Dictionary compression is based on the Lempel-Ziv (LZ) algorithm, which uses a dynamically encoded dictionary to replace a continuous bit stream with codes. The symbols represented by the codes are stored in memory in a dictionary-style format. The code and the original symbol vary as the data patterns change. Hence, the dictionary changes to accommodate the varying needs of traffic. Dictionaries vary in size from 32,000 bytes to much larger, to accommodate higher compression optimization. The compression ratios are expressed as ratio x:1, where x is the number of input bytes divided by the number of output bytes.

Dictionary-based algorithms require the dictionaries at the sending and receiving ends to remain synchronized. Synchronization through the use of a reliable data link such as X.25 or a reliable Point-to-Point Protocol (PPP) mode ensures that transmission errors do not cause the dictionaries to diverge.

Additionally, dictionary-based algorithms are used in two modes—continuous and packet. Continuous mode refers to the ongoing monitoring of the character stream to create and maintain the dictionary. The data stream consists of multiple network protocols (for example, IP and DECnet). Syn-chronization of end dictionaries is therefore important. Packet mode, however, also monitors a continuous stream of characters to create and maintain dictionaries, but limits the stream to a single network packet. Therefore, the synchronization of dictionaries needs to occur only within the packet boundaries.

Header Compression

TCP/IP header compression is supported by the Cisco IOS, which adheres to the Van Jacobson algorithm defined in RFC 1144. This form of compression is most effective with data streams of smaller packets where the TCP/IP header is disproportionately large compared with the payload. Even though this can successfully reduce the amount of bandwidth required, it is quite CPU-intensive and not recommended for WAN links larger than 64 Kbps.

To enable TCP/IP header compression for Frame Relay encapsulation:

```
router(config-if)# frame-relay ip tcp header-compression [passive]
```

(for interface configuration). Or, on a per dlci basis:

```
router(config-if)# frame-relay map ip ip-address dlci [broadcast] cisco tcp
header-compression {active | passive}
```

Another form of header compression, Real-time Transport Protocol (RTP), is used for carrying packets of audio and video traffic over an IP network, and provides the end-to-end network transport for audio, video, and other network services.

The minimal 12 bytes of the RTP header, combined with 20 bytes of IP header and 8 bytes of User Datagram Protocol (UDP) header, create a 40-byte IP/UDP/RTP header. The RTP packet has a payload of about 20 to 150 bytes for audio applications that use compressed payloads. This is clearly inefficient in that the header has the possibility of being twice the size of the payload. With RTP header compression, the 40-byte header can be compressed to a more reasonable 2 to 5 bytes.

To enable RTP header compression for PPP or high-data-rate digital subscriber line (HDSL) encapsulations:

```
router(config-if)# ip rtp header-compression [passive]
```

If the **passive** keyword is included, the software compresses outgoing RTP packets only if incoming RTP packets on the same interface are compressed. If the command is used without the passive keyword, the software compresses all RTP traffic.

To enable RTP header compression for Frame Relay encapsulation:

```
router(config-if)# frame-relay ip rtp header-compression [passive]

router(config-if)# frame-relay map ip ip-address dlci [broadcast] rtp
header-compression [active | passive]

router(config-if)# frame-relay map ip ip-address dlci [broadcast]
compress (enables both RTP and TCP header compression)
```

Link and Payload Compression

Variations of the LZ algorithm are used in many programs such as STAC (Lempel Ziv Stac, or LZS), ZIP and UNIX compress utilities. Cisco internetworking devices use the STAC (LZS) and Predictor compression algorithms. LZS is used on Cisco's Link Access Procedure, High-Level Data Link Control (HDLC), X.25, PPP, and Frame Relay encapsulation types. Predictor and Microsoft Point-to-Point Compression (MPPC) are only supported under PPP.

STAC (LZS) or Stacker was developed by STAC Electronics. This algorithm searches the input for redundant strings of data and replaces them with a token of shortened length. STAC uses the encoded dictionary method to store these string matches and tokens. This dictionary is then used to replace the redundant strings found in new data streams. The result is a reduced number of packets transmitted.

The Predictor compression algorithm tries to predict the incoming sequence of data stream by using an index to look up a sequence in the compression dictionary. The next sequence in the data stream is then checked for a match. If it matches, that sequence replaces the looked-up sequence in the dictionary. If not, the algorithm locates the next character sequence in the index and the process begins again. The index updates itself by hashing a few of the most recent character sequences from the input stream.

A third and more recent form of compression supported by Cisco IOS is MPPC. MPPC, as described under RFC 2118, is a PPP-optimized compression algorithm. MPPC, while it is an LZ-based algorithm, occurs in Layer 3 of the OSI model. This brings up issues of Layer 2 compression as used in modems today. Compressed data does not compress—it expands.

STAC, Predictor, and MPPC are supported on the 1000, 2500, 2600, 3600, 4000, 5200, 5300, 7200, and 7500 Cisco platforms. To configure software compression, use the **compress** interface configuration command. To disable compression on the interface, use the "no" form of this command, as illustrated in the following:

```
router(config-if)# compress {stac | predictor | mppc(ignore-pfc)}
router(config-if)# no compress {stac | predictor | mppc(ignore-pfc)}
```

Another form of payload compression used on Frame Relay networks is FRF.9. FRF.9 is a compression mechanism for both switched virtual circuits (SVC) and permanent virtual circuits (PVC). Cisco currently supports FRF.9 mode 1 and is evaluating mode 2, which allows more parameter configuration flexibility during the LCP compression negotiation.

To enable FRF.9 compression on a Frame Relay interface:

```
router(config-if)# frame-relay payload-compress frf9 stac
```
   or
```
router(config-if)# frame-relay map payload-compress frf9 stac
```

Per-Interface Compression (Link Compression)

This technique is used to handle larger packets and higher data rates. It is applied to the entire data stream to be transported—that is, it compresses the entire WAN link as if it were one application. The per-interface compression algorithm uses STAC or Predictor to compress the traffic, which in turn is encapsulated in a link protocol such as PPP or LAPB. This last step applies error correction and ensures packet sequencing.

Per-interface compression adds delay to the application at each router hop due to compression and decompression on every link between the endpoints. To unburden the router, external compression devices can be used. These devices take in serial data from the router, compress it, and send data out onto the WAN. Other compression hardware types are integrated on routers. Integrated compression software applies compression on existing serial interfaces. In this case, a router must have sufficient CPU and RAM for compression and dictionaries, respectively.

Per-Virtual Circuit Compression (Payload Compression)

Per-virtual circuit compression is usually used across virtual network services such as X.25 (Predictor or STAC) and Frame Relay (STAC). The header is unchanged during per-virtual circuit compression. The compression is therefore applied to the payload packets. It lends itself well to routers with a single interface but does not scale well in a scenario with multiple virtual circuit destinations (across a packet cloud).

Continuous-mode compression algorithms cannot be applied realistically due to the multiple dictionary requirements of the multiple virtual circuit destinations. In other words, it puts a heavy load on router memory. Therefore, packet-mode compression algorithms, which use fewer dictionaries and less memory, are more suited across packet networks.

Performing compression before or after WAN encapsulation on the serial interface is a consideration for the designer. Applying compression on an already encapsulated data payload reduces the packet size but not the number of packets. This suits Frame Relay and Switched Multimegabit Data Service (SMDS). In comparison, applying compression before WAN serial encapsulation will benefit the user from a cost perspective when using X.25, where service providers charge by the packet. This method reduces the number of packets transmitted over the WAN.

Hardware Compression

Cisco has developed hardware compression modules to take the burden of compression off of the primary CPU. On the 2600 and 3660 series of routers there is an Advanced Integration Module (AIM) slot, which currently can be populated with compression modules. For the 7000, 7200, and 7500 series routers there are Compression Service Adapters (CSAs) that offload the compression from the primary CPU. Note that CSAs require a VIP2 model VIP2-40 or above and that the 7200 VXR series does not support CSA-based compression.

The 2600 can populate its AIM slot with an AIM-COMP2= and increase its compression capabilities from 256 Kbps to 8 Mbps of compressed data throughput. On the 3660, if you populate the AIM slot with an AIM-COMPR4= module, the 3660 detects an increase from 1024 Kbps to 16 Mbps.

There are two available modules for the 7000, 7200, and 7500 series routers: the SA-COMP/1 and the SA-COMP/4. Their function is identical, but the SA-COMP/4 has more memory to maintain a larger dictionary. The SA-COPMP/1 and SA-COMP/4, while supporting 16 Mbps of bandwidth, can support up to 64 and 256 compression contexts, respectively. One context is essentially one bi-directional reconstruction dictionary pair. This may be a point-to-point link or a point-to-point Frame Relay sub-interface.

Selecting a Cisco IOS Compression Method

Network managers look at WAN transmission improvements as one of their goals. Due to ever-increasing bandwidth requirements, capacity planning is key to maintaining good throughput and keeping congestion to a minimum. Capacity planners and network operators have to consider additional factors when trying to add compression to their arsenal. Here are some of the considerations.

- **CPU and memory utilization** When utilizing link compression, Predictor tends to use more memory, but STAC uses more CPU power. Payload compression uses more memory than link compression; however, link compression will be more CPU-intensive.

- **WAN topology** With the increased number of remote sites (more point-to-point connections), additional dedicated memory is required due to the increased number of dictionary-based compression algorithms.

- **Latency** Latency is increased when compression is applied to the data stream. It remains a function of the type of algorithm used and the router CPU power available.

NOTE

Encrypted data cannot be compressed; it will actually expand if run through a compression algorithm. By definition, encrypted data has no repetitive pattern.

Verifying Compression Operation

To verify and monitor the various compression techniques, use the following Cisco commands:

For IP header compression:

```
router# show ip tcp header-compression
router# debug ip tcp header-compression
```

For RTP header compression:

```
router# show ip rtp header-compression
router# debug ip rtp header-compression
router# debug ip rtp packets
```

For payload compression:

```
router# show compress {detail-ccp}
router# debug compress
```

Summary

As a network grows in size and complexity, managing large amounts of traffic is key to maintaining good performance. Some of the many considerations in improving application performance and throughput are compression, queuing, and congestive avoidance techniques.

When selecting a queuing or congestion-avoidance algorithm, it is best to first perform a traffic analysis to better understand the packet size, latency, and end-to-end flow requirements for each application. Armed with this information, network administrators can select the best QoS mechanism for their specific environment.

There are three viable compression methods to increase network performance: header, payload, and link. These use various algorithms such as Van Jacobson algorithm for header compression, STAC, and Predictor for the payloads and link compression.

Hardware compression modules are used in the routers to offload CPU processing due to the heavy burden of compression algorithms.

FAQs

Q: Where can I find more information about queuing and QoS?

A: You can start online at Cisco's Web site: www.cisco.com/ univercd/cc/td/doc/cisintwk/ito_doc/qos.htm
Some related RFCs are:

RFC 2309: Recommendations on Queue Management and Congestion Avoidance in the Internet

RFC 2212: Specification of Guaranteed Quality of Service

RFC 1633: Integrated Services in the Internet Architecture: An Overview

Q: Are there any basic rules of thumb or "gotchas" that affect congestion management technologies?

A: Yes, some common rules of thumb are:

1. WFQ will not work on interfaces using LAPB, X.25, Compressed PPP, or SDLC encapsulations.

2. If the WAN link's average bandwidth utilization is 80 percent or more, additional bandwidth may be more appropriate than implementing a queuing policy.

Q: How can I verify queue operation?

A: The following debug commands can be useful (note that performing debug on a production router should be carefully weighed and the potential repercussions analyzed beforehand):

```
debug custom-queue
debug priority
```

Q: How can I verify queue operation?

A: The following show commands can be useful:

```
show queue <interface and #>
show queuing
```

where, for example, interface and # could stand for Ethernet 0.

Q: If both CBWFQ and CQ are available, which one should I use?

A: It is preferred you use CBWFQ over CQ because it will perform WFQ within each class-based queue. In other words, interactive applications such as Telnet are serviced before more bandwidth-intensive traffic within each statically defined queue. This results in better user response time than a custom queue using a FIFO method of draining the queue.

Q: When selecting a compression method, should I use hardware or software compression?

A: Use hardware compression over software compression when possible. Software compression can effect CPU utilization and needs to be monitored accordingly to avoid performance degradation. Hardware-based compression modules offload the main CPU by performing compression on a separate processing card. The end result is improved performance and throughput.

Index

G

N

Q

R

T

W

The Global Knowledge Advantage

Global Knowledge has a global delivery system for its products and services. The company has 28 subsidiaries, and offers its programs through a total of 60+ locations. No other vendor can provide consistent services across a geographic area this large. Global Knowledge is the largest independent information technology education provider, offering programs on a variety of platforms. This enables our multi-platform and multi-national customers to obtain all of their programs from a single vendor. The company has developed the unique CompetusTM Framework software tool and methodology which can quickly reconfigure courseware to the proficiency level of a student on an interactive basis. Combined with self-paced and on-line programs, this technology can reduce the time required for training by prescribing content in only the deficient skills areas. The company has fully automated every aspect of the education process, from registration and follow-up, to "just-in-time" production of courseware. Global Knowledge through its Enterprise Services Consultancy, can customize programs and products to suit the needs of an individual customer.

Global Knowledge Classroom Education Programs

The backbone of our delivery options is classroom-based education. Our modern, well-equipped facilities staffed with the finest instructors offer programs in a wide variety of information technology topics, many of which lead to professional certifications.

Custom Learning Solutions

This delivery option has been created for companies and governments that value customized learning solutions. For them, our consultancy-based approach of developing targeted education solutions is most effective at helping them meet specific objectives.

Self-Paced and Multimedia Products

This delivery option offers self-paced program titles in interactive CD-ROM, videotape and audio tape programs. In addition, we offer custom development of interactive multimedia courseware to customers and partners. Call us at 1-888-427-4228.

Electronic Delivery of Training

Our network-based training service delivers efficient competency-based, interactive training via the World Wide Web and organizational intranets. This leading-edge delivery option provides a custom learning path and "just-in-time" training for maximum convenience to students.

Global Knowledge Courses Available

Microsoft
- Windows 2000 Deployment Strategies
- Introduction to Directory Services
- Windows 2000 Client Administration
- Windows 2000 Server
- Windows 2000 Update
- MCSE Bootcamp
- Microsoft Networking Essentials
- Windows NT 4.0 Workstation
- Windows NT 4.0 Server
- Windows NT Troubleshooting
- Windows NT 4.0 Security
- Windows 2000 Security
- Introduction to Microsoft Web Tools

Management Skills
- Project Management for IT Professionals
- Microsoft Project Workshop
- Management Skills for IT Professionals

Network Fundamentals
- Understanding Computer Networks
- Telecommunications Fundamentals I
- Telecommunications Fundamentals II
- Understanding Networking Fundamentals
- Upgrading and Repairing PCs
- DOS/Windows A+ Preparation
- Network Cabling Systems

WAN Networking and Telephony
- Building Broadband Networks
- Frame Relay Internetworking
- Converging Voice and Data Networks
- Introduction to Voice Over IP
- Understanding Digital Subscriber Line (xDSL)

Internetworking
- ATM Essentials
- ATM Internetworking
- ATM Troubleshooting
- Understanding Networking Protocols
- Internetworking Routers and Switches
- Network Troubleshooting
- Internetworking with TCP/IP
- Troubleshooting TCP/IP Networks
- Network Management
- Network Security Administration
- Virtual Private Networks
- Storage Area Networks
- Cisco OSPF Design and Configuration
- Cisco Border Gateway Protocol (BGP) Configuration

Web Site Management and Development
- Advanced Web Site Design
- Introduction to XML
- Building a Web Site
- Introduction to JavaScript
- Web Development Fundamentals
- Introduction to Web Databases

PERL, UNIX, and Linux
- PERL Scripting
- PERL with CGI for the Web
- UNIX Level I
- UNIX Level II
- Introduction to Linux for New Users
- Linux Installation, Configuration, and Maintenance

Authorized Vendor Training
Red Hat
- Introduction to Red Hat Linux
- Red Hat Linux Systems Administration
- Red Hat Linux Network and Security Administration
- RHCE Rapid Track Certification

Cisco Systems
- Interconnecting Cisco Network Devices
- Advanced Cisco Router Configuration
- Installation and Maintenance of Cisco Routers
- Cisco Internetwork Troubleshooting
- Designing Cisco Networks
- Cisco Internetwork Design
- Configuring Cisco Catalyst Switches
- Cisco Campus ATM Solutions
- Cisco Voice Over Frame Relay, ATM, and IP
- Configuring for Selsius IP Phones
- Building Cisco Remote Access Networks
- Managing Cisco Network Security
- Cisco Enterprise Management Solutions

Nortel Networks
- Nortel Networks Accelerated Router Configuration
- Nortel Networks Advanced IP Routing
- Nortel Networks WAN Protocols
- Nortel Networks Frame Switching
- Nortel Networks Accelar 1000
- Comprehensive Configuration
- Nortel Networks Centillion Switching
- Network Management with Optivity for Windows

Oracle Training
- Introduction to Oracle8 and PL/SQL
- Oracle8 Database Administration

Custom Corporate Network Training

Train on Cutting Edge Technology

We can bring the best in skill-based training to your facility to create a real-world hands-on training experience. Global Knowledge has invested millions of dollars in network hardware and software to train our students on the same equipment they will work with on the job. Our relationships with vendors allow us to incorporate the latest equipment and platforms into your on-site labs.

Maximize Your Training Budget

Global Knowledge provides experienced instructors, comprehensive course materials, and all the networking equipment needed to deliver high quality training. You provide the students; we provide the knowledge.

Avoid Travel Expenses

On-site courses allow you to schedule technical training at your convenience, saving time, expense, and the opportunity cost of travel away from the workplace.

Discuss Confidential Topics

Private on-site training permits the open discussion of sensitive issues such as security, access, and network design. We can work with your existing network's proprietary files while demonstrating the latest technologies.

Customize Course Content

Global Knowledge can tailor your courses to include the technologies and the topics which have the greatest impact on your business. We can complement your internal training efforts or provide a total solution to your training needs.

Corporate Pass

The Corporate Pass Discount Program rewards our best network training customers with preferred pricing on public courses, discounts on multimedia training packages, and an array of career planning services.

Global Knowledge Training Lifecycle

Supporting the Dynamic and Specialized Training Requirements of Information Technology Professionals

- Define Profile
- Assess Skills
- Design Training
- Deliver Training
- Test Knowledge
- Update Profile
- Use New Skills

Global Knowledge

Global Knowledge programs are developed and presented by industry professionals with "real-world" experience. Designed to help professionals meet today's interconnectivity and interoperability challenges, most of our programs feature hands-on labs that incorporate state-of-the-art communication components and equipment.

ON-SITE TEAM TRAINING

Bring Global Knowledge's powerful training programs to your company. At Global Knowledge, we will custom design courses to meet your specific network requirements. Call (919)-461-8686 for more information.

YOUR GUARANTEE

Global Knowledge believes its courses offer the best possible training in this field. If during the first day you are not satisfied and wish to withdraw from the course, simply notify the instructor, return all course materials and receive a 100% refund.

REGISTRATION INFORMATION

In the US:
call: (888) 762–4442
fax: (919) 469–7070
visit our website:
www.globalknowledge.com

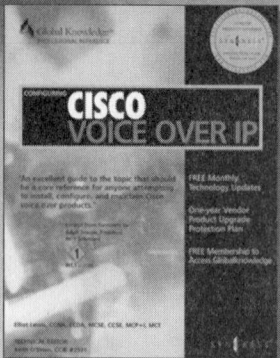